JESUS THE ONE AND ONLY

Beth Moore

LifeWay Press®
Nashville, Tennessee

Eighth printing June 2004

ISBN 0-7673-3275-X
This book is the text for course CG-0525
in the subject area Personal Life in the Christian Growth Study Plan.

Dewey Decimal Classification: 232.901
Subject Heading: BIBLE-STUDY AND TEACHING \ JESUS CHRIST-BIOGRAPHY

To order additional copies of this resource: WRITE LifeWay Church Resources Customer Service; One LifeWay Plaza; Nashville, TN 37234-0113; FAX order to (615) 251-5933; PHONE (800) 458-2772; E-MAIL to *CustomerService@lifeway.com;* ORDER ONLINE at *www.lifeway.com*; or visit the LifeWay Christian Store serving you.

Printed in the United States of America

Leadership and Adult Publishing
LifeWay Church Resources
One LifeWay Plaza
Nashville, TN 37234-0175

Dedication

To Marge Caldwell, my mother and teacher in ministry.
You were the first person whose passionate love for Jesus took my breath away.
I will never comprehend how I have been so blessed by God to know you,
love you, and learn from you. God has so tightly knitted the threads of our
ministries together that I'm not sure where one ends and the other begins.
Something of you is lived out in me every single good day. You taught me
countless things like how to be not only a woman in ministry, but also a lady.
Your love for Jesus the One and Only is wildly contagious.
I am only one of many who caught it feverishly.
How will I ever thank you for all you have invested in me?
I love you dearly.

The Author

Beth Moore realized at the age of 18 that God was claiming her future for full-time ministry. While she was sponsoring a cabin of sixth-graders at a missions camp, God unmistakably acknowledged that she would work for Him. There Beth conceded all rights to the Lord she had loved since childhood. However, she encountered a problem: although she knew she was "wonderfully made," she was "fearfully" without talent.

Beth hid behind closed doors to discover whether a beautiful singing voice had miraculously developed, but the results were tragic. She returned to the piano from which years of fruitless practice had streamed but found the noise to be joyless. Finally accepting that the only remaining alternative was missions work in a foreign country, she struck a martyr's pose and waited. Yet nothing happened.

Still confident of God's calling, Beth finished her degree at Southwest Texas State University, where she fell in love with Keith. After they married in December 1978, God added daughters Amanda and Melissa to their household.

As if putting together puzzle pieces one at a time, God filled Beth's path with supportive persons who saw something in her she could not. God used individuals like Marge Caldwell, John Bisagno, and Jeannette Cliff George to help Beth discover gifts of speaking, teaching, and writing. Seventeen years after her first speaking engagement, those gifts have spread all over the nation. Her joy and excitement in Christ are contagious; her deep love for the Savior, obvious; her style of speaking, electric.

Beth's ministry is grounded in and fueled by her service at her home fellowship, First Baptist Church, Houston, Texas, where she serves on the pastor's council and teaches a large Sunday School class. Beth believes that her calling is Bible literacy: guiding believers to love and live God's Word.

Beth loves the Lord, loves to laugh, and loves to be with His people. Her life is full of activity, but one commitment remains constant: counting all things but loss for the excellence of knowing Christ Jesus, the Lord, (see Phil. 3:8).

Beth's previous Bible studies have explored the lives of Moses, David, Paul, and Isaiah. In *Jesus the One and Only* she invites you along to study the life of our Lord Jesus Himself. May you be blessed by your journey as were those who traveled to Israel for the videotaping and those who have worked with Beth to bring you *Jesus the One and Only.*

Contents

Introduction

My romance with Jesus Christ began in a tiny circle of baby bear chairs in a Sunday School class of a small town church. My teachers were not biblical scholars. They were moms and homemakers. I'm not sure they ever delved into the depths of Scripture or researched a single Greek word. They simply taught what they knew. I don't know any other way to explain what happened next: I believed.

Because of the endless distractions, these women must have wondered if they were doing little more than babysitting while our parents went to big church. They were. Somewhere between twirling butter cookies on my fingers and spilling red fruit drink, I started falling in love.

I am quite certain my tiny childhood faith was a gift from God for at least two reasons. First, even as a preschooler, I already had reasons to disbelieve what big people said. Secondly, I made so few good decisions growing up that I can't imagine I made such a fine one on my own. No, I'm convinced that God intended to start this romance early and unexplainably.

I remember thinking how handsome Jesus was in those watercolor pictures and how I had never seen a man with long hair before. I wondered if my daddy, the Army major, would approve. My favorite picture was the familiar one with the children climbing all over Jesus' lap. As I recall, it was the only one I ever saw that captured Him smiling. I determined quickly that big people bored and upset Him and little people made Him quite happy.

My teachers said He was my very best friend. How funny to have a very best friend you've never even met. My teachers said Jesus thought all the things about us that I really wanted someone to think about me. I was raised in a big family. I dearly loved every member of that bulging household, but I wanted so badly to be special. My teachers used that word every single week. Special. Yep. I was starting to like Him. And it was just the beginning.

As I recount this simple, unexciting testimony to you, a lump wells in my throat and tears burn in my eyes. In a life history filled with so many regrets, I made one decent choice that has affected my life more profoundly than all my poor ones combined: I chose to believe Jesus. I can no longer hold back the tears. He is the most wonderful, most graceful, most exciting, most redemptive thing that has ever happened to me. Jesus is my life. I cannot express on paper my love for Him. It is a love that has grown in incongruous bits and pieces, baby steps, leaps, bounds, tumbles and falls, little-by-little, more then less, less then more…decade-after-decade. I cannot take an iota of credit for it. If possible, my shaky, inconsistent walk with Christ would have tested even a boundless supply of grace and mercy. I am proof God has not grown short on long suffering.

I was a troubled child who took her troubles smack into adulthood. I have no doubt I would finally have self-destructed if not for Christ. He continued to strive with me, forgive me, dress my wounds, and heal me, ever wooing me away from the familiar path of despair. I pray that those days of defeat are behind me, but if not, Jesus, my One and Only, will still be ahead of me, convincing me to walk again. This time a little closer.

A romance with Christ differs so dramatically from a romance between mortals. I do not wish any other woman to love my husband, Keith, the way I do. How different my romance with Christ! I want all of you to love Him … at least as much as I do. Then more and more and more. I can echo a hint of the emotion Paul felt when he claimed, "I am jealous for you with a godly jealousy" (2 Cor. 11:2). I want more of the abundance of Christ for you. No matter how much you have. More! I want you to be jealous for me to have His increasing abundance, too. I'm jealous for us to want Him more than we want blessing, health, or even breath. I want to know Him so well that my undivided heart can exclaim, "Because Your love is better than life, my lips will glorify You" (Ps. 63:3). Better than life! God invites mortal creatures—you and me—into a love relationship with the Son of glory. That, my friend, is the meaning of life. Let's partake. Fully. Completely.

We will never spend our time more valuably than in the pursuit of knowing Jesus Christ. My deepest prayer is that this offering would take you another step closer in the noblest pursuit of life. I have very little doubt that I will leave more lacking in this particular Bible study than any God has entrusted to me simply because there is no end to what could be said. And, indeed, must be said. If not by mortal creatures, then by those invisible to our eyes, encircling the throne and in a loud voice, singing, "Worthy is the Lamb!"

He is Jesus.
The One and Only.
Transcendent over all else.
To know Him is to love Him.
To love Him is to long for Him.
To long for Him is to finally reach soul hands into the One true thing we need never get enough of.
Jesus.
Take all you want.
Take all you need.
Till soul is fed.
And spirit freed.
Till dust is dust.
And Face you see.
Jesus Christ.
He's all you need.

Jesus the One and Only is written in an interactive format to enhance your learning and application of the truths of Scripture. I encourage you to complete all of the written work in your workbook. The Holy Spirit uses your efforts as you seek to answer the questions and respond to the activities in your own words.

On the introduction page of each week's study you will find five Principal Questions. Each Principal Question comes from one of the five lessons during the week. The Principal Questions deal with facts involved in the lesson. Your small group will discuss each of the Principal Questions each week.

In addition to the Principal Questions, you will find Personal Discussion segments identified with a symbol like this ❦. These learning activities help you personally apply the material by relating the events to your own life. Your small group will include time for you to share about your Personal Discussion responses as you wish. You will not be required to share unless you so desire.

I have used several resources for study of Greek and Hebrew words. Definitions taken from *The Complete Word Study Dictionary: New Testament* and the *Lexical Aids*[1] are enclosed in quotation marks with no reference. I have also used *Strong's Exhaustive Concordance of the Bible.*[2] Words taken from *Strong's* are enclosed in quotation marks with the word *Strong's* in parentheses.

---

[1]Spiros Zodhiates et al., eds., *The Complete Word Study Dictionary: New Testament* (Chattanooga, TN: AMG Publishers, 1992).
[2]James Strong, *Strong's Exhaustive Concordance of the Bible* (Nashville, TN: Abingdon Press, 1970).

Introductory Session

Today's focal passage: Amos 8:11-12.
Two Scriptures imply probable reasons why the Lord God instituted this kind of "famine."
Amos 2:11-12—God's people commanded His prophets to be silent (not to prophecy)
Zechariah 7:11-12—The hearts of God's people became as they would not listen and they God made their hearts hard as flint.
In essence, they stopped listening so God finally (though temporarily) stopped talking.

A Few Historical Events Affecting Israel During the Inter-Testament Era
Place the following events on the timeline below.

1. **The conquest of Alexander the Great.** In 336 B.C., Philip of Macedon's son, Alexander the III, took the throne at 20 years of age and proceeded to conquer much of the civilized world.
2. **The Greek translation of the Old Testament Pentateuch.** In 250 B.C. the Alexandrian Jews translated the Pentateuch into the Greek language. It was later called the Septuagint, Latin for seventy, traditionally believed to be the number of men who worked on the translation.
3. **The abomination of Antiochus IV.** In 168 B.C. he stormed Jerusalem, entered the temple, and stole the treasures. A year later, he banned obedience to the Jewish law.
4. **The rise of Herod the Great.** In 40 B.C. the senate in Rome appointed him "King of the Jews".

Malachi--Prophetic
Probably dated 336 BC. 300 BC. 250 BC. 200 BC. 168 BC. 100 BC. 40 B.C. Proclamation
between 433-400 B.C.

This was "not a famine of food or a thirst for water, but a famine of hearing the words of the Lord."
The original Hebrew word for hearing in Amos 8:11 is *shama*.

Two Primary Ramifications of "a famine of hearing the words of the Lord":
1. Unparalleled insecurity: Much of their identity was cast in hearing the words of the Lord (see Deut. 6:4-9). The ability to hear the words of the Lord was a critical part of what set them apart.
2. Unprecedented hunger: At least part of the overall plan was to invoke "a famine of hearing the words of the Lord" in order to provoke a hunger for "hearing the words of the Lord" (see Gal. 4:4). Note three components of this verse:

- **The time:** The word *kairos* inspired in Galatians 4:4 is the other word *chronos*, meaning the actual passing of moments or a period of measured time. season or opportunity
- **The fullness:** The original Greek word for *fullness* is *pleroma*, the noun form of the verb *pleroo* meaning to make full or "to fill up." The time wasn't full until their spiritual stomachs were empty.
- **The arrival:** The time didn't go. It came! Luke 15:13-17

In conclusion, consider the awesome plan of God: He used a famine to serve His purposes until the fullness of time. He used the withholding of His words to prepare for the revealing of The Word (His Living Word, Jesus: the expression of the heart and mind of God in human flesh.)

We have seen His glory, the glory of the One and Only,Who came from the Father, full of grace and truth.
(John 1:14, NIV).

WEEK 1

The Word Made Flesh

Day 1
Unexpected Company

Day 2
Give Him the Name Jesus

Day 3
Kindred Hearts

Day 4
His Name Is John

Day 5
A Savior Is Born

I am so glad to have you along on this ride, dear one! I would willingly have taken this particular journey all by myself, but you make it far more wonderful. We have several hundred miles ahead of us, so grab your Bible, a jug full of Living Water, and a durable pair of sandals. Our journey will take us all over Galilee, Jerusalem, Judea, and even across the lake to the "other side." Our goal is simply to walk with Jesus wherever He goes through the pages of Scripture during the next 10 weeks. You and I will drop in on His journey just a few months before His earthly arrival. Interestingly, His trek toward earth began much sooner—"In the beginning," in fact. God's perfect plan of redemption through the "Word made flesh" was already in motion before He breathed the first soul into man. May God astound you with a fresh glimpse of the greatest story ever told.

Principal Questions:

Day 1: Based on Luke 1:18-25, how did Zechariah receive Gabriel's news?

Day 2: Matthew 2:23 records an oral prophecy handed down through the generations. What was the prophecy?

Day 3: Based on Luke 1:39-56, what did Mary do after receiving Gabriel's news?

Day 4: According to Luke 1:78, why did God enact His intricate, redemptive plan?

Day 5: What two responses did Mary have to all the events that followed Christ's birth?

Commit, dear student of God's Word! Let's see this journey to the very last page! Let's welcome God to completely transform our image of His Son. Let's fall in love with Jesus all over again.

DAY 1

Unexpected Company

Today's Treasure
"Do not be afraid, Zechariah; your prayer has been heard" (Luke 1:13).

Please begin our study together by reading Luke 1:1-10.

Zechariah rose from his bed in a small room outside the temple, amazed at the once-in-a-lifetime privilege he feared would never come; after all, he was no spring chicken.

This was no time for marital preoccupation, but Zechariah's mind surely detoured to his wife of many years. Unlike most of the other priests, he had no children. When his temple service took him from home, Elizabeth was all alone. She handled her empty home with grace and dignity, but he knew her childlessness still stung terribly. Jewish homes were meant for children.

Zechariah took extra care to smooth out the white linen fabric and carefully tie the sash of his priestly garments. Not all the priests took their responsibilities so soberly, but Zechariah was a righteous man. He walked through the temple gate with all senses magnified and beheld a sight to take away a man's breath: the cream and gold temple bathing in the morning sun. A few early risers probably already gathered for worship in the courtyard. Little did Zechariah know that the gentle breeze was blowing in far more than just another morning.

I hope these descriptions help you to picture the Word rather than mechanically reading it. The Word of God is alive and powerful! It remains unexciting only when we remain detached from it. Attach yourself to it! Involve yourself in it. Abide in it for these 10 weeks. Every page of Scripture is about God's intervention in the lives of human beings like you and me.

Zechariah is not a character in a fiction novel. He was a real man who sought to serve a real God even in the midst of unanswered prayers, mystifying disappointments, personal weakness, mundane daily rituals, and anxiety-causing responsibilities. Can anyone relate? If so, a great adventure lies ahead of us in God's Word. Many noble things vie for our time, but nothing will affect our lives and the lives of those around us more powerfully and positively than an in-depth study of God's Word.

If you are fairly certain God has placed this study into your hands, would you be willing to write a brief prayer of commitment to see it through to the very last page? Use the space below.

Open my mind and heart to wisdom!!

Let's take a look at the Scriptures that provide the detailed background for Luke 1:1-10. Read 1 Chronicles 24:1-19. What is recorded in this segment of Scripture?

Aaron had many descendants. Each of the 24 divisions of priests served in the temple for one week twice a year and at major festivals. An individual priest could offer the incense at the daily sacrifice only once in his lifetime. Zechariah's only turn had come. Surely he was overwhelmed.

Although the courtyards of Herod's temple had already become a marketplace in Zechariah's day, you can be sure that Zechariah took the responsibility very seriously. He most likely spent the previous night in one of the rooms adjoining the outside wall of the temple. These rooms, also used for storage, are described in 1 Kings 6:5. One of the primary reasons for priests remaining on the temple grounds was to keep their minds and bodies sanctified. Even though God created marriage and blesses sexual intimacy between a husband and wife, priests were expected to have "one-track minds" when serving in the temple.

Based on your reading in Luke 1:1-10, why might we assume that Zechariah went to the fullest extent of preparation?

___

Verse 10 tells us that worshippers assembled outside the temple at the time for the burning of the incense. Their custom was to pray individually and simultaneously in the courtyard as the priest was praying for them corporately inside. After he finished his duties, he would come out to them and give them a blessing. Take a look at Psalm 141:2 and Revelation 5:8. The offering of the incense actually symbolized prayer.

In what ways can you imagine incense as symbolic of a believer's prayer?

___

___

With all these things in mind, continue reading Luke 1:11-17. What indicates that Gabriel didn't appear to Zechariah as a regular man?

___

Obviously, the fragrance of the incense wasn't the only thing that ascended to the throne of God that day. "Do not be afraid, Zechariah; your prayer has been heard." I do not want you to miss the significance of this statement. Please understand that the responsibility of the priest on duty was to offer the incense and to pray for the nation of Israel. His purpose was to offer a corporate prayer. Furthermore, the priest's intercession for the nation would have undoubtedly included a petition for the Messiah, Israel's promised Deliverer and King. Zechariah would have petitioned the throne of grace on behalf of the nation of Israel and for God to send its long-awaited Messiah.

The old priest could not know that God had purposely manipulated his appointment that day for a revolutionary reason. In the weeks ahead, we will see evidences that many of those who served in the priesthood were not like Zechariah. Numerous priests could have offered the incense that day with little respect and could have voiced a repetitious prayer utterly void of anxious expectation. Luke 1:6 tells us that Zechariah and Elizabeth were "upright in the sight of God." The Creator and Sustainer of the universe was ready to answer a prayer that had been prayed for hundreds of years, but He purposely chose a man who could pray an old prayer with a fresh heart.

I don't believe Zechariah's prayers that day were limited to corporate petitions. Whether or not he planned to make a personal request, I believe that he did. I think he poured the perfectly mixed ingredients on the fire, inhaled the aroma of incense rising toward heaven, asked God's blessing over the nation of Israel, passionately pled for the coming of the Messiah, then, before he turned and walked away, he voiced an age-old request from the hearth of his own home.

ILLUSTRATOR PHOTO/BOB SCHATZ

The Wailing Wall, for centuries revered by Jews as the only remaining wall of the ancient Temple area.

I will never forget the first time I had an opportunity to go into the "old city" in Jerusalem. As much as I had enjoyed the whole excursion, it would have been terribly incomplete without going inside the walls of the old Jerusalem and standing at the Wailing Wall. I knew from my studies that the Wailing Wall is considered to be virtually the most sacred place on earth to an orthodox Jew. As a portion of the sacred temple structure, it signifies the place of most intimate physical closeness to God. Droves of people pray at the Wailing Wall. Many write their requests on small pieces of paper and literally wedge the notes in the wall's crevices. I rose early that morning and had a lengthy time of preparation in prayer. I knew I would have only a very few minutes at the wall, and I gave serious thought to the petitions I would make there.

After deep consideration, I recorded the most important requests I could possibly make on a small sheet of paper. Several hours later, I stood at that wall as overcome in prayer as I have ever been. After I had voiced my petitions through sobs, I wedged my requests in a crack in the wall and left them there. Why did I take it so seriously when I can boldly approach the throne of grace 24 hours a day? Because in a common, godless world, I was standing at a uncommon, sacred place. A place where more collective petitions have been poured out to the One True God than any other in the world … and I had one chance.

I believe that's why Zechariah may have grasped the most sacred moment of his life to let his personal prayer ascend like incense to the throne of grace. The prayer at that exact moment may not have been for a son. At their ages, perhaps Zechariah and Elizabeth had given up. Or perhaps he remembered Abraham and Sarah, and he knew God could do the impossible. Either way, I believe Zechariah voiced something about the void in their lives and the hurt or disappointment of their own hearts. What the old priest could not possibly have known was how intimately connected would be his corporate prayer for the Messiah and his personal prayer for a son.

I wonder if you've almost given up on God answering an earnest, long-term prayer of your heart. Not growing stale, faithless, and hopeless over a repetitious request can be terribly challenging. God never missed a single, sincere petition from the children of Israel to send their Messiah; nor did He miss a solitary plea from the aching hearts of a childless couple. God does not have some limited supply of power necessitating our careful selection of a few choice things about which we can pray. God's power is infinite. God's grace and mercy are drawn deeply from the bottomless well of His heart.

When Zechariah stood at the altar of incense that day and lifted the needs of the nation to the throne, an ample supply of supernatural power and tenderhearted compassion remained in the heart of God to provide not just his needs, but the desire of his heart. God was simply waiting for the perfect time.

What long-standing prayer request have you continued to take to God's throne? Please write it in the space below:

___

If you have received a definitive "no" from God, pray to accept it and trust that He knows what He's doing. If you haven't, don't grow weary or mechanical. Like Zechariah and Elizabeth, continue to walk faithfully with God even though you are disappointed. Walking with God in the day-in/day-out course of life swells your assurance that God is faithful and inconceivably enjoyable even when a request goes unmet. Recognizing all the other works God is doing in your life will prevent discouragement as you await your answer. Zechariah waited a long time for God's answer, but when it came, it exceeded everything the old priest could have thought or asked.

What assurances was Zechariah given about his son (v. 14-17)?

____

____

Now read Luke 1:18-25. How did Zechariah receive Gabriel's news?

____

What happened as a result?

____

Something about this encounter makes me grin. Gabriel, the very angel who appeared to Daniel, meets Zechariah and tells him God has heard his prayer. The heavenly ambassador proceeds to give a very detailed prophecy regarding the child's life.

The first words out of Zechariah's mouth? "How can I be sure of this?"

Apparently Gabriel was in no mood for Zechariah's doubtful retort. Those were the last words out of the old priest's mouth for a while.

Zechariah's transgression wasn't terminal. The promise was still intact and the old man would still be a father. He just wouldn't have much to say until his faith became sight. As one commentator suggested, perhaps we all bear the signs of our doubts. Zechariah's sign just happened to be very obvious and conclusive. For many years, my young life bore the signs of doubt. I believed God could love me, but I'm not sure I really believed God could change me. It certainly showed, too.

Luke's account of Zechariah's news concludes with his return home and the record of Elizabeth's pregnancy. The woman in me fusses over the lack of details. How did Zechariah tell her what happened? What did she say? Did she laugh? Did she squeal? Did she cry? If age had already closed her womb, what was her first sign of pregnancy? And, anyway, why did she remain in seclusion for five months? Lastly, I wonder if Zechariah somehow shared with Elizabeth every last detail of the prophecy concerning their son. Can you even imagine being told in advance of your child's conception that he or she would bring joy and delight to you and be great in the sight of the Lord? We breathe a huge sigh of relief over a sonogram showing all the right appendages. What we'd give for a few guarantees about their character!

Without a doubt, Zechariah and Elizabeth would think this answer was one worth waiting for. God is so faithful. One reason He may have given them such assurances about their son's future greatness is because, foregoing a miracle, they would not live to see all the prophecy come to fruition. Like few of the rest of us, this set of parents would not die hoping. They would die knowing.

DAY 2

Give Him the Name Jesus

Today's Treasure
"You will be with child and give birth to a son, and you are to give him the name Jesus" (Luke 1:31).

Picture the omniscient eyes of the unfathomable *El Roi*—the God who sees, spanning the universe in panoramic view. Every galaxy is in His gaze. Imagine now the gradual tightening of His lens as if a movie camera were attached to the point of a rocket bound for planet Earth. Not a man-made rocket, but a celestial rocket—of the living kind.

Gabriel has been summoned once again to the imposing throne of God. Lightning flashes from the throne as peals of thunder pierce the angelic praises. Unearthly colors spray the heavenly city as light ricochets from His splendor.

Ezekiel used no small amount of ink to describe the cherubim, but when he tried to depict the One who sat on the throne, the inkwell dried quickly. Few words. If the created cherubim are so magnificent, what indeed is their Creator like? Even the creatures that never cease to praise God shield themselves with their wings from the blinding glory of His holiness.

Scripture names only two of the current angels: Michael, the warrior, and Gabriel, the bearer of God-news. At least six months had passed since God sent the ambassador Gabriel to Jerusalem. His previous assignment took him to Herod's temple, one of the wonders of the civilized world. This time heaven's lens focused north of Jerusalem. Imagine Gabriel searing earthward through the floor of the third heaven, breaking the barrier from the supernatural to the natural world. Feature him soaring through the second heaven past the stars God calls by name. As our vision "descends," the earth grows larger. God's kingdom gaze burns through the blue skies of planet Earth and plummets like a flaming stake in the ground to a backward town called Nazareth.

Read Luke 1:26-38. Try not to hurry. One of the delights of the Word is how the student can reap a fresh word from a familiar page. Before we begin to dissect this segment, does any particular element of the account seem to take a fresh leap off the page at you? Read it until one does, then note it below.

____

Based on the context of Luke 1, to what does the time frame "sixth month" refer? Check one.
- ❑ **the sixth month of Elizabeth's pregnancy**
- ❑ **the sixth month of the Jewish calendar**
- ❑ **the sixth month of the civil calendar**
- ❑ **the sixth month since Gabriel's last visit**

Miles and decades separated an expectant senior adult from her kid-cousin up north. Jewish families were close-knit, but these women, presumably related by marriage, inhabited very different cultures. A few constants would have permeated their family lives, however. The practices of the ancient Jewish betrothal were consistent.

Luke 1:27 tells us that Mary, a virgin, was "pledged to be married to a man named Joseph." *Pledged* or *betrothed* are the English translations from the Greek root word *mnesteuomai*, meaning "to remember." What a perfect expression of betrothal! When God instructed the Israelites to build the altar of sacrifice in the tabernacle courtyard so that

He could "meet" with them, He used no ordinary word (Ex. 29:42-43). The Hebrew word for *meet* (see Ex. 25:22) is *ya'ad,* which means to "betroth" *(Strong's).* Believer, you can rest assured that God remembers. He longs for us to act as if we do, too.

Betrothal compares more to our idea of marriage than engagement. The difference was the matter of physical intimacy, but the relationship was legally binding. Betrothal began with a contract drawn up by the parents or by a friend of the groom. Then at a meeting between the two families, in the presence of witnesses, the groom would present the bride with jewelry. The groom announced his intentions to firmly observe the contract. Then he would sip from a cup of wine and offer the cup to the bride. If she sipped from the same cup, she was in effect entering covenant with him.

The next step was the payment of the *mohar* or dowry by the groom. This occurred at a ceremony, ordinarily involving a priest. Other traditions were also practiced, but these were the most basic and consistent. By the time a couple reached this step, their betrothal was binding, though a marriage ceremony and physical intimacy had not taken place. An actual divorce would be necessary to break the covenant. Furthermore, if the prospective groom died, the bride-to-be was considered a widow.

Betrothal traditionally occurred soon after the onset of adolescence, so we are probably accurate to imagine Mary around age 13 at the time of the announcement. Remember, in that culture a 13- or 14-year-old was commonly preparing for marriage.

Don't miss the one fact we're told about Joseph in Luke's introductory account. What is the only elaboration on Joseph given in Luke 1:27?

____

How awesome of God to purpose that Christ's royal lineage would come through His adoptive father. We shouldn't be surprised at the profound significance with which God views adoption.

What does Ephesians 1:4-6 tell you about God's view of adoption?

____

In a peculiar kind of way, God the Father allowed His Son to be "adopted" into a family on earth so that we could be adopted into His family in heaven. Luke's Gospel doesn't tell us much about Joseph, but we have plenty of information to stir our imaginations about his bride-to-be. I love to imagine where Mary was when Gabriel appeared to her. I wonder if she was in her bedroom or walking a dusty path after fetching water for her mother. One thing for sure: she was alone.

No matter where the angelic ambassador appeared to Mary, he stunned her with his choice of salutations: "Greetings, you who are highly favored! The Lord is with you." Prior to Zechariah's encounter, centuries had passed since God had graced the earth with a heavenly visitation. I doubt the thought occurred to anyone that He would transmit the most glorious news yet heard to a simple Galilean girl.

How I love the way God works! Just when we decide He's too complicated to comprehend, He draws stick pictures.

I'm sure Mary wasn't looking for an angelic encounter that day, but if a town could have eyes to see, Nazareth should have seen. The word *Nazareth* means "watchtower."[1] A watchtower was a human-sized compartment built at a strategic place on the city wall for the designated watchman. He was one of the most important civil servants in any city. From the watchtower, the watchman stayed on red alert for friend or foe. Two thousand years ago, Nazareth received an unfamiliar friend.

Matthew 2:23 records a prophecy handed down orally through the generations. What was the prophecy?

____

Indeed, if towns could see, Nazareth would have been looking. But the recipient of the news was totally unsuspecting. Humble. Meek. Completely caught off guard. Luke 1:29 tells us "Mary was greatly troubled at his words." The phrase actually means "to stir up throughout." You know the feeling: when butterflies don't just flutter in your stomach but land like a bucket at your feet, splashing fear and adrenaline through every appendage. Mary felt the fear through and through, wondering what kind of greeting this might be. How could this young girl comprehend that she was "highly favored" by the Lord God Himself (Luke 1:28)?

The angel's next statement was equally stunning: "The Lord is with you." Although similar words were spoken over lives like Moses, Joshua, and Gideon, I'm not sure they had ever been spoken over a woman. I'm not suggesting the Lord is not as present in the lives of women as He is men, but this phrase was suggesting a unique presence and power for the purpose of fulfilling a divine kingdom plan. The sight of the young girl gripped by fear provoked Gabriel to continue with the words, "Do not be afraid, Mary, you have found favor with God" (v. 30). Not until his next words did she have any clue why he had come or for what she had been chosen.

"You will be with child and give birth to a son" (v. 31). Not just any son—"the Son of the Most High" (v. 32). Probably only Mary's youth and inability to absorb the information kept her from fainting in a heap!

My favorite line of all: "And you are to give Him the name Jesus" (v. 31). Do you realize this was the first proclamation of our Savior's personal name since the beginning of time? *Jesus.* The very name at which every knee will one day bow. The very name that every tongue will one day confess. A name that has no parallel in my vocabulary or yours. A name I whispered into the ears of my infant daughters as I rocked them and sang lullabies of His love. A name by which I've made every single prayerful petition of my life. A name that has meant my absolute salvation, not only from eternal destruction, but from myself. A name with power like no other name. Jesus.

What a beautiful name. I love to watch how it falls off the lips of those who love Him. I shudder as it falls off the lips of those who don't. Jesus. It has been the most important and most consistent word in my life. Dearer today than yesterday. Inexpressibly precious to me personally, so I am at a loss to comprehend what the name means universally.

You may feel as unable to express what His Name means to you as I do, but please try.

Life
____

____

Jesus. The Greek spelling is *Iesous*, transliterated from the Hebrew *Yeshu'a* (Joshua). Keep in mind that Christ's earthly family spoke a Semitic language closely related to Hebrew (called Aramaic), so He would have been called *Yeshu'a*. One of the things I like best is that it was a common name. After all, Jesus came to seek and to save common people like me. Most pointedly, the name Jesus means *Savior*. Others may have shared the name, but no one else would ever share the role. We have much to learn over the weeks to come about Jesus, the Savior. I can hardly wait!

God sent a message through Gabriel that could not have been accurately interpreted as anyone but the long-awaited Messiah.

Read Psalm 89:19-29. These words were attributed to King David in an immediate sense. In the margin write the phrases that no one but Jesus could have fulfilled.

What additional prophecy was Gabriel proclaiming would be fulfilled, according to Isaiah 7:14?

____

Look back at Luke 1:34-35. Like Zechariah, Mary also had a question. Compare her encounter with Gabriel to Zechariah's for just a moment (Luke 1:18). Why do you suppose the angel responded differently to the two questions? No right or wrong answer exists for this question.

____

____

____

Whatever the reason, Gabriel met Mary's question with a beautifully expressive response. "The Holy Spirit will come upon you, and the power of the Most High will overshadow you." The Greek word for *come upon* is *eperchomai*, meaning "to … arrive, invade, … resting upon and operating in a person." Only one woman in all of humanity would be chosen to bear the Son of God, yet each one of us who are believers have been invaded by Jesus Christ through His Holy Spirit (see Rom. 8:9). He has been invading the closets, the attic, and the basement of my life ever since. How I praise God for the most glorious invasion of privacy that ever graces a human life!

I wonder if Mary knew when He arrived in her life … in her womb. Our brothers in the faith might be appalled that we would ask such a question, but we are women! Our female minds were created to think intimate, personal thoughts like these! I have at least a hundred questions to ask Mary in heaven.

What would be a question you would want to ask the earthly mom of the infant Christ if you ever get the chance in heaven?

____

No doubt Mary would have some interesting stories to tell. Part of the fun of heaven will be hearing spiritual giants tell the details of the old, old stories. Mary certainly wouldn't have thought of herself as a spiritual giant, would she? I would love to know the exact moment this young adolescent absorbed the news that she would carry and deliver God's Son.

Gabriel ultimately wrapped up the story of the divine conception with one profound statement: "So the holy one to be born will be called the Son of God" (v. 35). The term *holy one* has never been more perfectly and profoundly applied than in Gabriel's statement concerning the Son of God. The Greek word is *hagios,* meaning "holy, set apart, sanctified, consecrated ... sharing in God's purity and abstaining from earth's defilement."

What does Hebrews 1:3 tell you about the holiness of Christ?

Could a teenager have fathomed that she was to give birth to the Son who was the radiance of God's glory and the exact representation of His being? Perhaps Mary's age was on her side. I still have one teenage daughter, and when she tells me something, I always have more questions than she has answers. I'll say, "Did you ask this question?" to which she'll invariably say: "No, ma'am. Never even occurred to me." I want to know every detail. She's too young to realize any were missing!

Mary only asked the one question. When all was said and done, her solitary reply was: "I am the Lord's servant. May it be to me as you have said." The Greek word for *servant* is *doule,* which is the feminine equivalent to *doulos*, a male bondservant. In essence, Mary was saying: "Lord, I am your handmaid. Whatever You want, I want." Total submission. No other questions.

We might be tempted to think: *Easy for her to say! Her news was good! Who wouldn't want to be in her shoes? Submitting isn't hard when the news is good!* Oh, yes, the news was good. The best. But the news was also hard. When the winds of heaven converge with the winds of earth, lightening is bound to strike. Seems to me that Gabriel left just in time for Mary to tell her mother. I have a feeling Nazareth was about to hear and experience a little thunder.

DAY 3
Kindred Hearts

Today's Treasure
"Blessed is she who has believed that what the Lord has said to her will be accomplished" (Luke 1:45).

Imagine again that you are Mary—still 13 or 14 years old, but in a very different culture. You awakened to the sun playing a silent reveille over the Galilean countryside. Among your first thoughts were a Hebrew benediction of thanksgiving for God's covenant reflected in another day. You are oblivious to the selection of this day on God's calendar.

You are an ordinary girl in a humble home. You dress in typical fashion, a simple tunic draped with a cloak. A sash wrapped around the waist allows you to walk without tripping over the long fabric. Still, the hem of your dress sweeps the dusty floor as you begin your morning duties. You are the virgin daughter of a Jewish father, so you have draped your veil over your head and crossed it over your shoulders for the duration of the day. You have never known another kind of dress, so you are completely accustomed to the weight and the constant adjusting of a six-foot-long, four-foot-wide veil. Beneath the veil, thick, dark hair frames a deep complexion and near-ebony eyes.

Without warning, a messenger from God appears and announces that you have been chosen among women to bear the Son of God. You can hardly believe, yet you dare not doubt. As suddenly as the angel appeared, he vanishes. You are flooded with emotions.

What do you imagine you would be thinking and feeling right now?

___

What in the world does a young woman do after receiving such life-altering news? Often God allows the space between the lines of His Word to capture our imaginations and prompt us to wonder. Not this time. He told us exactly what Mary did next.

Read Luke 1:39-56. What did Mary do after receiving Gabriel's news?

___

Glance back a moment to Gabriel's declaration. The most revolutionary news since Eden's fall: "the Savior is on His way." Announcing the soon-coming Messiah, he offered the stunned adolescent an almost out-of-place slice of information. By the way, "Elizabeth your relative is going to have a child in her old age … [she] is in her sixth month" (v. 36).

How like God! In the middle of news with universal consequences, He recognized the personal consequences to one girl. For years the scene of Mary running to Elizabeth has tendered my heart. I'd like to share my thoughts on this moment from my first book, *Things Pondered: From the Heart of a Lesser Woman.* These words were never meant to provide doctrinal exegesis, but to invite us to the momentary wonder of being a woman.

> How tender the God who shared with her through an angel that someone nearby could relate. The two women had one important predicament in common – questionable pregnancies, sure to stir up some talk. Elizabeth hadn't been out of the house in months. It makes you wonder why. As happy as she was, it must have been strange not to blame her sagging figure and bumpy thighs on the baby. And to think she was forced to borrow maternity clothes from her friends' granddaughters. But maybe Elizabeth and Mary were too busy talking between themselves to pay much attention. Can you imagine their conversation over tea? One too old, the other too young. One married to an old priest, the other promised to a young carpenter. One heavy with child, the other with no physical evidence to fuel her faith. But God had graciously given them one another with a bond to braid their lives forever.
>
> Women are like that, aren't they? We long to find someone who has been where we've been, who shares our fragile places, who sees our sunsets with the same shades of blue.[2]

Though wonderful, Mary's news was traumatic. How kind of God to provide someone to share her joy, her peculiarity, her belief in the impossible! I don't think Mary let the dust settle before she headed to Elizabeth's.

Verse 39 says, "At that time Mary got ready and hurried … ." The words *got ready* offer us a delightful possibility. The Greek word for this phrase is *anistemi,* meaning "to stand again; to cause to rise up." Certainly the word could mean Mary simply rose up and departed. The wording could also imply that she got up off her face where she had fallen after the angel departed. The rest of the definition adds "particularly spoken of those who are sitting or lying down; rising up from prayer." If she didn't fall on her face, she was the exception to the rule in such visitations. Both Ezekiel and John the revelator had to be placed back on their feet! Mary may not have taken the news standing up either.

Take a moment to appreciate Mary's challenge. Elizabeth lived 50 to 70 miles from Nazareth. Mary had no small trip ahead of her and no small amount of time to replay the recent events. She probably joined others making the trip to Judea, but we have no reason to assume anyone traveled with her. Can you imagine how different she was already beginning to feel? How did she feel to finally enter the village Zechariah and Elizabeth called home?

What do you imagine was going through Mary's mind as she passed village merchants and mothers with children as they surveyed produce for the evening meal?

____

Finally, Mary entered Zechariah's home and greeted Elizabeth. Mary's words of salutation may have been common, but Elizabeth's reaction was far from common. The infant John jumped within his mother's womb, and Elizabeth was suddenly "filled with the Holy Spirit" (Luke 1:41). The Greek word for *filled* is *pimplemi,* meaning "to be wholly imbued, affected, influenced with or by something." Elizabeth proclaimed Mary and her child "blessed" and asked a glorious question recorded in verse 43.

How does she refer to Christ in this question? ____________

Mary and Elizabeth shared not only tender similarities but also vital differences. Record below the similarities and differences between Elizabeth's and Mary's angelic encounters and subsequent situations:

Similarities	**Differences**
____________	____________
____________	____________
____________	____________

Elizabeth herself pointed out the most profound difference: she was expecting her son; Mary was expecting her Lord. The concepts seem almost unfathomable even with the complete revelation of the Word, so we might ask, "How did Elizabeth comprehend all this?" Remember, she was basically prophesying out of the fullness of the Holy Spirit. Don't miss the riches that follow Elizabeth's inspiring question in verse 43.

Read verses 43-45 and fill in the blanks.
"As soon as the ________________________ reached my ears, the baby in my womb leaped for joy. Blessed is she who has ____________ that what the Lord has said to her will be accomplished!"

Verses 46 through 55 comprise a segment of Scripture often called "Mary's Song." Many scholars also refer to this section as the Magnificat, derived from her words, "My soul glorifies the Lord" (v. 46). *Glorifies*, from the Greek *megaluno*, means "magnify." Mary's unparalleled experience caused her eyes to see evidences of God as if through a magnifying glass. Her wonderful words recorded for all of time offer us an opportunity to catch a glimpse of …

1. *Mary's excitement!* God used Elizabeth to confirm what Mary had experienced. Don't underestimate the weight of the news Mary received. Thus far she had absolutely no physical evidence to bring faith to sight. Imagine how many times on the way to Judea Mary replayed her angelic encounter. She probably wished she could tell everyone she saw, but wondered if they would think she was crazy. At times Mary may have wondered if she was crazy, too!

What confirmation when Mary heard Elizabeth's words! She had probably been too scared to celebrate, but Elizabeth's confirmation set her free! How do I know? Read verse 47 again. The original word for *rejoices* is *agalliao,* meaning "to exult, leap for joy, to show one's joy by leaping and skipping denoting excessive or ecstatic joy and delight. Often spoken of rejoicing with song and dance." Whether or not young Mary began physically jumping up and down with joy and excitement, her insides certainly did! I am totally blessed by the thought, aren't you? Nothing is more appropriate than getting excited when God does something awesome in our lives. I think He loves it! I think He smiled over Mary's sudden burst of enthusiasm … and maybe even laughed out loud.

How does James 5:13 substantiate God's invitation for us to go ahead and act happy in Him when we are?

___

The Magnificat shows us more than Mary's excitement. It also shows …

2. *Mary's love of Scripture.* Mary's song reflects 12 different Old Testament passages! She didn't just hear the Word, she held it to her heart and pondered it. Scripture draws a picture of a reflective young woman with an unusual heart for God.

3. *Mary's dreams of being a mother.* A young Hebrew girl believed nothing to be as important as motherhood. I believe she recalled a favorite Old Testament story when she received the news. The first chapter of 1 Samuel records a young woman's deep yearning to bear a child. God hears her prayer and gives her a son. Just as she promised, she dedicated her son to the Lord.

Read 1 Samuel 1:21—2:10. Pay particular attention to Hannah's prayer or song recorded in 2:1-10. What basic similarities do you see between Hannah's song and Mary's song?

___

I don't think anyone could doubt Mary's familiarity with Hannah's story and song. Surely it was one of the favorites among little Hebrew girls.

4. *Mary's humility.* Her statement "all generations will call me blessed" was not voiced in pride but from shock. Mary reminds me of David, who said: "Who am I, O Sovereign Lord, and what is my family, that you have brought me this far? … Is this your usual way of dealing with man, O Sovereign Lord?" (2 Sam. 7:18-19). In a way, the answer to his question is yes. God seems to love little more than stunning the humble with His awesome intervention.

You and I are not kings nor have we been chosen to bear the Son of God, but we can say that we are blessed, for the Mighty One has done great things for us. Notice that Mary said in verse 50, "His mercy extends to those who fear Him, from generation to generation." That includes ours. God is still mighty in the personal lives of His people.

When was the last time you were stunned by something God did for you and perhaps wondered, "Who am I that You would even look upon me?"

Please don't lose the wonder of Mary's experience. Marvel with me at the fact that she was plain, simple, and extraordinarily ordinary. I always felt the same way growing up. Still do deep down inside. That's part of the beauty of God choosing someone like you and me to know Him and serve Him. May we never get over it.

5. Mary's Hebrew social consciousness. Scripture taught the Hebrews to take care of the poor and be mindful of the oppressed. Mary was aware that God had promised her nation a special renown as a servant-ruler to the world. In verses 54 and 55, Mary is obviously aware of the covenant being fulfilled before her eyes. I'm not sure we can comprehend the mind-set of the ancient Hebrews. Their belief system was not just a religion to them—it was life. God was as much a part of their politics as their religious practices. We can't separate Mary from her culture. To get to know her is to gain insight into the home in which our Savior was reared.

Once again, Luke concluded the segment concerning Mary's time at Elizabeth's with the pen of a man rather than a woman. Verse 56 reads, "Mary stayed with Elizabeth for about three months and then returned home."

Wait a pair of minutes! Did Mary stay until John was born or not? Did Mary get to enjoy with her cousin the precious time of the birth? Did she see the baby? If not, why did she leave just before he was born? I feel like stomping my foot and demanding an answer. Wouldn't do me any good. The answer is not there. Add that to the list of things we want to ask in heaven. One thing for sure: During that three months Elizabeth and Mary had all the quality time in the world to share their hearts and chat about the babies. After all, Zechariah couldn't interrupt.

DAY 4

His Name Is John

Today's Treasure
"And you, my child, will be called a prophet of the Most High; for you will go on before the Lord to prepare the way for him" (Luke 1:76).

Time has a way of passing quickly ... unless you're with child. Pregnancy seems to expand everything—the calendar, the waistline, the hormonal anxiety—turning nine months into a lifetime. Finally the little one arrives and usually the only remaining trace of the longest tenure of a woman's life is stretch marks. Elizabeth's pregnancy flew by in our first week of study, but for her, no doubt time dragged its swollen feet. We're quite blessed to have all the information Luke provided about the two mothers and their extraordinary babies because the other Gospels have little to add. We also benefit from studying the account from the pen of a physician. How wise is our God to dictate four Gospel accounts from the ink of the Holy Spirit and the quills of very different men.

Our reading today will be divided into two parts. Begin by reading Luke 1:57-66. What event brought the relatives together after the child's birth?

What did this event represent to the Jewish people (Gen. 17:9-14)?

____

Can you think of a way in which circumcision, the representation of God's covenant with His people, had extra significance in the life of this child?

____

Nothing brings out family dynamics like a wedding, birth, or funeral. Perhaps God has given me a peculiar sense of humor, but Elizabeth's and Zechariah's run-in with the relatives makes me laugh out loud. Notice that the relatives took it upon themselves to name the new baby. Elizabeth spoke up: "No! He is to be called John" (v. 60). In Hebrew the name was *Johanan*, meaning "the Lord is gracious."[3]

How did the relatives respond to Elizabeth's unyielding response? "There is no one among your relatives who has that name" (v. 61). Listen closely to the narrative and you can almost hear those beloved busybodies whispering ear-to-ear: "John? Who's John?"

Names were not a particularly big deal in my family, so I didn't feel much pressure over naming our babies, but my husband's family had treasured certain names for generations. To make matters a little more emotional, Keith's dear grandfather was ill at the time of our first expectancy, prompting Keith to announce to me, "If the baby is a boy, I think we should name him after my grandfather."

I'm as sentimental as anyone, but Keith's grandfather's name was Leon. I have no idea what prompted me to think so quickly, but I came up with a retort immediately. "Honey, that sounds wonderful, but I think it's only fair that if the baby is a girl, we name her after my grandmother." Being the just man he is, Keith said: "OK, that sounds fair. What was her name?" Minnie Ola. The thought of naming our firstborn child Minnie Moore proved too much for Keith. The subject never came up again.

Elizabeth's relatives were not as easily dissuaded. They weren't taking the name John for an answer. I love verse 62: "They made signs to his father to find out what he would like to name the child." Right here in the introductory chapter of the Gospel of Luke, I believe we have our first recorded game of charades. Take a look back at Luke 1:22. They made signs to him because he made signs to them. The difference was, they weren't mute and he wasn't deaf! Makes me howl every time. Finally, "to everyone's astonishment he wrote, 'His name is John' " (v. 63). Subject closed.

What happened immediately following Zechariah's written statement?

____

Why wasn't Zechariah's tongue loosed the moment the baby was born? Wasn't that the implication of the angel? Look back a moment at Luke 1:20. Notice, Gabriel warned that Zechariah would not speak until the day this happens. Based on the outcome, "this" did not just refer to the birth but to the complete fulfillment of Gabriel's decree in Luke 1:13.

If you look through the entire prophecy issued to Zechariah by the angel, you will find only one specific instruction assigned to the aging priest. What was it (v. 13)?

____

You see, Zechariah could still have adjusted the details like names and lifestyles to his own tastes. He didn't dare. Nine months of silence taught him his lesson. "His name is John." Zechariah's mouth opened, his tongue was loosed, and he began to speak, praising God. The Judean hill country hadn't had this much excitement in years. Everyone got an ear full of good news … and had a mouthful to say about it.

Let's spend the remainder of our time surveying the words that fell from Zechariah's loosed tongue. Read Luke 1:67-80. Theologians often call Zechariah's psalm "the Benedictus." A benediction was a prayer that God might bestow certain blessings on a person or a people. Interestingly, a benediction was customarily spoken over the people by the priest performing the temple service. Don't miss the significance!

Glance back at the earlier segments of Luke 1. When was the last time Zechariah had spoken?

____

Take a look at verse 21. Do you remember why people were waiting for Zechariah? The priest performing the temple duties would customarily return to the courtyard after completing his tasks and bless the people. In other words, he would speak a benediction over them. Nine or so months earlier on Zechariah's big day, the people waited outside for a blessing they didn't get.

Verse 22 tells us that when he came out, he could not speak to them. Due to the number of priests, Zechariah probably received only one chance to perform those special duties. He had accomplished everything else, but he never got to speak that benediction. Months had passed. Elizabeth's tummy had grown. The house was finally filled with the furious screams of a healthy, circumcised son and the rejoicing of friends and relatives. For nine months a benediction had been mounting in the old priest with every fresh evidence of God's faithfulness. When God finally loosed that tongue, it was like a calf loosed from a stall.

Sometimes we praise because we choose to; other times we praise because we want to. Occasionally we praise because we have to—because, if we don't, the rocks will cry out! That's compulsory praise!

Like Mary's, Zechariah's psalm is replete with Old Testament quotations and allusions. Now I'm going to give you a chance to exercise your own expository skills. We don't need seminary degrees to organize biblical thought by outlining Scripture.

Read again verses 68 through 79. Using phrases or brief sentences, outline this portion of Scripture below and in the space on the next page. You may use any classifications or categories you see, filling in pertaining information underneath. I'll give you one idea. Zechariah's words include: a prophecy over the people of Israel, a prophecy over John, and a prophecy over the Messiah. You can use my idea, or you are welcome to categorize the Scripture in your own creative way.

____

____

____

Where do you see yourself in these words of prophecy? In other words, which parts pertain to you or have been fulfilled in your life?

Don't miss verse 78. Why did God enact this intricate, redemptive plan?

The Greek word for *tender* is *splagchnon,* meaning, figuratively, "the inward parts indicating the breast or heart as the seat of emotions and passions." The original word for *mercy* is *eleos,* meaning "mercy, compassion, active pity … special and immediate regard to the misery which is the consequence of sin."

God is many things: a ruling God, a righteous God, a judging God, a holy God. He is also a feeling God. Please meditate on the depth of feeling portrayed through the words *tender mercy.* He feels for us—not only when we are the innocent victims of a depraved world. He also feels for us when we are drowning in misery as a consequence of our own sin. He who knows no sin feels for us who do.

God possesses active pity—He not only feels for us, but also He does something about it. God throws out the Lifeline to every soul drowning in the consequences of sin—we have only to be willing to grab on for dear life. "Amazing grace, how sweet the sound that saved a wretch like me."

Listen closely as we conclude today's lesson. You are God's passion. God's tender mercy is as fresh today as it was in the home of an elderly set of new parents. Our Scripture today concludes with a profound synopsis of John's life: "And the child grew and became strong in spirit; and he lived in the desert until he appeared publicly to Israel" (v. 80). Please note: John was set apart from birth, yet God used time to mature him into a servant who knew how to wield the power of the Spirit he'd been given.

Based only on verse 80, can you see any parallels to the fact that you have likewise been set apart from the time of your "second" birth?

Beloved, God is into growth. We are set apart from our supernatural births, but God uses time to teach us what to do with all we've been given. God's Spirit is immutably and inconceivably strong, but we learn through many processes how to apply that strength to and through our own lives. John will prove to be a man worthy of our meditation. We have much to learn from him … for the Lord's hand was with him.

DAY 5

A Savior Is Born

Today's Treasure
"Today in the town of David a Savior has been born to you; he is Christ the Lord" (Luke 2:11).

As long as I live I will treasure the Christmas of 1981. Amanda was two years old and totally enraptured by the lights, ornaments, wrapping paper, and bows celebrating the season. Strangely, she also was swept up in the wonder of the story. She could have understood only the tiniest fragment, but true to her nature, she received what she knew with tender contemplation.

Melissa was tucked secretly inside me. The timing of the pregnancy was just right for a Christmas surprise. For Keith's grand finale a pair of booties lay strategically under the tree. My parent's small home bulged with excitement. Most of my family members share my personality. We are not small on enthusiasm … or volume. The swirling scents of baking turkey and sweet potatoes bathed in cinnamon, butter, and brown sugar filled the air. Someone announced, "It's time!" and all of us made our gleeful way to the living room and gathered around the tree to hear the old, old story.

I've heard the questions thousands of times: Why do we celebrate this time of year? How do we know when the birth of Christ took place? Why celebrate Christmas at a time originally set for ancient pagan celebrations?

The scrooges are right. We don't know when Christ was born, but I happen to think His is a birth worthy of celebrating at some time of year. God did not just tolerate celebrations and festivals commemorating His faithfulness—He commanded them. His idea! Some were solemn; others were for the pure purpose of rejoicing before the Lord.

On one such occasion Nehemiah said: "Go and enjoy choice food and sweet drinks, and send some to those who have nothing prepared. This day is sacred to our Lord. Do not grieve, for the joy of the Lord is your strength" (Neh. 8:10). The Book of Esther also speaks of an annual day set aside "for joy and feasting, a day for giving presents to each other" (Esth. 9:19).

Before we return to Christmas 1981, take a look at the most concentrated list of feasts and celebrations provided in the Old Testament. Glance at Leviticus 23. If your Bible has segment captions, you might see the chapter organized into seven different feasts. Take a look at the section on the Passover.

Read verses 4-5. What day was the Passover? ______________________

God chose the season of the Passover to be the first month on His own sacred calendar pertaining to planet Earth. The first month falls according to the new moon over the last half of March and first half of April. Look again at the wording in Leviticus 23:5. The timing God assigned to the Passover has significance to all of us who have carried children in our wombs. The 14th day of the first month is the day of conception. If by any chance our God, the God of perfect planning and gloriously significant order, happened to overshadow Mary on the 14th day of the first month of His calendar, our Savior would have been born toward the end of our December. We have absolutely no way of knowing whether or not He did, but I would not be the least bit surprised for God to have sparked His Son's human life on one Passover and ended it on another.

No, I don't believe in Easter bunnies, and I don't have much of an opinion on Santa Clauses, but I'm a hopeless romantic when it comes to celebrating Christmas, the birth of my Savior. Until a further "Hear ye! Hear ye!" from heaven, December 25 works mighty fine for me.

Back to 1981. It was my brother's turn to read the Christmas story. He was a college boy with a deep, passionate voice. Scarcely before he could say, "And it came to pass in those days," Amanda rustled to her knees, shut her eyes, and cupped her plump little toddler hands together as if praying a bedside prayer. She remained frozen in that position throughout the entire Christmas story, her eyes never opening, but her face changing expressions with every event. The tears streamed down our cheeks as we listened to the story as if for the very first time through her ears. Oh, yes, it's a wonderful story! Read the words with a fresh dose of wonder—Luke 2:1-20.

OK, I've had a chance to be nostalgic. What about you? What is your favorite part of this precious story? Use the margin if you need more room.

____

____

Factual to its finest detail, Luke's narrative places the dot on the time line. Caesar Augustus was the ruler of the Roman Empire. From Matthew we learned that Herod the Great was king of Palestine. Herod's reign ended in 4 B.C., so Jesus had to have been born prior to that time.

Why did Joseph leave Galilee at this time? ____________________

Look up the following Scriptures and comment on how they seem significant to the setting of our story.

Micah 5:2 ______________________________

1 Samuel 16:1,13 __________________________

Jeremiah 33:14-16 __________________________

Luke 1:31-33 ____________________________

Fulfilled prophecy demonstrates the incredible veracity of the Word of God. In the specific promises fulfilled by Jesus' birth, we have enough fact to build our faith from now till Christ returns. God purposed that His Son would come out of Nazareth but be born in Bethlehem. So He caused a census to require everyone in the Roman world to return to the place of his or her family's origin. Probably the timing was too close to the birth of the child for Joseph to leave Mary behind. One commentary tenderly suggested that Joseph may not have wanted Mary left behind and subjected to gossip. Remember, he was chosen, too. God looked upon his heart and saw a man who could fill a distinct and difficult role with integrity.

Bethlehem is about five miles south of Jerusalem. If you have a Bible map you'll see that Bethlehem is quite a distance from Nazareth, with chains of hills and mountains in between. Theirs was no easy trip.

We women could be tempted to picket the *New International Version* for leaving out one little detail that had a profound influence on Mary's trip: "Mary … being great with child" (v. 5, KJV). You and I have to appreciate the fact that the verb tense indicates a continuous action. We might say she was getting greater by the minute.

I certainly remember feeling that way. I'll never forget catching a glimpse of myself, great with child, in the distorted reflection of the stainless-steel faucet on the tub. My stomach looked huge, and my head and arms appeared like nubs. From then on I took showers. Taking "great with child" on the road is no easy task. Mary sounds like many of us. How many of our doctors told us to limit travel and certainly not to relocate during a pregnancy? Have you ever noticed how every cataclysmic transition seems to schedule itself strategically during those nine months?

Whether or not Mary and Joseph planned Christ's birth this way, God certainly did. One of my favorite phrases in the birth narrative is humbly tucked in verse 6: "The time came for the baby to be born." The time. The time toward which all "time" had been ticking since the kingdom clock struck one.

Time—the very first thing God ever created. All of Scripture unfolds from the words, "In the beginning, God created … ." Since eternity has no beginning, to what did the "beginning" refer if not to "time"? The words in Luke 2:6 refer to the most important segment of time since the first tick of the clock. The second hand circled tens of thousands of times for thousands of years, then finally, miraculously, majestically—the time came. God's voice broke through the barrier of the natural realm through the cries of an infant, startled by life on the outside. The Son of God had come to earth, wrapped in a tiny cloak of human flesh. "She wrapped him in cloths and placed him in a manger, because there was no room for them in the inn" (Luke 2:7).

Read again Luke 2:8-19. Who were the first to receive the glorious birth announcement?

____

Why do you think God first proclaimed the good news to a motley crew of sheepherders in a nearby field? We can't be certain, but in Scripture God consistently seems to enjoy revealing Himself to common people rather than those who feel most worthy. He often uses the foolish things of this world to confound the wise (see 1 Cor. 1:28). Maybe God had a soft place in His heart for the shepherds watching over their flocks.

Read Ezekiel 34:11-16. What significance do you see?

____

____

Until I researched Luke 2, I always pictured the shepherds in the fields as older men who leaned on their staffs. Maybe because of the shepherds in our Christmas programs when I was young. I definitely had the wrong picture. The youngest boy in the family usually became the shepherd. As a son grew up, he took on more and more of the farming responsibilities and passed the shepherding duties to the younger brother. This job transfer continued until the youngest son became the official family shepherd. The shepherds out in the field were old enough to brave the night with the sheep and young enough to make haste and find the One of whom the angels spoke.

Don't miss the fact that the announcement came to them while they were watching over their flocks at night. Sometimes in the contrast of the night, we can best see the glory of God. Verse 9 tells us that "the glory of the Lord shone around them." Notice the Scripture does not say that the glory of the Lord shone around the angel but around them, the shepherds. Compare verses 9 and 13. As you picture the scene, keep in mind that only one angel, an angel of the Lord, appeared to them first. The other heavenly hosts did not join the scene until after the birth announcement. Most definitely, the glory shone around the shepherds.

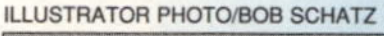

ILLUSTRATOR PHOTO/BOB SCHATZ

A modern-day Arab shepherd with his flock.

Try to imagine for a moment what happened. How do you think the glory of the Lord looked around the shepherds? We don't know for sure; I'm just asking you to express how you're picturing it in your mind right now.

____

____

I am convinced that God wants us to get involved in our Scripture reading. Using our imaginations and picturing the events as eyewitnesses can make black ink on a white page spring into living color. No matter how the glory of God appeared, it scared the shepherds half to death. The words of the angel that followed are so reminiscent of my Savior. Often He told those nearly slain by His glory not to be afraid.

Oh, how I love Him. The untouchable hand of God reaching down to touch the fallen hand of man. "I bring you good news of great joy that will be for all the people." I am convinced our witness would be far more effective if we brought our good news with great joy. Notice the shepherds wasted no time before embracing the news.

The angel then proclaimed the special delivery: "Today in the town of David a Savior has been born to you; he is Christ the Lord" (v. 11). In other words, He is the *Christos*, the *Anointed One*, the *Messiah*!

What was the sign?______________________________

I think you will cherish the meaning of the word *sign*. The Greek word *semeion* means the finger-marks of God, valuable not so much for what they are as for what they indicate of the grace and power of the Doer. You see, a sign is a fingerprint of God, given not so that we will be consumed by the sign itself but by the invisible hand that left the visible print. The angel sent the shepherds to embrace the Baby, not the sign.

The Scriptures tell us that suddenly a great company of heavenly host appeared with the angel, praising God and saying, "Glory to God in the highest, and on earth peace to men on whom his favor rests" (v. 14). Look carefully at those words and behold the awesome proclamation: Through this precious Child, the God of the highest heaven has graced the earth.

Carefully read verses 15-20. Beside each application below, write the portion of the verses that suggests the particular idea.

People who truly encounter Christ in their lives can hardly keep news of Him to themselves.

____

God does not mislead His children. If a message is from Him, it will undoubtedly bear true.

____

Authentic belief in the Word of God is best demonstrated by our actions. As James 2:17 says, "faith … not accompanied by action, is dead."

____

Our authentic testimonies about Jesus Christ can have a tremendous impact on those we tell.

____

At first glance, God seems to give more attention to the shepherds' responses to the birth of Christ than to Mary herself. On a more probing look, however, we discover that verse 19 describes what would have taken volumes to record.

In what two ways did Mary respond to all of the events following Christ's birth?

____

____

The Greek word *treasured up* is *suntereo,* meaning "to preserve." The concept embodies the idea of keeping treasure preserved or safe by holding it close. The word for *pondered* is particularly wonderful. *Sumballo* means "to throw or put together." It is the practice of casting many things together, combining them and considering them as one.

> A host of memories must have been dancing in her [Mary's] head: The angel's appearance. His words. Her flight to the hill country of Judea. Elizabeth's greeting. Their late night conversations. The first time she noticed her tummy was rounding. Joseph's face when he saw her. The way she felt when he believed. The whispers of neighbors. The doubts of her parents. The first time she felt the baby move inside of her. The dread of the long trip. The reality of being full term, bouncing on the back of a beast. The first pain. The fear of having no place to bear a child. The horror of the nursery. The way it looked. The way it smelled. The way He looked. God so frail. So tiny. So perfect. Love so abounding. Grace so amazing. Wise men bowed down. Shepherds made haste—each memory like treasures in a box. She gathered the jewels, held them to her breast, and engraved them on her heart forever.[4]

"In the beginning was the Word, and the Word was with God, and the Word was God. … The Word became flesh and made his dwelling among us. We have seen his glory, the glory of the One and Only" (John 1:1,14).

---

[1]Ronald F. Youngblood, ed., *Nelson's New Illustrated Bible Dictionary* (Nashville: Thomas Nelson Publishers, 1995), 883.

[2]Beth Moore, *Things Pondered* (Nashville: Broadman & Holman, 1997), 7.

[3]Youngblood, *Bible Dictionary,* 687.

[4]Moore, *Things Pondered,* 9.

VIDEO RESPONSE SHEET GROUP SESSION 1

Session 1

Event Timeline

Gabriel appears

Mary

Joseph

Shepherds

Read Matthew 1:18-25. Fill in your vertical timeline.

Event 1: Gabriel delivered the birth announcement to Mary in Nazareth (see Luke 1:26-38).

Event 2: Mary hurried to her relatives in the Hill country of Judean. She remained for "about three months" and then returned to Nazareth (see Luke 1:39-56).
The Greek work *egalio* means to skip, to leap, or to dance for joy.

Event 3: An angel delivered the birth announcement through a dream to Joseph in Nazareth (see Matt. 1:18-23). Consider the profound significance of the title *Immanuel*. The Greek *Emmanouel* is transliterated from the Hebrew *Immanu'el*. *El* means God. The rest of the word means *with us*. Literally, the term means the with us God.

Event 4: Joseph took Mary home as his wife. They remained a short time in Nazareth (see Matt. 1:24-25; Luke 2:4).

Event 5: Joseph and Mary traveled to Bethlehem to register for the census ordered by Caesar Augustus (see Luke 2:1-5).

Event 6: Jesus Christ was born in Bethlehem (see Luke 2:6-7).

Event 7: The angel proclaimed the birth of the Christ to the shepherds in a field near Bethlehem (see Luke 2:8-14).

Event 8: The shepherds hurried to find Mary, Joseph, and the Child in Bethlehem (see Luke 2:15-20).

Event 9: Jesus was circumcised at eight days old in Bethlehem (see Luke 2:21).

Event 10: Jesus was presented to the Lord in the temple in Jerusalem (see Luke 2:25-38).

Read Matthew 2:1-12.

Event 11: Mary and Joseph returned to Bethlehem where they received a visit from the Magi. (wisemen)

Read Matthew 2:13-18.

Event 12: Joseph and Mary took Jesus and flee to Egypt.

Read Matthew 2:19-23.

Event 13: Herod died and Joseph and Mary returned to Nazareth where Christ was raised to manhood (see Matt. 2:19-23; Luke 2:40,51).

WEEK 2

The Son of God

Day 1
The Lord's Christ

Day 2
The Child Jesus

Day 3
Picturing Jesus

Day 4
Wilderness Welcome to Ministry

Day 5
The Preacher

I hope the fresh reminder of the birth of Immanuel was as precious to you as it was to me. God is with us! May we never take the news lightly! Our second week of study unfolds while the Son of God is still wrapped in a tiny blanket of warm, wriggling flesh. Picture a newborn with me. Beautiful dark eyes and skin, squirming in a young mother's inexperienced arms. "Hear" the sounds He makes. Gurgles. Coos. Hungry cries. The Savior of the world has come. That's where we begin today. Our second week of study will accelerate quickly, however, because God chose to share only tidbits of information about the young life of Christ. Week 2 will conclude with Christ's induction into ministry at around 30 years of age. As you can see, we have lots of ground to cover this week and at times we'll have to use our imaginations, under the sound guidance of Scripture, to picture what Jesus was like. He was no doubt the apple of His Father's eye. May He become ours, too.

Principal Questions:

Day 1: According to Isaiah 49:6, why was Christ not sent for the nation of Israel alone?

Day 2: What are some of the inferences in Matthew 13:54-58 regarding a typical home life for Christ?

Day 3: What does Isaiah 53:2 tell us about Christ's physical appearance?

Day 4: If you were doing a character study on Satan (from Luke 4:1-13), what could you learn about him?

Day 5: Based on a comparison of Luke 4:18-19 and Isaiah 61:1-2, what are the phrases that detail Christ's God-given job description?

Babies have a way of grabbing your attention, don't they? I sense One in particular vying for ours this moment. Let's get started and give it to Him. I'll meet you in the Scriptures!

DAY 1

The Lord's Christ

Today's Treasure
"For my eyes have seen your salvation, which you have prepared in the sight of all people, a light for revelation to the Gentiles and for glory to your people Israel" (Luke 2:31-32).

We concluded our first week of study with Mary gathering memorable moments and holding them to her heart. Now the incarnate Christ is only a few days old. Picture Him with me. The infant Christ. Tiny. Deep olive skin. Ebony eyes. Soft, fuzzy hair, probably black as pitch. Fitting in one of Mary's small, young arms. No doubt she rubbed his soft, little head with her cheek, just as every mother nestles an infant.

Few things are sweeter than a new mom and her baby. Just a few days ago, I leaned over to peek at a total stranger's newborn in a stroller, and I looked back up at the mother and said, "Oh, how precious she is!" Tears welled in her eyes and she couldn't even respond. I embraced this darling mom and said, "I so remember how easily the tears come after the birth of a child." I think we are safe to picture Mary the same way. Not only had she experienced the miracle of childbirth with all the physiological changes that make a new mother so emotional, but she also was a virgin giving birth to the Messiah. Can you imagine being Mary—assigned to care for the Son of God? Every new mom battles fear and insecurity. Multiply the emotions many of us felt tenfold. After all, this days-old infant was God's only Son. Don't you imagine she felt pressure to get it right? An imperfect mom with a perfect child.

Our focal text for today is tucked in the center of Luke 2, but pop your knuckles and have your fingers ready to do some walking through the Word. Begin by reading Luke 2:21-39. You don't have to be a Bible scholar to deduce that several important occurrences in the life of a Jewish family are recorded in verses 21 through 24.

What distinct actions did Mary and Joseph take as a result of Jesus' birth?

Followed law ____

Each of the steps Mary and Joseph took after Christ's birth was typical of devout Jewish parents. What made these events altogether atypical is that their infant would ultimately fulfill the prophetic representation of each of these rituals. Let's take a brief look at all three rites: circumcision, redemption, and purification.

1. ***The rite of circumcision.*** Read Genesis 17:1-14.

According to verse 2, why did God appear to Abram?

- ❑ **to tell him he would have a son**
- ❑ **to confirm His covenant**
- ❑ **to rebuke him for turning to Hagar**

What was Abram's and Israel's part in keeping the covenant (v. 10)?

____

Circumcision was so important that verse 11 says, "it will be the sign of the covenant between me and you." Verse 14 says an uncircumcised male, "will be cut off from his people; he has broken my covenant." God told Abram that circumcision was a sign of the covenant; the Hebrew word for *sign* is *oth,* meaning a "mark, token—memorial—proof. It is an indicator or signal of something. It distinguished one thing from another. It was an inducement to believe what was affirmed, professed, or promised." The rite of circumcision was God's way of requiring the Jewish people to become physically different because of their relationship to Him.

Now read Colossians 2:9-15 very carefully. How would this infant later be used to fulfill a different kind of circumcision in believers?

____

In the margin describe how our spiritual circumcision should offer proof that we are different than the persons we originally were.

When the infant Jesus was circumcised at only eight days of age, I'm not sure His parents could fathom that He was the physical manifestation of the covenant God had made thousands of years earlier. Indeed, Christ Himself is God's greatest inducement to believe what was affirmed, professed, and promised.

Write your own paraphrase of 2 Corinthians 1:20 in the space below:

____

____

The Infant Joseph held during that circumcision was the very Yes of God to the promise of His covenant. But this Infant was more. He was also the fulfillment of:

2. ***The rite of redemption.*** Look back at Luke 2:22-24. In these verses two distinct rites were observed by Mary and Joseph. Before we research them, please note that a segment of time has passed between the events of verses 21 and 22.

Read Leviticus 12:1-8.
How many days would Mary and Joseph have waited before they came to bring a sacrifice for purification and present the Child in Jerusalem?______

Before we consider the rite of purification, let's walk through the events in the order Dr. Luke recorded them and consider what Luke 2:22 means. Eight plus 33 days after Christ's birth, Mary and Joseph took Him to Jerusalem to present Him to the Lord.

Read Exodus 13:1-2,11-16. Fill in the blanks using verse 15.

"This is why I _____________ to the Lord the first male offspring of every

womb and _______________ each of my firstborn sons."

Mary and Joseph went to Jerusalem in obedience to this command. Like all devout Jewish parents, they presented their infant to the Lord to depict sacrifice and redemption. When Jewish parents presented their firstborn son to the Lord, they were symbolizing the act of giving him up by saying, "He is Yours and we give him back to You." Then they would immediately redeem him or, in effect, buy him back.

According to Numbers 18:14-16, how much would Mary and Joseph have "paid" to redeem or buy back Christ? __________________

Few doctrines are more important and consistent in God's Word than the doctrine of redemption. The Hebrew word is *padhah*, meaning "to redeem by paying a price."

Read Ephesians 1:3-8. How did Christ come to fulfill for us the very rite Mary and Joseph observed as they presented the Christ child to the Lord?

___

Consider Ephesians 1:7 from the apostle Paul's Jewish perspective. He drew a glorious parallel related to our entrance into the family of God. Since most of us are Gentiles, we are considered the "adoption" in God's family. What was true in a tangible sense after the birth of a Jewish son is true of us in a spiritual sense after our rebirth as "sons" of God. We all must be redeemed. The wonderful picture for us, however, is that we are not bought from God by our natural parents. Rather, Christ buys us from our natural parentage, which is sinful flesh, in order to give us to His Father. If the concept is too confusing, just celebrate, adopted child of God, that Christ has redeemed you!

Before we turn our attention to the third rite Mary and Joseph observed, please look back at the last phrase of Luke 2:22: "Joseph and Mary took him to Jerusalem to present him to the Lord." Jewish families had presented their firstborn sons to the Lord since the giving of the law hundreds of years earlier.

Centuries of parents presented baby boys to the Father. He loved them all, but that day in Jerusalem two new parents presented God with His one and only Son. I'm about to cry just thinking about it. Do you think God smiled? Or do you think He cried? Don't you think He thought Jesus was the most beautiful baby He had ever seen?

An unimpressive looking couple walked into a temple built for the very presence of God—and God had never been more present. No cloudy pillar. No consuming fire. The Word made flesh first entered the temple wrapped in a baby blanket. His earthly parents lifted Him to His Father and, in essence, purchased Him from heaven—for a while—for a lost world. One day that Baby would buy them from earth for the glory of heaven.

3. *The rite of purification.* Read again Luke 2:24. The rite of redemption was distinct from the rite of purification. You actually read about this purification in Leviticus 12:1-8. Please give attention to this text once more. When we compare Leviticus 12:8 and Luke 2:24, it tells us something about the wealth of Mary and Joseph.

How were Mary and Joseph very fitting examples of James 2:5?

___

What does Christ's earthly poverty have to do with us (2 Cor. 8:9)?

___

___

Mary and Joseph offered the least sacrifice permitted by Jewish law for the rite of purification. How fitting that they held in their arms the greatest sacrifice a Holy God could ever make for their eternal purification. Titus 2:14 tells us that Jesus Christ "gave himself for us to redeem us from all wickedness and to purify for himself a people that are his very own." Now let's turn our attention to the touching scenes in Luke 2:25-38. Two deeply discerning people were at the temple the day Jesus was presented.

Describe a few things about each of them in the columns below:

Simeon	Anna
______________________	______________________
______________________	______________________
______________________	______________________

What hints are given in the passages as to why Anna and Simeon might have recognized an average-looking couple's infant son as the Messiah?

____

I hope you listed several possibilities, but one might be that they both were watching and waiting for the Messiah. In a spiritual sense, the same principle is true for us. God constantly reveals His glory to us. The more we prepare ourselves through devotion, prayer, worship, watching, and expectantly waiting, the more likely we will be to see the glory of God (see John 14:21). Let's conclude with Simeon's response and prophecy. One of my favorite titles for my Savior came from this devout man; He called Jesus the Lord's Christ (see Luke 2:26).

Search Simeon's proclamations of praise in verses 29-32. What evidence do you see that God's plan of redemption was offered to all people?

____

You simply must read Isaiah 49:6, a beautiful prophecy fulfilled only by Christ. Why was Christ not sent for the nation of Israel alone?

____

It would have been too small a thing for so great a Savior. God emphasized that the road to redemption would be costly and confrontational. Simeon didn't proclaim only the joy of Jesus as the Lord's Christ. He also spoke painful prophecy. Imagine all that Mary had experienced during the past year. How could she have understood that the infant Son of God would one day cause the piercing of her own soul? Surely the greatest callings of God are the gravest as well.

Are you wondering why we are researching Jewish customs that seem so irrelevant to our present culture? In today's focal text Luke stated our purpose: "according to the Law of Moses" (v. 22); "as it is written in the Law of the Lord" (v. 23); "in keeping with what is said in the Law of the Lord" (v. 24); and "what the custom of the Law required" (v. 24).

Luke was the only Gentile God inspired to write a Gospel, and he reminded his readers of something we must never forget: our incarnate Christ was Jewish. We cannot begin to picture Jesus' earthly walk without becoming a student of His world. This will be one of our chief goals during the next nine weeks.

Untold treasures await us. Some jewels will sparkle visibly like diamonds on red velvet; others will become obvious only by digging in the dark mines. But when our journey is complete, we will have arms filled with treasures to hold to our hearts forever. Come ye who are poor and needy. Unfathomable wealth is hidden in Him.

DAY 2

The Child Jesus

Today's Treasure
"Didn't you know I had to be in my Father's house?" (Luke 2:49).

Have you ever wondered what Christ was like as a child? Now that both my children are basically young adults, I treasure the moments when I catch glimpses of their childhood in something they do or say. Every now and then an expression crosses Amanda's face that looks exactly like when she was a toddler. Sometimes when I sit beside Melissa, stroking her long hair as she sleeps, I see her as a four-year-old all over again.

Today you and I will wonder together what Christ was like as a child. Did His adulthood reflect His childhood? We will attempt to draw a portrait of the child Jesus from Scripture, Jewish tradition, and supposition. We'll consider a few things that may have been typical in Christ's boyhood; then we'll consider a few that were obviously atypical.

In the margin list as many inferences as possible about what may have been Jesus' typical home life based on Matthew 13:54-58.

These verses remind us that Christ grasped average humanity by experiencing it. With the exception of Adam, all men were once little boys, including Jesus. He grew up in a small town with parents who possessed little wealth but came to be rich in offspring. We know Christ had at least four younger brothers and more than one sister. I'm no math whiz, but seven children would have filled Joseph's modest household to the brim.

Please read Luke 2:39-52.

These events that occurred in the temple demonstrate that Jesus was an exceptional child. Amazement over His miracles as an adult demonstrates that God shielded Jesus' young life from the complications of divine acts. Jesus probably did not walk until He was 10 or 12 months old, and He certainly didn't walk on His bath water. He probably gleefully splashed water all over His mother just like our children did us.

As the oldest child, Jesus probably begged to hold a baby brother or sister just like other preschoolers. I don't think Mary left Him to baby-sit from the time He was two or three just because He was the Son of God. I'm certain she watched Him cautiously as He played and explored the outdoors just as we watch our children. When He fell, He bruised. When He burst His lip, He bled. When He needed a nap, He cried.

Interestingly, other elements of Christ's childhood would be normal in a Jewish home but very atypical to Gentiles. Certainly Jesus was reared according to Jewish law and tradition. Joseph would have taken a primary role in His religious upbringing. Jesus read Scripture by the time He was five. At six He probably attended the school of the local rabbi. While still quite young, Christ began memorizing lengthy Scripture passages. One of the first segments of Scripture Christ most likely memorized was Deuteronomy 6:4-9. These passages probably tell us more about the strict Jewish home than any others.

Briefly describe a home that ascribed to these verses:

____

No doubt Christ grew up in a home where these verses were taken literally. At age 10 He would have begun training in the oral law. Long before Christ turned 12, He would have been reciting certain prayers as He arose in the morning, other prayers when He ate and dressed, and still others when He crawled into bed in the evening. I'm not sure we who are Gentiles can begin to comprehend Jewish religious life. Judaism was not a label used to identify where they attended church. Being Jewish was a completely unique way of life that permeated every move they made. Also, by the time we again catch up with Christ at 12 years old, He would already have begun learning His father's trade.

Compare the following two Scriptures. To whom does each refer?

Matthew 13:55 ________________ **Mark 6:3** ________________

Michael, our son of seven years, dearly loved a hammer, nails, and a piece of wood. Most little boys do. Little boys also tend to idolize their daddies. Jesus was probably little more than a toddler when He began to hang around His father's workshop and to hammer a nail into anything standing still. Some of the first blood ever drawn from Immanuel's veins may well have been when a hammer and a nail struck the tender flesh of a tiny apprentice.

Jesus was a little boy, a human little boy, with a little boy's childhood. But consider what made His childhood unique—the "otherness" of Christ. One of Mary and Joseph's children was God Incarnate. The rest were not. Can you imagine calling the Son of God for supper? Or telling Him to wash His hands? If you knew one of your children was the divinely born Son of God, would you want to be certain He ate His vegetables? How in the world would earthly parents rear the perfect Son of God in an imperfect household? When the Word was made flesh to dwell among us, He left a perfect, functional home behind. Far behind. No doubt sibling rivalry loomed.

You can imagine that Mary faced quite a challenge as she tried to give Jesus and His siblings equal attention. On a far more earthly level, you may be in a similar situation. Perhaps you have a child with unusual needs—talents and gifts that require cultivation—while your other children often find themselves as spectators. You may have a child with a superior intellect or one with learning disabilities. Or you may have a handicapped child who requires extra attention and your average children are learning to resent him. I don't believe there are any easy answers to this challenge.

Perhaps Proverbs 22:6 says it best: "Train a child in the way __________

______________ go, and when he is old he will not turn from it."

The verse does not say train all children in the way they should go. Rather, it says train a child in the way *he* should go. I believe this verse suggests that while certain parental principles apply across the board, each child is an individual with a unique emotional makeup and a personal set of needs.

Would you say that anything about your present home or your home of origin is atypical because of a certain family member's needs? ❑ Yes ❑ No If so, in the margin describe the situation.

The more I have opportunity to "interview" fellow believers, the more I'm convinced that often God allows circumstances to exist in our lives that drive us to dependency on Him. Today's text suggests another way Christ's boyhood was very atypical. I believe God orchestrated Christ's childhood to be as normal as possible, considering. Luke 2:41 tells us His family observed certain annual practices common to Jewish culture.

Strict Jews observed three annual pilgrimages to Jerusalem: Passover, Pentecost, and the Feast of Tabernacles. Virtually every Jewish family in a community made the trip. The trip was long, and parents allowed children to run between families and relatives, amusing themselves along the way. They didn't have televisions built into their SUVs in those days. Jesus was 12 years old—only a year from being considered a young man. Mary and Joseph simply assumed He was somewhere in the caravan.

I had the joy of raising my children alongside my best friend of 20-plus years. Numerous times we thought one of our children was with the other only to find the child in the dog bowl or splashing in the toilet. We feel fortunate we didn't leave any of ours while on a vacation somewhere. However, Scripture is clear: Mary and Joseph were frantic. When verse 45 tells us they were looking for Him, the verb comes from the Greek word *zeteo,* meaning "to seek after, look for, strive to find."

How long did they search for Him? ____________________

Where did they find Him? ____________________

I'm not sure anything prompts emotions like finding a lost child. Fear surges through your heart during the search. Relief floods over you when you find the child safe. Then if the child discounts parental concern, emotions surge to vengeance!

Luke 2:48 says, "When his parents saw him, they were ____________."

I think you'll appreciate what the word *astonishment* means. *Ekpletto:* "to strike out, force out by a blow, but found only in the sense of knocking one out of his senses or self-possession, to strike with astonishment, terror, admiration."

In the margin, explain what you think Mary and Joseph felt.

When one of our children does something we perceive as wrong, Keith or I will say, "What do you plan to do about your daughter?" Notice Mary and Joseph were both astonished, but Joseph may have given Mary that "go ahead and deal with Him" look.

Mary was understandably hurt and asked, "Why have you treated us like this?" (v. 48). Yep, this was their first brush with preadolescence. Mary was feeling a tiny prick of that sword Simeon prophesied. She had no idea how much deeper it would one day plunge.

Christ's response suggests that He was as mystified that they'd expect to find Him anywhere else as they were mystified to find Him there: "Didn't you know I had to be in my Father's house?" (v. 49). The words *had to* translate the Greek word *dei,* meaning "is inevitable in the nature of things." Likely this word has never been used more literally. After all, the Father and the Son had the same nature. Christ was drawn to God, not as a devout believer, but as an overpowering magnet—as two pieces of the same whole.

Even though I feel compassionate concerning Mary's and Joseph's fear, I love what they found their Son doing! "After three days they found him in the temple courts, sitting among the teachers, listening to them and asking them questions" (v. 46).

"Listening." I'm so thankful Christ not only speaks, but also He listens. We don't know if God allowed 12-year-old Christ to exercise His full omniscience or to unleash just enough wisdom to astound His listeners. I love the fact that Christ still listens—but not to learn, since He knows all things. Rather, He allows us to pour out our hearts.

"Asking them questions." Christ not only listened but also He asked questions. Contrary to popular belief, faith is not the avoidance of questions. Our faith grows when we seek answers, and we find many between Genesis 1:1 and Revelation 22:21. We may hear a gentle, "Because I said so," to those God chooses not to answer, but I don't believe our Heavenly Father is offended by questions. Part of Christlikeness is learning to listen and ask appropriate questions, even of those you respect in the faith.

"His answers." My favorite part! Not only did Christ listen and ask questions, but Luke 2:47 tells us He answered them! As we study we may see several examples of Him posing a question that only He could answer. Christ certainly uses that teaching method with me. Sometimes He'll cause me to dig through Scripture for a question He seemed to initiate. Other times the question may come as a personalized whisper in my heart: "Beth, why are you acting that way?" Often my honest answer is: "I don't know, Lord! Can You tell me why?" If I really search His heart, sooner or later He'll give me insight into my reactions. As He reveals my insecurities and fleshly defense mechanisms, understanding makes me more cooperative with the subsequent changes.

Can you relate? If so, note ways in the margin.

If the boy Christ could answer difficult questions, surely we can trust the immortal One seated at the right hand of God to make intercession for us (see Heb. 7:25). Whether or not you receive a speedy answer, I believe you are always free to ask questions.

How does asking questions of God differ from questioning God?

___

Before we close, please understand one more thing about questions and answers. In verse 48, Mary asked Christ a question. In verse 49, Christ gave her an answer. Verse 50 tells us, however, that she didn't understand the answer He supplied. There you have it. Another very real possibility: we might ask Christ a question and receive an answer, though we still may not understand the answer—until later. Maybe much later.

In my opinion, Christ's response was quite interesting. I've searched every Greek translation I can find and none of my resources have an original word that directly translates to *house* (NIV) or *business* (KJV). From what I can gather, a more precise translation of Christ's response might be: "Didn't you know that I had to be about my Father?"

That question implies the desire of my heart more than any other I can imagine. I just want to be about God. Not about ministry. Not about my own agenda. Not about writing Bible studies. Not about me at all. When all is said and done, I would give my life for people to be able to say, "She was just about God." That would be the ultimate legacy. "Not that I have already obtained all this … but I press on" (Phil. 3:12).

Dear student, may we live lives that would cause others to be surprised to find us any other place than to "be found in him" (Phil. 3:9).

DAY 3

Picturing Jesus

Today's Treasure
"And Jesus grew in wisdom and stature, and in favor with God and men" (Luke 2:52).

This is an important day in our study because we will begin to form mental images of what Jesus was like physically and personally. My hope is that the pictures we create will remain with us throughout the study.

We will tread carefully because we want to capture an accurate visual even though we will be using our imaginations. I don't want the Jesus we study to remain faceless and devoid of personality. I am asking the Holy Spirit to help each of us form some kind of image of Jesus that we can picture throughout our study. I am praying that you will picture a face and imagine its changing expression with each encounter in Scripture. I believe we have God's full approval to use our imaginations and picture His Son as real and vivid flesh and blood. After all, that's what He sent Christ here to be.

When we first began planning this study, my editor asked, "Beth, have you given some thought to what your primary goal will be as you write about the life of Christ?" I have pondered the question. This is my response: I want you, the reader, to feel like an eyewitness to the life of Christ. I want you to feel the arid Middle-Eastern breezes in your face as He teaches and ministers and to imagine the expressions on His face.

With all my heart I believe God approves of this type of approach because it reflects the very mind-set He seemed to birth in His own people. Ray Vander Laan described a major difference between Western and Eastern thought. He said: "A Westerner like me learns in the Greek way, in the Greek tradition. Truth is presented in words and in careful definitions and explanations. We love bullets … lists and points. An Easterner, however, is much more likely to describe truth in pictures and in metaphors, in the meaning of places and structures. For example, a Westerner might describe God as powerful or loving or all-knowing. An Easterner would be much more likely to say God is my Shepherd or a Rock or Living Water."[1]

During my first tour of the Holy Land, I devoured everything our Jewish tour guide told us and asked him countless questions. Toward the end of the trip, he admitted that at first he could not imagine a woman Bible teacher "knowing anything about the Scriptures," but, as he overheard our teaching segments, God softened his heart and kindled his interest. I was touched when I said good-bye and saw his eyes glistening with tears.

He said: "Miss Beth, continue your digging. There is much to discover. Consider studying the Hebrew language and our approach. You cannot fully picture this Jesus you love so much until you picture Him Jewish in His thinking, teaching, and acting."

I hope, like proper Westerners, we learn through our bullet points and word definitions, but let's also seek to learn through pictures and metaphors. Today let's try to imagine Christ as an Easterner might. Our purpose in using our imaginations is to picture Christ and His encounters as real and vivid, not to worship an inaccurate image. We cannot begin to picture Christ as He is this moment, seated at the right hand of God. We have absolutely no reference point to imagine His holiness. His earthly stature, however, is different. We do have a few reference points to help us create His human visage. Our goal is to lightly sketch a possible picture, not to draw one with permanent ink. Now let's settle into the proper context for today's study.

How old was Jesus at the conclusion of day 2 (Luke 2:42)? ________

How old was Christ when He began His ministry (Luke 3:23)? ________
Luke supplies only two verses spanning those 18 years. Glean every piece of information you can from Luke 2:51-52 and note them in the margin.

During these years, Christ Jesus went from boy to mature man. Verse 52 appears brief and to the point, but actually broadens dramatically our concept of Christ.

Jesus grew in wisdom. The Greek word for *wisdom* is *sophia*. Consider two different segments of the definition because each applies to Christ in Luke 2:52: (1) *Sophia* is skill in the affairs of life, practical wisdom, wise management as shown in forming the best plans and selecting the best means, including the idea of sound judgment and good sense. (2) *Sophia* is in respect to divine things, wisdom, knowledge, insight, deep understanding, represented everywhere as a divine gift, and including the idea of practical application. *Sophia* stands for divine wisdom, the ability to regulate one's relationship with God. As you seek to formulate an impression of what Christ was like in His earthly form, please view Him as completely practical and deeply spiritual. In fact, Christ came to show us that the deeply spiritual is very practical.

God is indeed Spirit (see 1 John 4), but He never intended Himself to be viewed within church walls alone. The fact that He is Spirit enables Him to permeate every level of our lives. If you leave God at church, your life will remain unchanged. God reveals His Word to us through His Spirit (see 1 Cor. 2:10) that we may know a Heavenly God intimately and live an earthly life victoriously.

I am affectionately teased at times by those who love me for not necessarily being the poster child for common sense. I can spend hours researching ancient language translations, then get lost on my way home from work. In fact, the verse they sometimes laughingly apply to me around my office is Luke 1:20: "Behold, thou shalt be dumb" (KJV). I, on the other hand, simply say I am blonder than I pay to be.

When it comes to the Word, however, I have learned both the hard way and the delightfully pleasant way that the spiritual is deeply practical. I encourage you to avoid imagining Christ as so deep you'd have to dig to find Him or so spiritual His head is in the clouds. He came bringing heaven to earth. In today's terms, He was a man who could preach an anointed sermon, then change a flat tire on the way home from church.

Here's the type assignment I love. Read Proverbs 2:6-20. It describes Christ's kind of wisdom. Compare the verses in Proverbs to the two definitions of *sophia* given previously. Classify the verses as describing practical or divine wisdom. Note results in the margin or in your Bible.

No wonder Christ became such a rare teacher! Believing people are starving for a wisdom that is both deeply spiritual and vastly practical. Christ embodied every dimension of wisdom in His earthly life, even before He officially began His public ministry.

Jesus grew in stature. The original word for *stature* is *helikia,* meaning "adulthood, maturity of life, mind or person ... vigor, stature, size." This phrase tells us the obvious: Christ grew physically (and mentally) in the vigor and stature of a man. What is, of course, less obvious is what He grew to look like. God's Word lets us use our permanent markers only once as we try to imagine Christ's appearance. Our solitary source happens to be one of my least favorite verses. God knows my heart and why I feel this way.

What does Isaiah 53:2 tell us about Christ's physical appearance?

____

I simply cannot imagine Christ not being beautiful, but I also believe beauty is in the eye of the beholder. All of us can think of people who are beautiful to us, but whose faces might never be chosen for a magazine cover. Don't read more into Isaiah 53:2 than is there, however. The intent of the original terms is that He didn't have a magnificent, godlike physical appearance that attracted people to Him. The descriptions don't imply that Christ was unattractive, but that His looks were most likely ordinary.

Now let's put down the permanent marker for a moment and pick up our light lead pencils. We can sketch a few more details on our mental canvas through supposition.

His people and part of the world offer a few clues about His physical appearance. His skin was most likely very brown as were His hair and eyes. The men of His culture and era usually wore their hair almost touching the shoulders. They wore it longer if they had taken a vow of consecration (see Num. 6). The texture of their hair was probably as varied as the Caucasian of the Western world. Christ's hair could have been wavy or straight, thick or thin. The most common appearance was probably dark, thick, and wavy hair to the shoulders. Jesus almost certainly wore a beard. His facial features were probably strong, bony, and masculine. The biggest error many painters have probably made in their interpretations of Jesus is a small, almost scrawny stature. In *Jesus the Messiah: A Survey of the Life of Christ*, Robert H. Stein writes:

> Jesus was a carpenter by occupation … . This term can refer not only to a worker of wood but also to a craftsman who worked with stone or metal. Justin Martyr in the second century referred to Jesus' having made plows and yokes. Whether he had additional information for saying this or inferred it from the biblical reference is impossible to determine. As carpenters Jesus and his father, Joseph, were part of the working poor, although it would be incorrect to describe them as destitute. Jesus' occupation required of him physical labor, so the later art of the church that tended to portray Jesus as skinny and weak is clearly in error.[2]

Jesus' daily dress was much like you probably imagine. He would have worn the traditional tunic, girded with a belt, and at times a large cloak called a mantle, which served somewhat as an overcoat. The climate and terrain meant His feet and sandals were more often dusty than muddy. In public Jesus probably wore a turban made of linen. The colors men most often wore on a regular day were tan, beige, brown, and amber tones. Right about now, our men readers are wondering who cares, while our women readers are wondering what He wore to church! So I'll stop while everyone is dissatisfied.

Is anything I've suggested different than you pictured? If so, describe:

___

Jesus grew in favor with God. Oh, how I love picturing the relationship Christ shared with His Heavenly Father. I will limit my comments for now because I don't want to steal the joy of discovery as we search out dimensions of their relationship in the weeks to come. For now, note what the word *favor* means. The Greek word is *charis,* which is often translated *grace* in the New Testament. If you'll refer to Luke 2:40, you'll see the word applied to Christ as early as His boyhood: "the grace of God was upon him."

Charis means "*grace*, particularly that which causes joy, pleasure, gratification, favor, acceptance." Jesus growing in favor with God basically implies that their relationship became an increasing delight to both of them. Among many things I'm anxious to see in heaven, I can hardly wait to see the Father and the Son together. Without a doubt, the relationship between God the Father and God the Son is totally unique.

In the margin write a statement reflecting the common denominator in each of the following Scriptures: John 1:14; John 3:16; John 3:18; John 6:46; 1 John 4:9.

Indeed Jesus is the One and Only—the only begotten of the Father. And the relationship the two of them shared while Christ was earthbound is unparalleled.

Jesus grew in favor with men. As we attempt to formulate a picture of Christ's stature and personality, this description is extremely important. Earlier you read in Isaiah 53:3 that He was despised and rejected by men. Please understand that He was not despised and rejected until He became a complete threat to the establishment. Actually, His popularity was the driving force behind Jesus' opponents' lust for His blood.

In Luke 2:52, God states Christ's favor with men, but throughout the Gospels He demonstrates it. Fishermen don't leave their nets to follow someone void of personality. People didn't just respect Him—they liked Him. The word *favor* is undeniably related to the word *favorite*. One of my daughters dated a wonderful young man for months before she went to college. For some reason, neither of them wanted to be considered boyfriend and girlfriend. When their friends tried to get them to define the relationship, they would simply describe the other as being one of their very favorite people on earth. As a result of that description, they began to refer to each other as "Favorite." They signed cards to each other with that endearment. I would hear her answer the phone and exclaim, "Hi, Favorite!" I loved it. I don't believe we are stretching the text in the least to say that Christ was a favorite of many who knew Him.

Spend a few moments identifying the different characteristics of people who tend to capture your favor. List below some of those characteristics.

____

____

Unless the characteristics you listed are inconsistent with godliness, in all likelihood Christ possessed them. I can readily share a few of my favorite characteristics in people: godly, warm and personable, at least somewhat demonstrative, knowledgeable in a specific area so I can learn from them, trustworthy, and funny!

Let's explore some of our favorites for a moment, assuming we probably share a few of the same ideas. I have the utmost respect for anyone who characterizes godliness, but if they don't also possess some semblance of warmth, my feelings toward them may not progress much further than respect. I know lots of people who are funny, but if their humor is unkind or inappropriate, I am very resistant to choose their company.

Although God's Word tells us that we are not to show favoritism, all of us have favorite characteristics we enjoy in people. I think you can safely assume that Christ possessed many of the dimensions you would favor most. Work with me here while I make one more suggestion that you may or may not choose to sketch on your pencil portrait.

I believe Christ had a warm smile and a great sense of humor. If you can't imagine a godly person as funny, I know some folks you need to meet. The older I've become, the more I've asked God to purge my personality of anything that is inconsistent with godliness. I stopped giving place to inappropriate humor a long time ago, yet dozens of times a week I laugh so hard I can't sit up. Not only are my husband and children hilarious, but also my coworkers, and I laugh hysterically over things that are neither off-color nor unkind. I am convinced laughter is as much a gift of expression as tears.

What does Proverbs 17:22 say about humor?

____

____

Can you imagine that Christ, the Great Physician, would not have used such an effective medicine? Good humor and laughter are far too wonderful not to come straight from the heart of God. One of the surest characteristics of a healthy little one is cackling laughter and smiles. Christ dearly loves for us to come to Him as little children.

I pray that today's lesson will help you pencil a picture of Christ on the canvas of your mind. He was real. His sandals flapped when He walked down the road. His hair was misshapen when He awakened. He had to brush the bread crumbs off His beard after He ate. The muscles in His arms flexed when He lifted His little brothers and sisters. He had hair on His arms and warmth in His palms. He was the Son of God and the Son of man. Fathom the unfathomable.

DAY 4

Wilderness Welcome to Ministry

Today's Treasure

"Jesus, full of the Holy Spirit, returned from the Jordan and was led by the Spirit in the desert where for forty days he was tempted by the devil" (Luke 4:1).

Today we reach a pivotal point in the life of Christ: His 30th year on planet Earth. Suddenly, as if Christ's ministry had been contained in an alabaster box, God broke the seal and began to pour Him forth like fragrant oil.

Based on Luke 2:52, I don't believe Christ was sitting by idly until God took the box off the shelf. We can more accurately picture Christ being suddenly thrust from private ministry to the public domain. The fragrance that had been favored by those closest was about to splash all over Judea. The first splash came from the waters of the Jordan River.

Today we will purposely limit our comments about Christ at the Jordan because I want to share that moment with you "face-to-face" (1 Cor. 13:12) via video in session 2.

Read Luke 3:1-23 and answer just one question that will have your mental wheels turning for our time together:

What did John mean by "fruit in keeping with repentance" (v. 8)?

___

Compare verses 15 and 16. The people were "wondering in their hearts," apparently not aloud, yet John "answered them all" in such a way as to correct and redirect them. Although John was filled with the Spirit, he could not literally read their minds.

How do you think John knew what they might be wondering? Explore as many possibilities as you can.

___

___

Verse 21 says of Jesus, "And as he was praying." About what do you think He might have been praying?

___

Press the hold button on this topic and keep it blinking until you view session 2. Now take a look at Luke 3:24-38. What do these verses record?

____

Let's compare Luke's version of Jesus' genealogy with Matthew's. Refer to both Matthew 1:1-17 and Luke 3:23-38. Where does each writer begin and each writer finish based on the following verses?

Matthew 1:2,16 _______________

Luke 3:23,38 _______________

What do you notice about the order of these genealogies? Choose one.

- ❑ **Both genealogies begin in the past and end with Jesus.**
- ❑ **None of the names in the genealogies overlap.**
- ❑ **The genealogies are in reverse order. One ends with Christ and the other begins with Christ.**

Since Matthew was a Jew and Luke was a Gentile, in the margin describe any conclusions you can make from the fact that one traced Christ's roots to Abraham and the other to Adam.

For the remainder of our lesson, we will discuss the first order of business God ordained for Christ on His messianic mission. Please read Luke 4:1-13 and complete the following:

Why did Christ go into the desert according to verse 1? _______________

If you were doing a character study on Satan from these verses alone, what could you learn about him? Be as thorough as possible.

____

____

If you were doing a character study on Jesus from these verses alone, what could you learn about Him? Again, be as thorough as possible.

____

____

Luke included the genealogy of Christ between the account of Christ's baptism and His temptation in the desert. Mark's Gospel helps us to specifically pinpoint the timing.

Read Mark 1:9-12. What was the time relationship between these two critical events in the life of Christ?

____

My first question about the temptation is, Why did God lead Christ into the desert immediately following His baptism? Likely God's purpose was multifaceted, but I want to offer one possibility: before Christ went public, He had to already determine what type of Messiah He was going to be.

Christ's baptism represented His initiation into public ministry. God was about to present Jesus as His Son and Israel's Messiah. These specific temptations are not those you and I typically fight. Satan probably won't tempt you to turn stones into bread, assume authority over the kingdoms of the world, or throw yourself off the highest point of the temple. Satan is very shrewd. He tailors the temptations to each person's challenges. I believe we would be inaccurate to assume that this encounter between Jesus and Satan represents the sum total of Christ's temptations. I believe we also go to unnecessary lengths to categorize every conceivable sin into the three areas of Christ's temptation. I'm not sure God's Word was meant to be "packaged" so neatly. The rough edges of interpretation keep us learning.

What do Hebrews 2:17-18 and 4:15 tell us about Christ and temptation?

____

I believe that long before He was 30 years old Christ had numerous other temptations exactly like those we face in our day-to-day struggles. God's Word says He was tempted in all ways like us, yet was without sin. What 30-year-old hasn't been tempted? Let's resist seeing this encounter as Christ's all-encompassing grapple with temptation. Christ's experience in the desert represented an intense season of temptation that was tailored by the enemy for the challenges of messiah-ship that lay ahead. I believe some issues were meant to be settled from the very beginning of Christ's ministry. God placed Jesus with His adversary in a lab of sorts to establish the ground rules. With this idea in mind, let's briefly consider each temptation in Luke 4:1-13.

*1. **"Tell this stone to become bread" (v. 3).*** Could Christ? Undoubtedly! So why shouldn't He? After all, He was famished. Matthew 4:2 probably holds the key that unlocks the understanding to this temptation.

Why was Jesus hungry? ____________________________________

Nothing is wrong with eating when a person is hungry, unless a greater issue is involved. Luke 2:37 beautifully describes the most probable purpose for the kind of fasting Jesus practiced in the desert. It describes Anna, the prophetess, who "served God with fastings and prayers night and day" (KJV). No doubt Christ's fast was for similar purposes. Most likely His intent was to seek God and refrain from all distractions. Since we know He was filled with the Spirit and led by the Spirit, we can assume the Spirit prompted the fast; therefore, the fast wasn't over until God said so. What did this temptation have to do with Christ's imminent ministry?

Robert Stein says the issue was whether or not Christ would use His power for His own ends. "Would he live by the same requirements of faith and dependence on God as everyone else in the kingdom?"[3] Satan's strategy wasn't all that different from what he used tempting Eve in the garden (see Gen. 3:1). Think with me about the similarities of the two temptations. In both cases, Satan wanted to sow doubt … but certainly not because he had any. He knew word for word what God said to Adam and Eve and he definitely knew Christ was the Son of God. We can understand why Eve would have bought into doubt, but why in the world would Satan have tried sowing doubt in Christ?

It's at this point in Christ's wilderness temptation that I can really relate. Think of the questions we would have if we encountered an intense battle right after we entered a place or time of ministry.

- Did I misunderstand God?
- If He really loves me, why would He appoint me to such a struggle?
- How could this happen right after my finest moment with God?

We see a second similarity in that the temptation involved food. Christ was hungry. Eve was hungry for something different. Our physical appetites are ferocious. They are fodder for much temptation. Amen?

I find Paul's description of the enemies of the cross of Christ very interesting in Philippians 3:19. He not only says their minds are on earthly things, but he also says "their god is their stomach." Although you and I are not enemies of the cross, we certainly know the temptation of making our stomachs gods. Christ didn't fall to the temptation. Return to Luke 4:4 now and answer this question:

What Scripture did Christ use as an offensive weapon against the enemy?

____

2. ***"If You worship me, it will all be yours"*** *(v. 7)*. This one causes chills up my spine. As my grandmother would say, "The very idea!" We cannot imagine Christ ever being the least bit tempted to worship Satan, but can we not imagine that He might have been tempted to rip Satan's authority out of his hands?

How do the following Scriptures refer to Satan?

John 12:31 ______________________________________

2 Corinthians 4:4 ________________________________

Christ didn't challenge Satan's ability to make such an offer. We can assume Satan had the authority as the prince of this world. It's true the authority God has allowed Satan is limited and temporary, but it is nonetheless very real.

Can you imagine how Christ must feel as He watches the state of the world under the influence of the evil prince's authority? Oppression, violence, and deception characterize the world God loves. Surely Christ is counting the days until He can grab the deed restriction to the world and reign in righteousness.

Satan was hoping Christ would be so anxious to secure the world in the right hands that He'd worship him. Needless to say, Satan was wrong. Christ will most assuredly reign over this world system, but not until all things have happened according to God's kingdom calendar.

How did Christ respond to His adversary in this temptation?

____

Christ adamantly resisted worshiping Satan as a way to gain the world. In the margin describe what Christ's attitude says about the phrase, "the end justifies the means."

3. *"Throw yourself down from here" (v. 9).* Based on Christ's response to this temptation, we know that at least one of Satan's intentions was to tempt Christ to put God to the test.

What do you think "putting God to the test" means?

___

I'm pretty confident that you have the general idea. One way of putting God to the test might be disguising a dare by calling it faith. Challenging God is not only void of faith; it is also foolish.

Consider each of the following scenarios. Which could be examples of testing God? More than one answer may be correct.

- ❑ **a self-prompted refusal to seek medical attention for serious illness, followed by a public proclamation of God's obligation to heal you**
- ❑ **racing a car and saying God is responsible for keeping you from injury**
- ❑ **believing certain rules of propriety and accountability don't apply to you because you're in church leadership**

I believe any of these examples could put God to the test. Now let's think of an example that represents a risk in our own lives. This exercise will alert us to ways Satan might tailor our temptation to put God to the test.

Describe a way Satan has tempted or might tempt you to put God to the test.

___

___

Satan may have had a second intention in this particular temptation. The placement of the temptation at the temple suggests that the enemy may have been hoping a dramatic scene would cause the Jews to hail Jesus as their king before He faced the cross.

How might John 6:14-15 support this possibility?

___

___

If Christ had foregone the cross, He would have been no less God, but we would be lost. In conclusion, I believe our hypothesis was correct. These were no ordinary temptations. They appear to be direct assaults on the messiah-ship of Christ. We can, however, draw a few closing applications.

- First, seasons of intense temptation are not indications of God's displeasure.
- Second, Satan is tenacious. Don't expect him to give up after one or two tries.
- Third, Scripture is the most powerful tool in our fight against temptation. Don't fight back with *your* words, fight back with God's!

DAY 5

The Preacher

Today's Treasure
"The Spirit of the Lord is on me, because he has anointed me to preach good news to the poor" (Luke 4:18).

Today's Scripture reading is so dear to me. I was a mess before the Savior set me free. That's why my dearest life passages are the ones found in Isaiah 61:1-2 and quoted again in the Gospel of Luke. Please read this passage with me: Luke 4:14-21. Do you know this Jesus? Once you do, you can't get over Him. God allowed me to write an entire study based on these verses; yet even now as I read them, I cannot help but cry. I owe Jesus everything. Every breath. Every word out of my mouth. Not because I can repay Him, but because I love Him so. Even as a believer, I continued to live in defeat. Abundant life was not mine until I let the Healer set me free, not just from hell but from myself.

OK, I'll get a grip and we'll see what fresh word God will bring us today. First consider verse 14: "Jesus ... returned to Galilee."

Where had He been (Luke 4:1)? ______________________

How does verse 14 describe His state of being? ______________________

Don't miss the significance! Jesus went into His wilderness temptation full of the Holy Spirit. He returned from the wilderness in the power of the Spirit. After all He had suffered? We picture ourselves emerging from intense seasons of temptation or trial "by the skin of our teeth." Wounded. Half dead. Limping forever.

Jesus, on the other hand, came from the battle with an annointing of power. Scripture tells us He taught in various synagogues and word of Him spread through the whole countryside. Christ then set His sights on Nazareth—His hometown. I wonder what He was thinking as He rounded those familiar hills and gazed upon the village, no longer as a fellow citizen but as a saving Servant.

No doubt Jesus received warm embraces, even kisses on His cheeks, as He walked the village streets. Merchants probably called His name and welcomed Him back, not because He was the Son of God but because He was a native son. We can safely assume Christ ducked His head through His family's own front door and probably slept there until He went on the road with His disciples.

By this time most of His siblings probably were also grown with families of their own. His brothers' homes were most likely "add-ons" to their father's. Jesus' family members probably had feelings toward Him ranging from curiosity and confusion to animosity and jealousy. A single Jewish man making the road His home was highly irregular. They probably loved Him, but they most assuredly didn't understand Him.

Jesus returned to Nazareth with power He had never manifested there. Still, He didn't throw the defining explosive until the next Sabbath. Although Jesus regularly went to the synagogue, on that day a fresh breeze blew in. He stood up to read.

Based on verse 17, what obvious differences exist between our Bibles and their scrolls?

____

Old Testament Scripture, which included the five books of the Law and probably the Psalms and the Prophets, were meticulously copied by hand onto parchment, usually by scribes. The parchment was then rolled into scrolls and placed in cabinets or what is called a Torah ark. They removed one scroll of Scripture at a time. Luke's description accurately reflects the custom of the designated reader. Jesus stood up to read. He was then handed the scroll that, not coincidentally, was the Book of Isaiah, the book containing more prophecy about the earthly venture of Christ than any other.

Picture the scene. The synagogue was the center of Jewish community life, so it was undoubtedly buzzing with activity. The structure was rectangular and its typically ornate triple doors usually faced Jerusalem. As Christ walked through the doors, He passed three or four pillars and several stone benches on the edges of the room. Most of those attending sat cross-legged in the floor. Undoubtedly, many of them knew Him personally. Customarily, the designated reader was handed the scroll chosen for the day and, after reading the passages at a lectern, he handed the scroll back to the attendant, sat down in front, and offered instructional commentary. Imagine the authority and power that must have accompanied Christ's voice that day.

What were the people doing when He sat down?

____

With every eye glued to Him, Jesus began with a stunning eight-word synopsis: "Today this Scripture is fulfilled in your hearing" (v. 21). The Greek word for *fulfilled* is *pleroo*, meaning "particularly, to fill a vessel or hollow place." To demonstrate His play on words, go back and read aloud Luke 4:18-19 and insert the name *Jesus* every time you see the word *me*. Could anyone else in all of history fill this position? No matter how many priests, prophets, and kings had served the nation of Israel, this calling was Christ's alone. Until then, the long-awaited position remained unfilled. How aptly this applies to us as well. We remain hollow until the only One suited for fulfillment is allowed to take His proper place. Luke 4:18-19 constitutes somewhat of the job description God assigned to His chosen One.

Compare the Luke 4:18-19 list with the original in Isaiah 61:1-2. You will notice a few differences. In the margin list every descriptive phrase compiled from both lists.

One very clear difference between the two texts is that Jesus abruptly stopped reading without saying "and the day of vengeance of our God" (Isa. 61:2). He had a very good reason. He read only what God was immediately fulfilling through Him. When Christ returns, He will come for His own, but He will also come with a vengeance. In His first advent, however, God purposely sent Christ with a different agenda.

Let's practice a little creative thinking. Based on Christ's job description, what would have been a good name for His ministry? For instance, because I am such a recipient of Christ's grace, I call my ministry "Living Proof." I hope I'm living proof God can forgive, transform, and use anyone! Give His ministry a name that summarizes Luke 4:18-19.

____

I think you'd have fun sharing these in small group. I wish I could hear them! Now let's briefly discuss each description:

1. *"The Spirit of the Lord is on me, because he has anointed me to preach the good news to the poor"* (*Luke 4:18*). Christ didn't mean the financially destitute. The Greek word for *poor* is *ptochos,* indicating "utter helplessness, complete destitution, afflicted, distressed." I think God is far too faithful to let anyone make it through life without confronting seasons of utter helplessness. Look at the remainder of the definition: "subsisting on the alms of others." We know what that means in the physical and monetary sense, but since we know Christ was referring to far more than finances, let's think about another application.

God created us to need something or someone else. Sooner or later, any healthy individual discovers that autonomy doesn't cut it. Once we confront our need for someone or something beyond ourselves, we will subsist on the alms of others if we don't discover Christ. Like beggars we go from person to person with our empty cup, crying, "Can't you add anything to my life?" They might throw in a coin or two. In fact, a few may be weekly … and probably weary … tithers. But when we shake the cup, the tinny echo reminds us how empty we remain. Until we allow Jesus to fill our cups daily, we simply subsist. The good news Christ may want to preach to you today is that you don't have to subsist. You were meant to thrive.

In the margin write the names of a few of the tithers to your cup. In other words, who makes fairly regular contributions to your life?

How did you last discover that their contributions were not enough?

____

Sooner or later, God will make sure we confront the poverty of living on the alms of others so that we may learn to feast on Him.

2. *"To heal the brokenhearted"* (*Isa. 61:1*). Unless you're using a *King James Version,* this phrase probably came from the Isaiah reference. Some New Testament translations include it, while others don't. Either way, the phrase was in the original job description and is worthy of our consideration. The original word for *brokenhearted* is *suntribo,* meaning "to break, strike against something … break in pieces … to break the strength or power of someone." The Greek word for *heal* is *iaomai,* meaning "to heal, cure, restore." I love the Hebrew word translated *heal* in Exodus 15:26 when God introduced Himself by a new title: "I am the Lord, who heals you." The word *raphah* means "to mend (by stitching), repair thoroughly, make whole" (*Strong's*).

Visualize this divine ministry for a moment. What things are implied in mending a broken heart by stitching?

____

I'd love to know your thoughts. Perhaps you thought of many other things, but I picture God focusing steadily on the object of repair. One stitch follows another. It takes time. I picture painful penetrations of the healing needle. I don't know about you, but I'm quite sure if my healing processes had been painless, I would have relapsed.

3. *"To proclaim freedom for the prisoners"* (*v. 18*). Is anybody but me giving this a hearty "Amen"? In many ways I was like the prisoners in Psalm 107:10-16,20—long after my salvation.

Why were they in chains? ______________________________

How were they set free? ______________________________

Many people sincerely love God, but I don't think anyone stands to appreciate the unfailing love of God like the believer finally set free from failure. This captive can undoubtedly testify: He sent forth His Word and healed me. Stitch by stitch. Please notice that Christ proclaimed freedom. He didn't impose it. It remains an offer.

4. "Recovery of sight for the blind" (v. 18). Although Christ would heal many from physical blindness, I believe His intent here was a far more serious kind of blindness.

Second Corinthians 4:4 describes this blindness. What is it? __________

____

I found the original word for *blind* in both Luke and 2 Corinthians to be so interesting. *Tuphlos,* from the word *tuphloo,* means "to envelop with smoke, be unable to see clearly." This definition implies far more than the blindness of the unbeliever. Can you think of a few things the enemy has used to keep you from seeing clearly at times?

Perhaps there is no time when the enemy attempts to cloud our vision like our fiery trials. His job is to keep us blinded to the One who walks with us through the fire. Oh, believer, He's there whether or not our spiritual eyes discern Him.

5. "To release the oppressed" (v. 18). I looked up every single definition for *oppressed* in the Greek and Hebrew dictionaries. A half dozen original words are translated in the Bible with our single word *oppressed,* and all but one have the word *break* in the definition. So why would that be significant? Because I'm becoming more and more convinced that heavy-duty oppression, which in essence is external oppression with the intent of breaking its object, is Satan's counterfeit for biblical brokenness.

At times I've fought back the tears as I've heard testimonies of people who had been utterly unable to function, describing themselves as broken by God. I don't think God's brand of brokenness is total emotional wreckage. God's intent in breaking us is bending our stiff knees so that we will submit to His authority and take on His yoke. His aim is our abundant and effective life. Being totally unable to function because the mind and emotions are in shambles is Satan's counterfeit. Praise God, Christ can certainly use Satan's counterfeit brokenness to bring us to a place of accepting His own, but I think we credit some things to Christ that He didn't do.

6. "To proclaim the year of the Lord's favor" (v. 19). That year those gathered in the Nazarene synagogue were staring in the face of the Lord's favor—His blessed gift of grace, Jesus Christ. The word *year* can be translated as "any definite time." God places before each of us a definitive period of time to accept the Lord's favor. He wills for none to perish, but for all to come to repentance (see 2 Pet. 3:9). The world has until His return. The individual has a definitive period of time known by God alone. I am not a "hellfire and brimstone" teacher, but I am not past begging people not to wait too long-for salvation, because eternal life in heaven is at stake, and for freedom, because abundant life on earth is at stake. He longs to be your Champion now.

---

[1]*Faith Lessons on the Life and Ministry of the Messiah,* prod. and dir. Bob Garner and Stephen Stiles, vol. 3, video one, "In the Shadow of Herod," 77 min., Focus on the Family, 1996, videocassette.

[2]Robert H. Stein, *Jesus the Messiah: A Survey of the Life of Christ* (Downers Grove, Ill.: InterVarsity Press, 1996), 84.

[3]Ibid., 106.

VIDEO RESPONSE SHEET GROUP SESSION 2

Session 2

Introduction: This week we watched Mary and Joseph present the infant Christ, the Son of God, to His Father at the temple. We also appreciated the anxiety these chosen parents experienced when the 12-year-old Jesus remained in Jerusalem after they departed for Nazareth. We then considered what the unrecorded years of Christ's adolescence and young manhood might have been like. Day 4 centered on His wilderness temptation and day 5 pictured Him at the podium in the Nazarene synagogue reading His own job description from the Book of Isaiah. This session focuses on the ministry of John the Baptist and the baptism of Jesus.

Read Luke 3:1-23.

1. A task of Preparation.

John's primary task was to make straight paths for the coming Messiah. The original Greek word for *paths* in Luke 3:4 is *tribos*, which means a beaten pathway

2. A significant location.

Matthew 3:5 states the people went out from Jerusalem and all Judea and the whole region of the Jordan and were baptized by John in the Jordan River.

The name Jesus is Joshua in Hebrew.

The word for consecrate (or sanctify) in Hebrew is qadhash, which means to be clean, dedicated, declared holy, treated as holy.

The Hebrew word pala means wonders or "to be separate, distinguished, singular, extraordinary, marvelous, miraculous."

3. An unexpected visitation.

(See Luke 3:21; Matt. 3:13-15.)

4. A glorious representation

Confession means

- Acknowledgement
- Agreement

5. A divine demonstration.

(See Luke 3:22; Matt. 3:16.)

6. A paternal proclamation

(See Luke 3:22; Matt. 3:17.)

WEEK 3

The Way and Life

Day 1
"What Is This Teaching?"

Day 2
A House Call

Day 3
A Catch in Deep Waters

Day 4
If You Are Willing

Day 5
The Lord of the Sabbath

Ministry is never easy. It's also rarely uncomplicated. You and I are called to ministry whether or not it is a full-time vocation. Keep in mind a point so obvious it's almost obscure: Christ was the first person God ever assigned to "Christian" ministry. He set the precedent. We can learn much from watching how He handled fickle crowds and difficult circumstances. That's what our third week of study is all about. Mark 10:45 tells us Christ didn't come to be served but to serve. However, not everyone Christ met wanted what He had to serve. We can certainly expect the same response at times. But we'll never see a single situation cause Christ to flinch from what His Father called Him to do. He had a "made-up mind." His example will challenge us this week as we take deep stock of His goals and His methods. May "His way" become ours.

Principal Questions:

Day 1: What is your understanding of the events in Luke 4:22-30? How did the crowd's mood change when Christ confronted them?

Day 2: Why do you think healing the sick was not the absolute priority work Christ came to accomplish?

Day 3: What conclusions can you draw from the kinds of people Christ called to do things His way?

Day 4: How did Jesus see the faith of the paralytic and his friends (Luke 5:20)?

Day 5: Based on Luke 6:7, what were the Pharisees and teachers of the law looking for?

I love this point in a Scripture journey. After two weeks of study, the foundation is poured and fresh habits are forming. Let's not miss a single truth this week, beloved. Let your mind and heart be completely immersed by the Spirit of God through His Word.

DAY 1

"What Is This Teaching?"

Today's Treasure
"All the people were amazed and said to each other, 'What is this teaching? With authority and power he gives orders to evil spirits and they come out!' " (Luke 4:36).

Our previous lesson centered on the glorious job description of the Anointed One. In an ideal world, a gracious offer made would be an offer received ... but this is no ideal world. Before the dust of a rolled-up scroll could settle, the fight was on. Glance back at Luke 4:17-21 to refresh your memory; then begin your reading with Luke 4:22-30.

After your reading, check any of the following statements which reflect your reaction to Christ's statements in the passage.
- ❑ **Jesus didn't seem to even give them a chance.**
- ❑ **Jesus seemed to be picking a fight with them.**
- ❑ **The listeners must have been faking their initial favorable responses.**

If I hadn't studied Scripture for a number of years and learned to recognize behavior that was characteristic of Christ, I might have marked the first two statements. I tend to cheer for the underdog, and strictly from appearances, I might have been tempted to think Jesus didn't seem to give them a chance. Since we know His heart was perfect and patient, something more was going on in that encounter than meets the eye. Murky waters like these force us to dive in and see what's stirring on the bottom. Two considerations may help us to understand Christ's prophetic confrontation.

First consider the original wording. Verse 22 tells us that "all spoke well of him." The words *spoke well of* come from the Greek word *martureo,* meaning "to be a witness, bear witness ... to be able or ready to testify." The word *amazed* is the Greek word *thaumazo,* meaning "struck with admiration."

Either of these words could be used by spectators after attending any rock concert and being impressed by a talent. The wording suggests that they were impressed by Christ's delivery—not so much what He said, but how He said it. Galileans were not known for smooth speech. Quite the contrary, they were considered by many in the other provinces to be uneducated and crude. The crowds who heard the apostles preaching in foreign languages on the Day of Pentecost said, "Are not all these men who are speaking Galileans?" (Acts 2:7). The crowd at the synagogue in Nazareth was reacting similarly when they asked, "Isn't this Joseph's son?" in Luke 4:22.

Let me draw on my experience and offer a possible explanation. After delivering a message, nothing hits me like cold water more than someone saying, "You are a great speaker." First of all, I know better than that. I have a thick accent and use tons of country colloquialisms. Far more importantly, though, if someone makes a statement like that, I know either I failed miserably or the person didn't get it.

Jesus can't fail, so obviously, they didn't get it. Personally, I believe He may have been responding to their grading His speech with an "A" rather than receiving His message.

Grab a spiritual stethoscope and perform a quick heart check. When you hear a message, do you tend to grade it or receive any possible insight, no matter how elementary the message or unpolished the messenger?

Like those who gathered in the Nazareth synagogue, we could be impressed with a message but never let it beat past our eardrums into our hearts. Notice a second consideration: the velocity of the crowd's change of mood.

Fill in the following blanks from your understanding of the events:

The crowd's mood went from __________________________ to

____________________ in the moments of Christ's confrontation.

The word in the text for *furious* comes from the word *thuo,* meaning "to move impetuously, particularly as the air or wind, a violent motion or passion of the mind." The north wind of their admiration suddenly reversed into a south wind of tornadic proportions. When a mood can change in a matter of moments from admiration to murderous fury, something is amiss.

I have learned some very hard lessons in ministry. One is that some people in the religious world make idols or stars out of Christian speakers or singers. A fan can turn to foe with mind-boggling velocity. You don't have to be in a ministry that places you in front of people to know what I'm talking about.

Have you seen a dramatic and sudden mood swing in an individual or group? ❑ Yes ❑ No If so, what were you thinking as you witnessed it?

____

Unsettling, isn't it? Don't forget that the people Christ addressed in Luke 4 were very religious. Unchecked anger can easily lead to uncontrolled behavior regardless of how much we attend church. The synagogue members tried to kill Jesus.

Please fill in the following blank according to verse 30: "But he walked right through the crowd and ______________________________________."

Allow these words to represent far more than a simple getaway. Based on what follows in the chapter, I believe Christ's experience in Nazareth was a pivotal moment in His life. He had to choose to either perform ministry their way or His way.

What do you think their way would have been?

____

The types of crowds Christ encountered two thousand years ago still fill many churches today. Many congregations want to hear impressive A+ messages, but the messenger better keep his confrontational thoughts to himself. The same committee that throws out the red carpet to a new preacher may eventually roll him out the door in it! Meanness at church sometimes exceeds anything that occurs in secular surroundings. As James 3:10 says, "My brethren, these things ought not so to be" (KJV).

For the remainder of today's lesson and this week's study, we're going to watch Jesus do things His way. You can be sure His way won't likely be conventional.

Read Luke 4:31-37 and complete the following:

Where did Christ go after departing His hometown? ____________________

These verses constitute the first account of Christ's miraculous works recorded in the Book of Luke. According to John 2:11, Christ's first miracle was performed at the wedding in Cana. But I believe we are safe to assume the miracle Luke mentioned here is among the earliest of Jesus' signs and wonders.

Christ's earthly ministry was hardly launched before the demonic world confronted Him—in a synagogue, no less. Thank goodness, Christ isn't spooked by the demonic world. No matter what authority Satan and his subjects have been temporarily allowed in this world system, Christ can pull rank any time He wants. On that day in Capernaum, He wasted no time.

Take a moment to note the specific demonic actions. Which of these words characterize the demon's reaction to Christ? (Check one or more.)

❑ **fearful**	❑ **arrogant**	❑ **contemptuous**
❑ **loud**	❑ **attention getting**	❑ **intimidating**

Compare this demonic encounter with one the apostle Paul experienced in Acts 16:16-18. List every similarity in the two encounters.

____

____

Among your comparisons, you may have noted that both encounters occurred in places meant for practices of devotion to God such as prayer, worship, and study. Another similarity is that both demons appeared to desire attention. We can assume the demon was loud in Luke's account because Christ adamantly told him to "Be quiet!" Acts records the demon shouting. I'm certainly not suggesting that all demonic activity is loud. I am asking you to consider that when allowed to penetrate a place meant for practices of devotion to God, one of their chief tactics is to divert attention.

I have witnessed this tactic. At a recent conference a woman began to shriek right after someone prayed and before I was to speak. The wise and godly woman leading the conference immediately went to the microphone and dealt graciously but firmly with the outburst. Although I've not often observed that type behavior, the few times I've experienced it, I discerned a tactic of the demonic world to divert attention. I'm not talking about precious children rattling papers or innocent babies crying. I'm talking about intrusive disruptions that leave little doubt of origin.

You may have noted at least one more similarity between the two demons in Luke 4 and Acts 16. Both seemed to be telling some semblance of the truth. John 8:44 tells us that there is no truth in the devil, and we can assume this applies to all his unholy flock. We see a distortion, or misuse of the truth, in both these accounts. Both were acting as counterfeit preachers of sorts. They could not stop the truth so they hoped to disqualify the message by the instability or insanity of the apparent messenger.

Some years ago, a strange thing happened at our church. Each Sunday, for six or seven weeks, a man who appeared to be mentally ill would stand outside the main doors and "preach" to us using a megaphone as we left the building after worship. Some of the statements he made were technically scriptural, but his appearance and his approach demonstrated such instability that he did more to detract people from the truth than attract. The typical listener's tendency would be to disbelieve anything he said simply because he was the one saying it. I have no idea if he was demon-possessed, but I would not be surprised, even though many of the things he said came from Scripture.

A new dimension of spiritual warfare was erupting as Christ began His earthly ministry. Let's have a quick history lesson so we can recognize the new dimension introduced today. Thousands of years ago, war was declared in the heavenlies when Satan was booted out of heaven. I believe that each of the following Scriptures portrays aspects of the origin and nature of Satan. Begin by reading Ezekiel 28:11-17.

Who was Satan originally (v. 14)? ______________________________

What was he like (vv. 12-13)? ______________________________

Why was he cast from heaven to earth (vv. 15-17)? ______________________

Now read Isaiah 14:12-15. What did Satan want before he fell from heaven?

____

Many biblical scholars believe Revelation 12:3-4 also speaks of Satan's banishment from heaven.

Who are we told the dragon symbolizes in Revelation 12:9? ____________

Obviously the dragon in Revelation represents the devil. Many commentators also believe that the "third of the stars" in verse 4 represents a third of the angels in heaven. They believe these fallen angels are now called demons. Remember, unlike God, Satan cannot be in all places at once; therefore, many demons do his worldwide bidding.

In week 2, day 4, we established that Satan is presently the "prince of this world." Although war was declared in the heavenlies at the moment of the angelic division, Christ had not come in human form to challenge the devil on his own turf until now. We don't even have to wonder how unwelcome Christ's presence was to the demonic world. Christ's transcendent power is obvious in Luke 4:35. The moment He commanded the demon to "come out," the demon received a compulsory expulsion.

Compare Luke's version of these events with Mark 1:21-28. What one piece of information supplied in Luke 4:35 is not included in Mark 1:26?

____

I think this is one of many times we profit from Luke's perspective as a physician. He couldn't help telling us that the man wasn't injured. Matthew, a former tax collector, had much to say about stewardship. In the same way, Dr. Luke, more than any other Gospel writer, pointed out more about the physical condition of the people Christ encountered.

Christ's encounter with the demon-possessed man concludes with the introduction of a vital word. Both Mark and Luke record the crowds remarking that Jesus' teaching possessed a totally distinctive element. He taught with authority.

No greater concept exists where you and I are concerned than the authority of Jesus Christ. Even the atonement. For if He has no authority, His act of atonement would have been sacrificial, but powerless. The life of Christ unfolding in our study during the weeks to come will say volumes about authority. From this point forward, be on the lookout because what we do with Christ's authority determines what He does with us. He's not just good. He's God.

DAY 2

A House Call

Today's Treasure

"He bent over her and rebuked the fever, and it left her. She got up at once and began to wait on them" (Luke 4:39).

This Bible study is the first God has given me that focuses entirely upon the life of Christ. *A Woman's Heart* revealed Christ through the Old Testament. *A Heart Like His* reflected the heart of Christ through King David. *To Live Is Christ* showed what can happen when the worst of sinners abandons his life to Christ. *Living Beyond Yourself* woos believers to live in the fullness of the Spirit of Christ. *Breaking Free* portrays an impossible dream without the power of Christ. But this is the first one I've written that is Christ and nothing but the Christ. And it's a problem.

Do you know why? Because every day, after studying the text, I stare at the computer and want to begin the entry with, "Oh, how I love Him." No new words. Nothing creative, nor even particularly profound. Just true. I keep telling myself, "You can't start with the same words every single day!" Fine, then. But that's what I'm thinking.

Please read Luke 4:38-44. Also look back at Luke 4:15-16,31 and refresh your memory about the places where we've "seen" Christ teach and minister so far. Now compare it with Luke 4:38 and complete the following:

What very significant place has now entered the picture? ____________

What ministry did Christ perform there? ____________

What did she do after Jesus healed her? ____________

What happened when the sun was setting? ____________

Based on our discussions in the previous lesson and any new insights you gain from today's text, why do you think Jesus silenced the demons?

____

Why do you think Jesus went out to a "solitary place" (v. 42)? List as many possibilities as seem reasonable to you.

____

____

Why do you think the people tried to keep Jesus from leaving them? List as many possibilities as you can.

____

____

Why was Christ sent? ____________

These passages lend themselves to at least five insights into the life of Christ.

1. *Jesus made house calls.* We see the platform for Christ's ministry broaden from the synagogue to include the home. What a relief to know that God doesn't just go to church, He goes to our homes! When I was a little girl, I was fairly certain God lived in our church baptistry. My vivid imagination turned dressing-room doors into secret doors that led into the mysterious dwelling of the divine boogie man. I am happy to report that God doesn't live in the baptistry. He lives in the hearts of those who trust Him and in the homes of those who provide Him room. Sometimes we don't bother to summon Jesus Christ into our homes until we are overwhelmed by threatening circumstances.

One person suffering in a home is enough to affect all who live within. Simon's mother-in-law was suffering from a high fever and "they," not she, asked Jesus to help her. Our assumption is that *they* are her family members. Understandably, she would not have been in a position to seek help for herself.

Aren't you thankful we can summon Christ's intervention on another person's behalf? Aren't you also thankful that others have summoned Him on ours? Our homes today are threatened by fevers of all sorts—far beyond the physiological: unresolved conflict, unforgiveness, unfaithfulness, compromising media communications, pornography, and more. We need Jesus in our homes.

Do you have a sense of Christ's activity in your home? ❑ Yes ❑ No
If so, what set of circumstances led to the invitation for Him to come?

____

I've a good reason for asking you this question. Almost every spiritual marker of Christ's heightened activity in my home came as a direct result of some threatening situation. Right now both my daughters are walking with God, but I assure you this did not simply happen in the natural evolution of their lives. I've watched their relationships grow through situations in which some threat convinced them to cleave closer to Christ.

Can you relate? In the margin share your thoughts (discreetly if necessary).

God is so faithful. He can use the worst of circumstances to introduce us to the best of relationships. Don't miss the fact that Simon's mother-in-law immediately began serving Christ and the others. Few people are more compelled to serve than those who have experienced the healing power of Christ.

2. *Jesus engaged Himself in the lives of those He helped.* Look at Luke 4:39. Christ "bent over her." I don't think I'm reading too much into the picture to imagine a close encounter suggesting deep concern. I react in a similar way any time one of my children is sick. I don't remain upright and stoic, checking off a list of symptoms. I bend over them and draw close. I learned from my mother how to better gage a temperature with my cheek on their foreheads than with a thermometer. I cannot keep my distance from a sick child even if her malady is contagious. Christ could have healed Simon's mother-in-law from the front porch. He didn't. He came to her and drew down close. Also, don't miss the strong inference that Christ involved Himself one-on-one with those He helped.

Read Luke 4:40 carefully, then compare Mark's version, chapter 1, verses 32-34. What description of these exact events is recorded only by Luke?

____

Why might this fact have been of special interest to Dr. Luke?

___

We will study several encounters in which Christ healed people. Be forewarned against drawing a particular formula for healing based on any one incident. For now, the point is that Christ Jesus had a hands-on approach to ministry—just like He does today. His hands may currently be invisible, but His prints appear in countless restored lives.

*3. **Jesus rebuked the fever, not the patient.*** Not all illnesses are the patient's fault. I oppose teaching that suggests the opposite. Sometimes we do things or fail to do things that cause poor health. At those times, we probably could use a good rebuke. Often, however, the cause and effect is something only God understands. Thank goodness, the only One who knows absolutely is the One who reigns absolutely.

*4. **Jesus encountered much desperation.*** Our passages today give us two snapshots of desperation that no doubt pierced the heart of Christ. First take a look at verse 40: "The people brought to Jesus all who had various kinds of sickness."

At what time of day did they come? ___

Why did they wait until sundown to suddenly bring the sick?

___

To those of us who are Gentiles, the reason is not very obvious. Verse 38 tells us Christ had previously left the synagogue when He went to the home of Simon.

Look back at verse 31. What day was it? ___

Remember, at this point Christ primarily has been ministering in various synagogues to Jews. Additions to God's law did not permit Jews to carry the sick on the Sabbath. The Jewish "day" ends at sundown; therefore, a God-fearing, law-abiding people counted the moments until the sun would set over the Sea of Galilee. As the darkness of a new day fell, they bundled their sick and brought them to the Light. The thought almost makes me cry. It was as if they watched the clock of man's law tick until it finally struck grace … and they raced to Him with their need. How blessed we are to live in the liberty of a completed Calvary! The pharmacy dispensing God's grace is open 24 hours a day.

A second snapshot of desperation appears in today's reading. Study the picture in verse 42. Once again we are given a time frame.

What time of day was it? ___

Mark's version tells us exactly what Christ was doing in that solitary place before the camera flashed on the people's desperation.

Read Mark 1:35. What does this verse tell you? ___

I wish I had words to express the feelings scriptural moments like these stir in me. The thought of Christ ducking out the door while it was still dark to find a place to be by Himself with God floods my soul with emotion. I love every glimpse of the unique relationship they shared while Christ was on earth and His Father was in heaven. Never before had such a bridge connected the celestial and the terrestrial. I always wonder what Christ said to His Father in those intimate moments and what He saw. Did God the Father speak audibly to Him? Or, did He speak in His heart like He does to you and me through His Word? I can't wait to find out someday in glory.

We have no idea how many moments Jesus got to steal with His Father, but Scripture seems to imply He was soon interrupted: "When they came to where he was, they tried to keep him from leaving them" (v. 42). I'm convinced we don't give enough thought to how challenging a prison of flesh must have been to Christ. Prior to His advent, He was completely unencumbered by the natural laws governing the human body. Suddenly He experienced for Himself the pull to be in many places at once and the challenge to prioritize not just the good but the goal.

What was the goal according Luke 4:38-44? ________________________

Healing the sick seems like an awfully important ministry to me. Why do you think it was not the absolute priority work Christ came to accomplish?

____

5. Jesus was determined. Luke 4 concludes with a definitive statement in verse 44: "He kept on preaching in the synagogues of Judea." He kept on—no matter how many directions He felt pulled. No matter how many needs remained in each town He departed. No matter what others prioritized for Him—He kept on. Why? Because every other need humanity possessed was secondary to the need to hear and receive the gospel. Not unimportant, mind you. Just secondary. Physical healing affects this life alone.

How long is this life according to Psalm 39:5? ____________________

The kingdom is forever. Then why did Christ spend time and energy performing miracles of healing on such temporal bodies? Probably for three primary reasons:

- Because He could. He can do whatever He wants and He wanted to. Before that fact makes you nervous, remember: what He wants is always consistent with who He is. Among many other wonderful things, He is the Healer. In one way or another He heals every single person who comes to Him by faith.
- Because He is compassionate—beyond anything we can imagine.
- Because the miracles helped authenticate the Messenger.

Preaching the good news of the kingdom of God was Christ's absolute priority. One of the biggest temptations even mature believers face is being sidetracked by the urgent. Many situations need our attention. They tempt us to let them steal our focus. Christ may have faced the same temptation when the people came to Him and tried to keep Him from leaving. The word for *keep* is *katecho,* meaning "to hold fast, retain, or hold down, quash, suppress."

The people's attempts to hold onto Christ may not have been limited to the vocal and emotional. They may have hung onto Him physically, too. How His heart must have broken for them. I believe He may have been torn emotionally, but He was not dissuaded. The best thing He could do for them was to stay true to the goal.

Can you imagine how Jesus longed for the time when His work would be accomplished and He could dwell within the hearts of all who would receive Him, never to leave them? Until then, He had a job to do. Christ ignored neither the urgent need nor the ultimate goal—but He never allowed the former to hinder the latter. Oh, how I love Him.

As we conclude today's lesson, I feel He's speaking to you about a few things just as He is to me. Take time to listen as He whispers in your heart and through His Word.

Glance back over the lesson. In the margin note what you believe God is saying to you most clearly today.

DAY 3

A Catch in Deep Waters

Today's Treasure
"Then Jesus said to Simon, 'Don't be afraid; from now on you will catch men' " (Luke 5:10).

Today we get to celebrate a fact that continually staggers my imagination—Christ calls mere mortals to join Him in His work. What stuns me most is that He doesn't need our help. Christ could save the world through dreams and visions, but He doesn't. Instead, He delights in asking us to join Him. I am convinced that every believer is summoned by Christ to work with Him here on earth. His is the only work we do for keeps.

I love my family so much, but sometimes after I have worked maniacally on the house and 24 hours later it is a wreck, I want to bawl! Other times at the office I'll finally get through a stack of paperwork and clean off my desk just in time for another stack to appear in its place. You can no doubt relate. My tasks at home and at work are important, but when I pour my life into God-things, such as boasting in the Lord with my children or teaching a Bible class on Sundays, those activities are for keeps.

Before we study our passages in Luke today, please read John 5:17. What does this verse say to you personally?

____

____

I believe Christ calls disciples not so much to work *for* Him as *with* Him. In the margin note the differences this approach could make.

Throughout week 3 we are emphasizing how Christ did things His way, especially who He called to join Him. I want you to read all three segments in Luke pertaining to the call of His disciples. After a brief consideration of all three, we will focus on the first segment for the remainder of today's lesson.

Please read Luke 5:1-11,27-32; 6:12-16 and answer: How do we know Christ's encounter with Simon (Peter) at the Lake of Gennesaret was probably not the first time the two met? (Reflect on previous lesson.)

____

We don't know the previous vocations of each of Christ's twelve apostles, but what two vocations do we know for certain were among them?

____

What conclusions can you draw from the kinds of people Christ called to do things His way?

____

How did Christ respond to the Pharisees and the teachers of the law when they complained He fraternized "with tax collectors and sinners" (Luke 5:30)?

____

What did Christ do prior to calling the twelve to be apostles (Luke 6:12)?

____

Note the distinction Luke 6:13 draws between the disciples and apostles. The Greek word for *disciples* is *mathetes*. "*Mathetes* means more in the New Testament than a mere pupil or learner. It is an adherent who accepts the instruction given to him and makes it his rule of conduct."

We have no idea how many disciples Christ had at this point, but He must have had enough to draw out the twelve from among them after an intense night of prayer. The twelve did not cease being disciples, but they had an additional function. The Greek word for *apostles* is *apostolos,* meaning "one sent, apostle, ambassador … it designates the office as instituted by Christ to witness of Him before the world (John 17:18). It also designates the authority that those called to this office possess." We will most often see them referenced as the twelve disciples, but keep in mind that their distinction was an apostolic ambassadorship and authority assigned them by Christ.

More than any other one-on-one relationship in his Gospel, Luke developed the relationship between Christ and Peter. Let's focus now on their first encounters. Earlier I asked how we know that Luke 5:1-11 most likely does not represent their initial meeting. Hopefully you remembered that Christ was in Simon's home and healed his mother-in-law. Actually, even Luke 4:38 does not represent their first encounter.

Read John 1:35-42. Briefly describe the events that surrounded Christ and Simon Peter's very first meeting.

____

By the time Jesus taught on the shore in Luke 5:1, Christ and Peter had already shared at least two encounters. This one, however, was more than an encounter. It was a call. Peter's call took place at the Lake of Gennesaret, which is also called the Sea of Galilee. This body of water is actually called by four different names at different times. In addition to the two above, it was also called the Sea of Tiberias and the Sea of Chinnereth.

This harp-shaped body of water is a beautiful freshwater lake. I've had the privilege of standing barefoot in those waters and I long for you to see it, too. Picture Christ on the shore, pressed from all sides by people listening to the Word of God.

Can you see Him? In an attempt to capture His meekness, artists and filmmakers often portray Jesus as a skinny, mealy-mouthed weakling. Biblical meekness never equals weakness. The Bible's concept of meekness is submission to the Father's will. Few things require more strength than submission. The incarnate Jesus, preparing to teach the crowds, was a powerful and authoritative orator. He was a man's man.

ILLUSTRATOR PHOTO/BOB SCHATZ

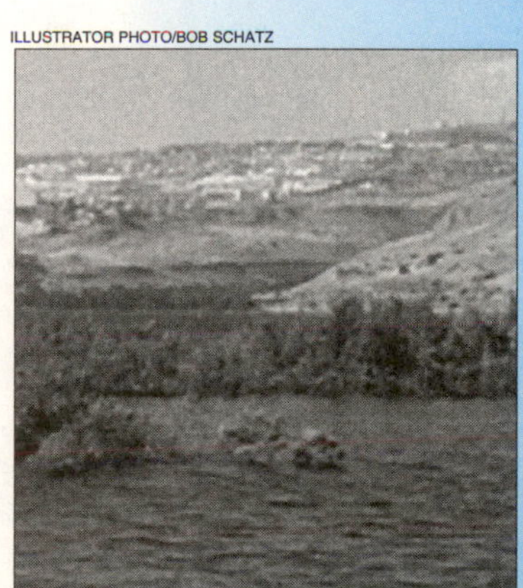

One of many inlets on the Sea of Galilee. Modern Tiberias can be seen on the slopes above.

Luke 5:2 tells us Jesus saw two boats at the water's edge, one of which belonged to Simon Peter, who was rinsing his nets. Jesus got into the boat and asked Peter "to put out a little from shore. Then he sat down and taught the people from the boat" (v. 3). Two reasons probably exist for Christ teaching from the boat: the boat provided a platform that made Him more visible, and the breeze coming off the lake provided acoustics that made Him more audible. Obviously, the spiritual does not always operate apart from the logical.

Although hearing Christ teach the Word would have been wonderful enough, what happened when He finished speaking was transforming to a certain fisherman.

Why did Peter do what Christ requested in verse 4?____________________

Why was he reluctant?____

What was the result? ____

Let's draw a series of applications from the events that unfolded on the lake that day:

1. Christ knows more about our jobs than we do. In our previous lesson, we learned that Christ makes house calls. Now we see Him expand His ministry into the workplace. He told Peter how to fish. Had Peter not already known Christ, he might have thought: *Me fisherman, you carpenter. I won't tell you how to build and you don't tell me how to fish.* Instead, he submitted one brief disclaimer: We've done this all night and caught nothing.

One of the most critical reasons believers experience defeat is because we categorize only a few areas of our lives as Christ's arena. Many believers think Christ's jurisdiction doesn't extend into certain areas. Many don't even get out of the church parking lot with Him on Sundays. As if to save Him the extra trouble of dealing with things that don't concern Him, they leave Christ at church to deal with areas related to His expertise.

Satan is greatly defeated when we start living our lives based on the truth that every area is Christ's specialty. Let's each take an inward look and try to determine how much we allow Christ to move from our church life into our home and work life.

What is your occupation? __________________ If your primary job is homemaking you certainly work hard, so don't hesitate to list it.

Have you ever thought that Christ knows every single detail associated with your job? ❑ Yes ❑ No

Have you ever really acknowledged that He knows more about your job than you do? ❑ Yes ❑ No

Jesus knows accounting, movie-theater managing, banking, drafting, engineering, nursing, real-estate brokering, and anything else we could do. For crying out loud, the One who knows the numbers of hairs on your head could also style them if He wanted. With all due respect, not one of us does anything for a living He can't do better.

2. Christ honors our submission even when our only motivation is obedience. If there was one phrase I wasn't going to say as a parent, it was "because I said so." I heard those words from my Army-captain Dad more times than I could count. I wasn't about to repeat them. After all, I studied child development. I vowed to explain things to my children as if they were little adults. I almost got away with it, too. Then I had Melissa—

the proverbial "but, why?" child. One day she pushed me too far. Something in me snapped. I suddenly exploded, *"Because I said so!"* Not just once. I screamed it over and over like a mad bull on a rampage. I even screamed it at the dog. Four-year-old Melissa shrugged her shoulders and retorted, "OK!" and then skipped off happily.

I called my Dad and thanked him. Sometimes God allows us to explore the "whys" of His instructions. Other times He wants us to obey "because He said so." Has God asked you to obey in a specific matter that still awaits your obedient response? (Always remember, He never leads us to do anything inconsistent with His character as expressed through His Word.)

Would you consider filling in the blank: "Master, I've had a lot of excuses for doing this my way, but because You say so, I will ________________."

Follow through, then wait upon the Lord to bless your act of obedience, no matter how long it takes. He is faithful.

3. ***The same job subjected to Christ's authority can yield entirely different results.*** Peter had no doubt fished in every level of water in the lake. The key to his enormous catch was not the deep water. It was the authority of Christ. Beloved, if your job has grown stale, you may not need a new occupation. You may need a new Partner.

What does Colossians 3:23 have to say about your job? ________________

____

What do you receive if you have this attitude toward your work (Col. 3:24)?

____

Every hour you do your job as working for the Lord gets punched on a time clock in heaven. You, sister, are getting paid by God Himself for the hours you work as unto the Lord. I'm not being cheesy. Our future inheritance is real, and it far exceeds minimum wage. You possess a heavenly bank account in which He is making divine deposits for every moment you work as unto Him. As you partner with Christ at your job, you will be more efficient. No matter whether your new efficiency increases your earthly dividends, it most definitely will increase your eternal dividends where moth and rust cannot destroy or thieves break in and steal (see Matt. 6:19).

4. ***Christ's willingness to empower us should occasionally overwhelm us.*** Simon Peter knew Jesus possessed extraordinary power. Christ healed his mother-in-law, and he may have witnessed the subsequent healings in Luke 4:40.

Why do you think Simon Peter suddenly fell at Jesus' knees and said, "Go away from me, Lord; I am a sinful man!" (Luke 5:8)?

____

The moment Peter realized he had been touched by such holiness, his knees buckled with unworthiness. He was far more comfortable with Jesus' power before God allowed it to rub off on him. The instant it touched him, he realized that holiness had met unholiness. "Go away from me, Lord!" Like Isaiah at his call (see Isa. 6:1-5), Peter suddenly couldn't bear Christ's presence. When Christ draws near, His brilliance always sheds light on our secret chambers. Isaiah encountered the Lord on His throne. Peter encountered the Lord Incarnate on earth. Both encounters summoned the common to the work of the sacred.

What blessed condescension that the God of glory would use us! What humility the realization should bring! Isaiah cried, "Woe to me! ... I am ruined" (Isa. 6:5). Peter cried, "Go away from me, Lord; I am a sinful man!" (Luke 5:8). Both men were overwhelmed, not just by what they had done. They were overwhelmed by what they were: sinful men. Do not miss the fact that neither was prepared to receive their call until they confronted their sin.

I've certainly never experienced an encounter like Isaiah's or Peter's, but I have assuredly faced moments of such stark realization of my own sin that I felt unbearable pain. Interestingly, those moments did not come during times of rebellion, but rather, they came during close encounters with God when I drew close enough to get an eyeful of myself.

I will never forget the realizations that brought me to surrender to the crucified life. Suddenly I realized that even if I could cease all sinful behavior, I would continue to battle sin throughout my life because I don't just *commit* sin. Apart from God, I *am* sinful. My problem is not just what I do, it's who I am without His nature.

Those realizations were both harrowing and liberating. The surrender resulting from the realization of my own innate unholiness did more to activate the holiness of God in me than anything I've ever experienced. How like God! Even our painful realizations of sinfulness are to mortify us to new life.

In conclusion, if you've had an encounter with Jesus that shed a harrowing and liberating light on you, please describe it in the margin.

DAY 4

If You Are Willing

Today's Treasure
" 'That you may know that the Son of Man has authority on earth to forgive sins' " (Luke 5:24).

As much as I wish we could, we won't be able to delve into every segment of Luke. Instead, I am praying for God to draw out specifically the precepts that are critical to accomplishing His goals for us. If I pass over a Scripture passage you were hoping we'd dissect, slice into it yourself and ask God to tutor you. He wants to talk just to you!

Today's Scripture reading involves two miracles of healing. Either could teach volumes, but the second introduces concepts so critical that we dare not miss them. Let's spend a couple of minutes on the first segment, then move into the heart of today's study.

Please read Luke 5:12-16. How would you describe the leper's approach?

____

Interestingly, the leper's approach revealed more insight into God and His complex ways than he probably intended. He simply wanted to be healed, but the means by which he sought the miracle underscored the bottom line in the issue of physical healing.

Notice first of all that the leper humbly approached Christ in absolute belief: "You *can* make me clean" (v. 12). The leper was convinced Jesus possessed all the necessary power. He had no doubt Christ could heal him. He just didn't know if He would—which brings us to our second consideration.

The leper also realized another issue was at stake: was this healing God's will? "Lord, if you are willing" (v. 12). The word for *willing* is *thelo*—"implying active volition and purpose. To will, i.e., to have in mind, purpose, intend ... seeing one's desire to its execution." The most critical word in the definition is *purpose*. In essence, the leper said: "Lord, I have no doubt You possess the power to heal me. If You, in Your wisdom and plan, see purpose in it, please do it."

I believe with all my heart that eternal purpose is the central issue involved in whether or not God heals a believing (see Matt. 9:28) and requesting (see Jas. 4:2) Christian's physical illness. Although I don't pretend to understand how or why, some illnesses may serve more eternal purpose than healing, while other healings serve more purpose than illness.

Oh, Beloved, in no way do I desire to minimize the issues involved in physical healings. Like you, I cannot imagine what purpose some illnesses and premature deaths possibly serve, but, after years of loving and seeking my God, I trust who He is even when I have no idea what He's doing. Above all things, I believe God always has purpose in every decision He makes.

How like the leper are you? Are you convinced that Christ can do absolutely anything, and are you also seeking His purposes in everything? If so, in your present challenges, how would you complete this sentence?

Lord, if You are willing, you can ______________________.

Don't lose courage. As long as this remains the desire of your heart, come to Christ as the leper did—humbly making your request while seeking His purposes for your life.

If these concepts are critical to you right now, meditate on them after you conclude today's lesson. Allow God to continue to speak to you even though we are moving on to the next segment of Scripture. Keep in mind, you never have to stop where I do! Go on with God wherever He leads you in each study.

Now read our central passage for today: Luke 5:17-26.
Who was Christ's identified audience that day according to verse 17?

____

Don't miss the interesting words, "And the power of the Lord was present for him to heal the sick." What do you think these words mean? Do you think Christ sometimes lacked the power to heal?

____

____

Luke 5:20 says of the paralytic and his friends, "Jesus saw their faith." How had they shown their faith?

____

What was the nature of the conflict that evolved? ______________

____

Two concepts surface in this account. Consider each one with me:

The power of the Lord. I hope the question I asked earlier concerning the power of the Lord being present caused you to really think. A good student is not afraid to ask questions and explore challenging passages. This statement causes us to wonder if times existed when Christ did not have the power to heal the sick. Dissecting the original language provides a key to understanding this statement. The word for *power* in this statement is *dunamis*, meaning "power, especially achieving power." Another Greek word often translated *power, strength*, or *might* in Scripture is *ischus*. This word will help us understand what *dunamis* is and is not. "Contrast *ischus* which stresses the factuality of the ability, not necessarily the accomplishment." *Ischus* expresses the fact that God possesses divine power. *Dunamis* expresses God's earthward application of His divine power. *Dunamis* is divine *ischus* applied in order to achieve certain earthly results.

Let's make sure you understand the concept. In your own words, write what each term means:

Ischus: ______________________________

Dunamis: ______________________________

Now read again Luke 5:17. What do you think the statement "the power (*dunamis*) of the Lord was present for him to heal the sick" means?

____

I hope you caught the inference that Christ was ready and willing to apply His *ischus* to specifically achieve (*dunamis*) healing that day. Christ healed many times, but the implication is that healing was a far more specific agenda in certain instances. We can break it down this way: Christ is always able. He is often willing. Sometimes He is more than willing—He is utterly resolved.

Our fresh insight makes the scene with the paralytic even more provocative. Do you remember the identified audience? The *King James Version* offers an interesting twist that changes the climate of the room. "There were Pharisees and doctors of the law sitting by, which were come out of every town of Galilee, and Judea, and Jerusalem: *and the power of the Lord was present to heal them*" (v. 17, italics mine). Take another look at the final word in this statement: *them!* The Greek word for *them* is *autos*, meaning "self ... the same." In other words, *them* referred to those identified in the preceding phrases. The power of the Lord was present to heal the Pharisees and teachers and anyone else who would fall under the power of His Word in that place!

Christ hadn't just come to heal those who were physically sick. He came to heal those who were sick with sin! We can be sure because of the nature of the conflict that ensued. Are you with me? Then let's continue with the next concept:

The authority of the Lord. Do you love picturing the paralytic being lowered through the roof into the crowded home-classroom? When was the last time you were trying to concentrate on a sermon when something terribly distracting occurred? Imagine the Pharisees trying to look scholarly while the roof is falling on their heads.

How long do you think they waited before looking up? Doesn't the thought make you grin? Then imagine the paralytic descending into the distinguished crowd like a puppet on a string. You can be fairly certain that the smell of a man unable to bathe himself was unwelcome (many believed this to be true about him). In their culture, the chronically ill or debilitated also tended to be the chronically outcast and poor. What a contrast of characters! Before their proper eyes, the paralytic dropped smack in front of Jesus.

Luke recorded no conversation between Doctor and patient. Christ took no history. He required no pulse. All Christ took was the vital sign of faith … and it was soaring.

How did Christ proclaim healing to the paralytic in verse 20?

____

Another troublesome passage! Does Christ's statement mean that all sickness results directly from the individual's sin? Take a look at John 9:1-3. Many people in that ancient culture presumed that chronic illnesses or handicaps were somehow related to sin.

How does comparing John 9:1-3 and Luke 5:20-24 refute some of our pat answers, or our use of the words "always" and "never"?

____

The only absolute connection between sin and physical infirmities is that we live in a fallen world. Our assumption from Scripture is that problems such as disease and poverty resulted from the fall into sin. Beyond that we can make no other assumptions.

Sometimes Christ emphasized forgiveness of sin when He healed and other times He didn't. In one of our two passages from Luke 5, Christ raised the issue of forgiveness of sin (the paralytic) but not in the other (the leper). None of the Gospels record Christ telling the leper to leave behind his life of sin. Perhaps our safest supposition is that sometimes sin was an issue and other times it was not.

Obviously Christ had an important point to make concerning healing and the forgiveness of sin in Luke 5:17-26. Whether or not sin has ever made you physically ill, couldn't we each say that we've been somehow paralyzed by it at one time or another? One situation involving sin in my past literally paralyzed me with fear. Would you like to know how I found healing and began to walk as a healthy believer again? I finally "heard" Christ say, "Friend, your sins are forgiven" and accepted His gift of grace. Christ's forgiveness caused me finally to be healed from the crippling fear that resulted from sin.

How about you? Have you ever been paralyzed by sin? Write your explanation in the margin. Use as much discretion as you feel is necessary.

For the remainder of our lesson, we'll concentrate on Christ's declaration in verse 24. Jesus said to the paralyzed man, "I tell you, get up, take your mat and go home." What we're about to discuss was pivotal to me after an unexpected and harrowing detour into sin years ago. I would still be paralyzed except for the truth God presented to me out of this exact Scripture. I'd like to share with you what He taught me:

Jesus came as the Son of man to rescue us from the plight of man. Christ is not only the Son of God but also the Son of man. In other words, He came to share our plight so that He could save our lives. We have a sin problem. We are powerless to help ourselves. Given the right set of circumstances and the wrong state of mind, each of us is capable of just about anything. If we could get our external lives under perfect and legalistic control, we'd probably rot on the inside with the heinous sin of pride. Let's face it. Given enough time, circumstances, and opportunity, we're all hopeless—except that Jesus came as the Son of man. Hallelujah!

Relish Hebrews 4:14-16. How do these verses capture the mission of the specific title, *Son of man?*

"The Son of Man has authority on earth to forgive sins" (Luke 5:24). The word for *authority* is *exousia,* meaning "permission, authority, right, liberty, power to do something." It comes from the word *exesti*, an authority that "denies the presence of a hindrance. The words *exesti* and *exousia* combine the two ideas of right and might."

I can remember being so devastated over a sin I had allowed to ensnare me that I repeatedly begged God to forgive me. I was repentant the very first time I begged. I confessed my sin with great sorrow and turned radically from it. Still I continued to plead for forgiveness.

One day in my Bible reading, God revealed these Scriptures to me. He spoke to my heart and said: "Beth, My child, you have an authority problem. You think you can do your part, which is repent. You just don't think I can do My part, which is forgive."

I was stunned. I began to realize that my sin of unbelief was as serious as my prior sin of rebellion. I wept and repented for my failure to credit Him with the authority He possessed to forgive my sins. It was eye-opening!

In *I Know I Should Forgive, But…*, Dr. Chuck Lynch says when we keep confessing the same sin "each subsequent time that sin is confessed, rather than the confession bringing relief, it only reinforces the false belief that it has not been forgiven. Double, or re-confession, only deepens the false belief that we have not been forgiven."[1] I know he's right because my constant re-confessions did not bring me relief. They only made me more miserable and self-loathing! Relief came when I decided to take God at His Word!

If you have truly repented—which means you have experienced godly sorrow and a subsequent detour from the sin—bathe yourself in the river of God's forgiveness. The Son of man has authority to forgive sins right here on earth. You don't have to wait until heaven. You can experience the freedom of complete forgiveness right here. Right now. Fall under Christ's authority and accept His grace. You've been paralyzed long enough, child of God. Hear Him say to you this day: "Friend, your sins are forgiven. … I tell you, get up, take your mat and go home" (Luke 5:20,24).

DAY 5

The Lord of the Sabbath

Today's Treasure
"Then Jesus said to them, 'The Son of Man is Lord of the Sabbath' " (Luke 6:5).

In Luke 5:17-18 the Pharisees and doctors of the law were "sitting by" (KJV). Matthew Henry wrote: "How many are there in the midst of our assemblies, where the gospel is preached, that do not sit under the word, but sit by! It is to them as a tale that is told them, not as a message that is sent them; they are willing that we should preach before them, not that we should preach to them."[2]

Can you recall a time you attended a Bible study or church service that profoundly affected a few of the people you were with, while others were completely unmoved, almost as if they hadn't attended? ❑ Yes ❑ No

Perplexing, isn't it? Sometimes the explanation is more than the lost condition of the unaffected because the Holy Spirit faithfully convicts and woos the lost when they are willing to hear the truth. Let's face it, believers can sometimes be as unaffected by a powerful message as any unbeliever. Like the Pharisees and teachers of the law, sometimes the unaffected can be the most "religious" people in the room. Could the difference be sitting by rather than sitting under the raining power of God's Word?

Several months ago this remarkable difference became crystal clear to me. One of my favorite congregations to visit is an African American church in New Orleans. I've fellowshipped with these wonderful people after a number of services and not one of those times has a solitary person been critical or even untouched by the message. You may be thinking, *They must have a great preacher.* It's not the preacher because I've never heard the same person preach there twice. What, then, is the difference? The listeners involve themselves in the message. They are not spectators. They take responsibility for the effectiveness of the message by actively engaging themselves in it.

I've been in many other settings where members basically gave the preacher an anointing rating over lunch. This discovery startled and affected me. I began praying that God would motivate me to actively engage myself in every message that I hear or read. Since that time, and not accidentally, I've not heard or read a single ineffective message. The teaching of God's Word is life-changing and healing! Who wants to sit *by* when we could sit *under* and be showered by His power!

Today's text shares two more prime examples of the attitudes that can be developed by people who sit *by* rather than sit *under* the power of God's activity.

Read Luke 6:1-11. These Scriptures describe two different scenes involving the same general issue. What was it?

____

I would love to have been a Jew who received Christ, but most of us working on this Bible study have Gentile roots. No matter how long we've studied Scripture, I'm not sure we can understand the significance in Jewish life of observances like the Sabbath. Let's do a little research into the significance of the Sabbath. Read Exodus 20:8-11.

Who first observed the Sabbath (v. 11)? ____________________

What was the basic point of the Sabbath? Circle the one best answer.

inactivity	**sleep**	**rest**
productivity	**meditation**	**quiet**

The Hebrew word *Shabbath* means "intermission … the day of rest. The Sabbath was a covenant sign of God's authority. It was a way of showing their trust in God, that He would honor their labors with fruit." The Sabbath had two primary purposes:

- First, its observance demonstrated that the people may plant and water the seed, but only God can bring the increase. The Sabbath was a way to practice trust. Even today in a ferociously competitive marketplace, many Jewish and Christian proprietors close their businesses one day a week to honor and trust God.
- Second, the Sabbath enforces regular intermissions of rest following work. God created us and knows our needs: physically, emotionally, mentally, and spiritually. The rest God proposes restores. Exodus 20:11 says God "rested on the seventh day."

I believe God was making a point concerning work followed by regular intermissions of rest. The Hebrew word for *rested* in Exodus 20:11 is *nuwach,* meaning "to rest, i.e.

settle down, to dwell, stay, let fall, place, let alone, withdraw, give comfort, etc." *(Strong's)*. The words *let fall* refer mainly to the hands relaxing from the plow or any other means of work. Also notice the word *withdraw*. Glance back at Luke 5:15-16. When God zipped up the coveralls of human flesh on His beloved Son, He allowed Him to experience various limitations of our physical bodies—like exhaustion.

Why would crowds of people be exhausting? ______________________

____

How did Christ practice *nuwach* or rest? ______________________

____

With a little background under our belts, turn back to Luke 6:1-2. What were the Pharisees labeling "unlawful"?

____

Try to fathom the pettiness of their complaint. Basically, they were charging the disciples with threshing wheat because they were rubbing it in their hands. They preferred the disciples ache with hunger rather than break the law as they knew it.

Read Isaiah 1:11-17. How were the Pharisees in Luke 6:2 displaying similar attitudes to those God addressed in these passages?

____

What was God's basic message to them? ______________________

____

Jesus is His Father's Son. He had no opinion or action independent of His Father. His attitude would have been no different as the Pharisees sunk their proud feet into the quicksand of legalism and stood their sinking ground. What a ridiculous scene they created. They presumed to tell the Lawgiver Himself how to obey the law.

Those who caught Christ's disciples threshing grain in their own palms weren't the first to be presumptuous. Through the centuries religious leaders had taxed God's laws with so many of their own that God's original purposes were often obscured. By the time Christ came to earth to accomplish His work, the Pharisees and teachers of the law had turned the Sabbath into the hardest day of the week. They twisted and turned the law until the people had to work to rest! The energy required to obey every single "don't" of their "man-made brand of Sabbath rest" took work.

Like yours, my job can be exhausting. Those who think ministry is easy would be wise to keep that opinion to themselves lest they be hit by a Catholic candlestick, a Lutheran communion plate, or a Baptist hymnal. Exhaustion is an interdenominational, equal opportunity vocational hazard. The travel this ministry necessitates is one of the biggest contributors to exhaustion. Strange hotel rooms are not conducive to sleep, especially when you're accustomed, like I am, to sleeping with a fan on.

Just as I was preparing this lesson, my staff gave me a delightful gift they knew I could use to make a hotel room "sound" more like home. It is a compact noise-maker. You can choose from several "tranquil" sounds such as rain or gentle wind. We nearly died laughing when we discovered that one of the tranquil sounds was a vacuum cleaner! What a perfect example of a way to make your rest remind you of work!

How do you tend to make rest more work than work?

___

Remember, God established the concept of regular work/rest cycles during creation. The need for authentic rest and the demonstration of trust in God is for all people, not just the ancient Jews. For the remainder of our lesson, let's draw our attention to the second sabbatical situation in today's text.

What was the malady of the man whom Christ encountered at the synagogue on the Sabbath (Luke 6:6)?

___

What kind of jobs would have been difficult, if not impossible, for this man?

___

A shepherd had to be adept at using a rod and a staff. A farmer needed both hands to plow. A carpenter had to hold a hammer in one hand and a nail in the other. A merchant would have had a difficult time securing and displaying goods with only one hand. Even a tax collector needed his right hand! In a discourse on rest versus work, I don't think it's a coincidence that the man involved had lived a humiliating life of unwelcome, imposed rest from any effective labor. Christ granted him a rest from his incapacity and futility. The One who created the Sabbath used it to bring restoration to a man weary of uselessness. Few things could be more reflective of the heart of God.

What were the Pharisees and teachers of the law looking for (Luke 6:7)?

___

The Pharisees' and teachers' primary reason for attending that day was to see if Jesus would heal. I love the fact that they were convinced Christ would heal, even on the Sabbath, if He encountered a need. What a Healer He is! No amount of laws could keep Him from being Himself! The Pharisees and teachers of the law caught Christ in the act of being God. Hallelujah!

The most merciful people are those who have been sitting *under* the faucet of God's mercy instead of sitting *by* with a critical eye. Please note this sad fact which was emphasized by the events following the Pharisees' and teachers' speculations: those who look for reasons to accuse will undoubtedly find some.

In Luke 6:7, the word for *accused* is *kategoria,* which involves the concepts of "accusation, incrimination … public condemnation." Being accused doesn't necessarily mean being found guilty. Christ was perfect in every way. In our admittedly imperfect states, how much sooner would you and I be accused or condemned by onlookers, even when actively pursuing godliness? We'd better learn what to do when it happens.

In my own life and ministry, I've accepted that, sooner or later, anyone looking hard enough to condemn will be accommodated. I really do believe that more people in the body of Christ are generally accepting than accusing, but one mean-spirited person is practically enough to ruin anyone's day. Francis Frangipane wrote something so powerful on the subject, I immediately committed it to memory. He said of the Lord:

To inoculate me from the praise of man,
He baptized me in the criticism of man,
until I died to control of man.[3]

In your own words, what does this quote mean?

____

____

____

Beloved, one thing I know for sure on this subject: nothing will squelch our efforts to seek the approval of others as not receiving it! Furthermore, those who approve one day can be the same ones who accuse the next day. I encourage you to break free from the traps set by approval and accusation. We are called to live our lives above reproach, but expect it anyway. Christ was blameless yet was blamed continually. And I think you can trust me on this one: blameless people are rarely those who cast blame.

When the man with the shriveled hand stood before Him on the Sabbath, Jesus knew the Pharisees and teachers of the law were looking to accuse Him. Remember, He could read their minds. (Incidentally, aren't you glad we can't?) Christ did not allow Himself to be controlled by potential accusations nor even by the law that He, Himself, instituted. He was indeed the Lord of the Sabbath.

Anyone who tried to put Christ on the hot seat usually ended up getting burned. (Thankfully, not necessarily in the eternal sense.) His public question to His accusers made them look terribly foolish: "I ask you, which is lawful on the Sabbath: to do good or to do evil, to save life or to destroy it?" (v. 9). Picture the scene described in verse 10: "He looked around at them all." Eye to eye. Just waiting for someone to give Him an answer. They were struck dumb. Or maybe dumber. Then He said to the man, "Stretch out your hand" (v. 10). And he did. Right there in front of all those perfect and pious-looking people, the man—who all his life had probably hidden his handicap under the sleeve of his garment—stretched forth his humiliating infirmity—and was healed.

"Now, Lord, … stretch out your hand to heal and perform miraculous signs and wonders through the name of your holy servant Jesus" (Acts 4:29-30).

---

[1]Dr. Chuck Lynch, *"I Should Forgive, But …"* (Nashville: Word Publishing, 1998), 33-34.
[2]Matthew Henry, *Matthew Henry's Commentary on the Whole Bible* (New York: Fleming H. Revell, Co., n.d.), 634.
[3]Francis Frangipane, *Exposing the Accuser of the Brethren* (Cedar Rapids, IA: Arrow Publications, 1991), 37.

VIDEO RESPONSE SHEET — GROUP SESSION 3

Session 3

Introduction: This week we had the opportunity to see Christ in the thick of ministry. On day 3 we studied the call of His disciples. They were eyewitnesses to concrete events that we hope somehow to capture in our imaginations. In this session we will join Christ and His disciples on the side of a certain mountain for a slice of a very important sermon. We can be certain this message was ingrained in their memories forever.

Read Luke 6:17-36.

- **The Timing:** According to Luke's Gospel, Christ's Sermon on the Mount followed the designation of the twelve apostles. (See Luke 6:12-17.)

- **The Setting:** Their introduction into ministry included encountering a sea of human suffering. (Compare Matthew 4:23—5:1.)

- **The Introductory Theme:** An antithetical and exceeding __future__ awaits the willing recipient who __suffers__ now. The original Greek word for *blessed* is *makarios*, meaning "blessed, possessing the favor of God, that state of being marked by the __fullness__ from God." (See Luke 6:20-23.)

A hint of the __unfair__ future for those with an __unfair__ present

1. "Blessed are you who are poor, for yours is the __Kingdom__ of __God__" (v. 20).
2. "Blessed are you who hunger now, for you will be __filled__" (v. 21).
   The Greek word for *hunger* is *peinas*, meaning to be __hunger__, to be __famished__ to be __starved__
3. "Blessed are you who weep now, for you will __laugh__" (v. 21).
4. "Blessed are you when you are __Appreciate__, __cursed__, and __excluded__" (v. 22). The original Greek word for *exclude* is *aphorizo,* meaning "to __seperate__ from or __cast__ __out__ of society."

Until heaven, how do we show we are children of the Most High God (v. 35)?

- Love our __enemies__. Romans 12:9 adds a little footnote: love __must__ be __sinere__
- Do __good__ to those who hate us.
- Bless those who __curse__ us.
- __Pray__ for those who mistreat us. It's for us as well as them.
- First Peter 3:8-9 offers a revolutionary perspective: "to this you were __Called__."

WEEK 4

The Esteem of Man

Day 1
Amazing Faith

Day 2
Compassion Without Restraint

Day 3
A Bout with Doubt

Day 4
Loving Much

Day 5
His True Brothers and Sisters

I'm already finding myself completely immersed in our story line. Are you? I hope so. Let's be willing to go even further, asking God to involve us emotionally, mentally, and spiritually in every single Scripture and to help us picture each scene with the spiritual sight of an eyewitness. We have an extremely interesting week of study ahead. I love watching Christ operate in relationships. Christ did not come to redeem the earth. Sand and water were not His priority. He came to redeem people. Study Him carefully this week. Watch the kinds of things that impressed Him. Let's allow Him to move us, to change us. As remarkable as this may seem, you and I can have lives that "impress" Christ. This week we'll learn how.

Principal Questions:

Day 1: How did the centurion's occupation lend him insight into Christ's ability?
Day 2: What differences can you identify between the two miracles recorded in Luke 7:1-17?
Day 3: According to Mark 6:17-18, why was John the Baptist in prison?
Day 4: Can you summarize, in one sentence, the parable Christ told the Pharisee in Luke 7:41-42?
Day 5: According to Luke 8:19-21, what was the sudden development in Christ's family dynamics?

Let's dive in even deeper this week. If I don't go as deep as you desire, take off with Jesus on your own! Allow my commentary to be a catalyst for your own encounters with Jesus. Ask Him questions and search for the answers. Hold nothing back from Him. Treasures await you, my friend.

DAY 1

Amazing Faith

Today's Treasure
"I tell you, I have not found such great faith even in Israel" (Luke 7:9).

One of my most heartfelt personal petitions to God is to develop His taste. I want to grow to love what He loves, hate what He hates, and marvel at the things He finds marvelous. I'm a long way from His gloriously discriminating palate, but today's lesson gives a refreshing bite of heaven's taste. Let's begin by asking ourselves what kinds of things amaze, astonish, or impress us. What's your taste in amazement? Today, and most of this week, we're going to learn what impresses Christ. As we grow in grace, may we each develop His taste and marvel over the things He considers marvelous.

Please read Luke 7:1-10 and complete the following:
How would you state in one sentence the theme of these verses?

____

Upon what basis were the elders pleading earnestly in the centurion's behalf (v. 4)? Circle the most accurate word, then explain your answer.

worthiness **desperation** **proximity** **affection**

____

Why didn't the centurion want Christ to come to his house?

____

How did the centurion's occupation lend him insight into Christ's ability?

____

Why do you think Christ was so amazed?

____

Awesome story. I love the way Christ could know all things, yet be amazed. Christ almost seems delightfully shocked in this encounter—almost caught off guard by such faith. I'm so glad God purposed for Christ to know all things, yet also know the thrill of sudden amazement. It's one of life's sheerest joys. Don't you agree?

The original word for *amazed* in verse 9 is *thaumazo,* meaning "to wonder, marvel, be struck with admiration or astonishment." Perhaps you've bought into the "wretched worm that I am" mentality enough to be uncomfortable thinking about Christ being impressed by anything wretched man can do. Since we're attempting to develop God's taste, perhaps we could all use a little adjustment in our perception of the divine.

Take a look at Isaiah 66:1-2, then fill in the missing word:

"This is the one I ________________" (v. 2).

This word meaning may blow your mind. *Nabat* means to "regard with pleasure, ... have respect" *(Strong's)*. God is clearly saying that He respects certain people.

According to Isaiah 66:2, what about a person impresses God?

____

Do you see the like-mindedness of Christ and His Father? Our difficulty imagining that God could have respect for a mortal is because we confuse attitudes of respect with feelings of inferiority. We tend to view respect as a feeling we have for those we perceive as superior to us, and on our best day, we are so inferior to Christ that, if not for the Lord's great love (see Lam. 3:22), we would be consumed by holy fire.

If we're to have a balanced perception, however, we must keep in mind that God created us. We are His "workmanship" (Eph. 2:10). He loves us. At times, He actually delights in us. God could have created us void of weakness and with a complete inability to sin. He didn't. He purposely created us with free will and affections so that we could choose Him and love Him in the midst of many options and much opposition.

God didn't create robots. He created humans. We humans happen to be His prize creation and an important part of a work He looked upon and considered "very good" (Gen. 1:31). When God sees humans cooperate with His good work and fulfill what they were created to be, He still sees something very good. Perfect? No. Respectable? Yes. When the Father sees a human who is prone to selfishness, pride, and arrogance humble him or herself and tremble at God's Word, He esteems that person. Hallelujah! Oh, how I want to be someone God could respect!

Christ's encounters on earth show our mortal minds the stuff of heaven by transplanting them onto the soil of earth. In essence, Luke 7:1-10 is an earthbound interpretation of Isaiah 66:1-2. Let's spend the remainder of our lesson considering two amazing things about a man whose faith amazed the Son of God.

The centurion valued his servant highly. Please don't miss this! The person who was dying was not a family member or a good friend. He was a servant! In fact, the original word is *doulos,* meaning "a slave, one who is in a permanent relation of servitude to another, his will being altogether consumed in the will of the other. Generally one ... bound to serve." Slaves were certainly not hard to come by under the Roman rule of that day. The typical mentality in that culture was the immediate replacement of an infirm slave. The attitude of the centurion, however, was that his servant was virtually indispensable to him. In fact, the words *valued highly* are translated from the Greek word *entimos,* meaning "honored ... dear, precious, costly." Look at another place in Scripture where *entimos* is used but rendered with a different English word.

Fill in the missing word from 1 Peter 2:4.
"As you come to him, the living Stone—rejected by men but chosen by God

and ________________ to him—you also, like living stones, are being built into a spiritual house to be a holy priesthood, offering spiritual sacrifices acceptable to God through Jesus Christ."

Years ago a friend discerned that I was beginning to be overwhelmed by the sudden demands of a writing ministry. She said something that made both of us laugh: "I can't write the Bible studies for you, but I could answer some of your mail. All I'd have to do is say precious a lot." Ever since I've been aware of how much I say and write the word precious! But you see, it's a very biblical word. First Peter 2:4 tells us that Christ is precious to God. Keeping this fact in mind, read John 15:9 and John 17:23.

How can you accurately conclude that you are also precious?

____

The centurion revealed a dimension of godly character in the high regard he felt for his servant. Christ, however, doesn't just display godly character. He *is* godly character. Be blessed by knowing that Christ Jesus values His servants highly. We are precious to Him. Even in our frailties. Even though we can't reach perfection in this lifetime.

How does Luke 7:8 define a highly valued servant?

____

The centurion valued a readily obedient servant. His slave was so important because he revealed his complete devotion through obedience. Likewise, Jesus Christ is building a spiritual household out of devoted servants willing to offer spiritual sacrifices. These living stones are as precious to Jesus as He, the Chief Cornerstone, is to His Father.

The centurion was a man of good works. Take another look at Luke 7:4-5. Keep in mind that the centurion was a Gentile, yet the Jewish elders pled with Jesus on his behalf. They said he deserved to have his servant healed. Thank goodness, our works do not measure how much we "deserve" the activity of Christ in our lives. We couldn't possibly muster enough works to deserve the attention of Jesus. His grace is entirely unmerited favor. He loved us long before we loved Him. He worked for us long before we dreamed of working for Him. No, works don't reveal worthiness, but according to Luke 6:43-45, they can reveal something else.

What did the centurion's good works probably reveal about his character?

____

Have you noticed that all three of our primary texts have raised issues of building a kind of "house" for the presence and activity of God (see Isa. 66:1; Luke 7:5; 1 Pet. 2:4)? Yes, the centurion had built something wonderful, but his works did not compare to Christ's nor earn His graceful attention. We're reminded that God is the Builder. We could spend our life's blood, sweat, and tears building for God, but it would never be big enough to hold Him nor worthy to deserve Him. The mind blower is not what we're building for God but what He's building with us.

The centurion didn't believe his own press. No matter what he had accomplished nor how others viewed him, the centurion knew himself. Apparently the more he thought about what he sent the elders to request, the more overwhelmed he became. Having no idea the elders would tell Christ how deserving he was, the centurion sent his friends with the opposite message: I do not even deserve to have You come under my roof. The word for *deserve* in this verse is *hikanos,* meaning "sufficient, … enough, … adequate, competent." He was saying, "I'm not even competent for You to walk through my front door!"

Don't overlook the fact that Christ was not far from the house when the centurion sent this message. I can't help drawing this parallel: the closer Christ's presence comes to us, the more humble a discerning person becomes.

Have you ever noticed how what seemed like a good idea can look so different in retrospect? Suddenly our audacity hits us like a slap in the face. I have the privilege of knowing personally the president of the International Mission Board of the Southern Baptist Convention and his wonderful wife. They insisted I call them by their first names in our personal visits. However, recently when I wrote them a letter and stared at my salutation using their first names, I was horrified at my audacity! On a far grander scale, I believe the centurion had a similar realization. In fact, he appears to have been so humiliated that he did not even consider himself worthy of Christ's presence.

Please notice that even though the centurion was greatly humbled, he still presented his request! Again, let's keep a balanced perspective! The "wretched worm that I am" mentality might say, "I can't even ask such a thing," then end up having not because he asked not (see Jas. 4:2). Those who are truly humble and discerning know that we can approach Christ with our petitions, not because we deserve to approach, but because He has graciously made Himself approachable!

Surely the most impressive statement made by the centurion was, "Say the word, and my servant will be healed" (Luke 7:7). The centurion's understanding of authority may be unparalleled in the Gospels. He seemed to be saying, "If I am who I am and people under my authority do as I say, You, being who You are, need simply say the word and the act is accomplished." I seriously doubt the centurion knew Jesus' full identity. All he probably understood was that Jesus possessed an authority that seemed to be ignited into action by His word.

Look up each of the following Scriptures and complete the sentences:

Genesis 1:3: "And God said, 'Let there be light,' and ________________

____."

Mark 4:39: "He got up, rebuked the wind and said to the waves, 'Quiet! Be still!' Then the wind ____

____."

John 11:43-44: "When he had said this, Jesus called in a loud voice, 'Lazarus, come out!' The ____, his hands and feet wrapped with strips of linen.

Child of God, Christ's Word is action. What He commands He also accomplishes. That is a fact. What impresses Christ, however, is when we believe it's a fact. In one way, we face a situation similar to the centurion. We are challenged to believe what Jesus Christ can do without seeing Him with our own eyes. The centurion never laid eyes on Christ, but he witnessed His incomparable power as suddenly as his dear servant sat up in the bed, fully recovered. I have a feeling it may have taken the centurion a little longer to get up. I can almost picture the blood returning to the servant's deathly pale cheeks while it drained from the centurion's.

Somehow, even if we've asked and believed, God also allows us the wondrous delight of total amazement when He works. We simply weren't meant to recover from certain things. A miracle of God is one of them.

DAY 2

Compassion Without Restraint

Did you happen to skip over Today's Treasure? If so, please take a moment to read it slowly, even meditatively. Sometimes one sentence of Scripture speaks scrolls to the soul without one even knowing the context.

Today's Treasure
"When the Lord saw her, his heart went out to her and he said, 'Don't cry' " (Luke 7:13).

Without knowing anything about the circumstances surrounding this sentence, based on these few words, what can you deduce about Christ?

____

I'm having one of those "Oh, how I love Him" moments and we haven't even gotten to the heart of the lesson. One of the things that moves me so much about Jesus Christ is that He allows us to get to His heart and move Him. Let's read our text for today: Luke 7:11-17. After reading today's text, let your thoughts return to the miracle in Capernaum from our previous text, Luke 7:1-10. In both accounts Christ performed amazing deeds, but the circumstances present interesting contrasts.

What differences can you identify between the two miracles?

____

Keep those differences in mind as we picture the events at the city gate of Nain. Verse 11 tells us that after Christ healed the centurion's servant, He and His disciples went to the town of Nain. Forgive me if this seems unimportant, but I can't help noting their physical condition. Nain was 25 miles southwest of Capernaum. No short walk.

Not only did Christ and His disciples walk a great distance to get to Nain, but also the large crowd. Perhaps the view kept their minds occupied on the long walk. Nain enjoyed a panoramic portrait of Mount Tabor. Surrounded by plains, "it rises steeply to form a dome-shaped summit."[1] The word *Nain* actually means *beauty*. Not hard to imagine why—whitewashed by the sun and rolled against the vivid blue Middle Eastern sky. Picture the scene with me. Two crowds met that day in Nain. Christ, His disciples, and a large crowd approached the town gate just as a funeral procession was leaving the city.

ILLUSTRATOR PHOTO/BOB SCHATZ

Mount Tabor, as viewed from Nain, rises steeply from the surrounding plains.

Western funeral customs leave us little to compare to those of the ancient East. For us, even in the most tragic situations, cries of any volume are rare, and when they occur, their sounds are almost more than a Western soul can bear. Contrast that to the scene Christ met. In the ancient East, the depth of concern for the dead and the grieving could be measured by the volume of the wails and the physical demonstrations of grief.

I can't think of a situation they would have considered more tragic in those days than a widow losing her only son. Her double portion of grief would have been compounded by an utterly hopeless future. The sound of the processional would have been as unsettling as the sight.

Christ may have been more unsettled by the sight and the sound than anyone present. This kind of funeral processional was the people's custom, but I'm not sure Christ has ever grown accustomed to death, no matter how many millions of times He's seen it. It's too contrary to His nature. He is Life (see John 14:6). He is the One who came to save life, not destroy it (see Luke 6:9).

Read 1 Corinthians 15:25-26. What is death called? ______________

Although Satan is certainly Christ's animate foe, I believe Scripture suggests that His ultimate archenemy is death. He hates it. He longs for the time when death will be swallowed up in victory and we will sing, "Where, O death, is your sting?" (1 Cor. 15:54-55).

With His transcendent hatred of death, Christ had an entirely different angle on the sight in Nain. The crowds that met at the town gate were most assuredly moved but not in the same way. Since the creation of man Christ viewed death from a heavenly perspective: earthly life is but a breath. Eternity holds incomparable riches for the trusting. He possessed incomprehensible compassion combined with a constant eternal perspective in which death, for the faithful, is the door for a greater reality of life. I have a feeling, however, that occupying a cloak of human flesh and staring grief straight in the face from street level might have been momentarily staggering for Christ. In fact, I believe Scripture suggests such a thing. Let's look again at the verse: "When the Lord saw her, his heart went out to her and he said, 'Don't cry'" (Luke 7:13).

By what name is Christ called in Luke 7:13? ______________
How would you describe what this particular title represents?

____

God the Father, Son, and Holy Spirit are called by many titles in Scripture. Each title fits the context like a hand in a glove. Not coincidentally, Jesus is called *Lord* in a verse in which He is entirely moved over the reverberations of death.

How hard must it have been for Christ to possess all authority but stick to a kingdom plan requiring its timely exercise? He could sneeze on Satan and blow him to oblivion, but that's not the plan. Satan's prompt demise would spare us trouble, but it would also spare us tremendous growth resulting in many rewards. Until the right time for Satan's disposal, Christ restrains Himself. Other areas of restraint must have also been challenging for Jesus as He walked on this pavement. Imagine the thoughts a funeral procession provoked in the mind of the Author of Life.

I think the very lordship of Christ overwhelmed Him at that moment in Nain. No one else in the crowd could do anything about the widow's plight. They possessed no power. Christ was the only one present who had lordship over the quick and the dead. *His heart went out to her.* The Greek word for this phrase is *splagchnizomai,* meaning "to feel deeply or viscerally, to yearn, have compassion, pity." We're going to learn that Christ didn't just feel. He felt deeply. He spoke only two words to her: "Don't cry." We've all said those two words to someone who was brokenhearted, but I believe Christ probably meant something a little different.

What do we fellow humans usually mean when we say, "Don't cry"?

____

I don't know about you, but most of the time when I've said those words, my heart was saying: "Please stop crying. I can't bear to see you in so much pain!" They are usually the words of one who can't stand to see the hurt because she is powerless to help. Christ, on the other hand, is never helpless. When He said, "Don't cry," He meant, "Not only do I hurt for you, but also I'm going to do something about the cause of the hurt."

Verse 14 records Jesus' initial action: "He went up and touched the coffin." Picture the structure more like a stretcher than our Western concept of a coffin. The body was placed on a board and shrouded with burial linens. Now imagine Christ walking up and touching this burial slate.

The first thing we read after Christ touched the bier is that "those carrying it stood still" (v. 14). They probably stood there bug-eyed. You see, for anyone unnecessary to the interment process to risk touching the dead body was a serious "no-no." Jesus was ritually defiling Himself. What they couldn't have realized is that the Son of God could not be defiled no matter what He touched. One day soon He would literally take on the sins of the entire world while still remaining the perfect Lamb without spot or blemish.

We've already established that Christ did not need to touch to heal. He did not even need to be present. He seemed to touch because it came natural to Him. I'm anxious to share with you what *touched* means in today's context. The word is *haptomai*, from the word *hapto,* meaning "to connect, bind." *Haptomai* means "to apply oneself to, to touch. Refers to such handling of an object as to exert a modifying influence upon it." Christ Jesus literally connected Himself to the situation. He applied Himself to it, hallelujah! We apply all sorts of medication for hurts. Christ took one look at this woman's grief and applied Himself.

I hope you'll be as blessed by the Greek antonym or opposite term as you are the original. The antithesis of *haptomai* is *egkrateuomai*. You will find the English translation of this word at the very end of the list of the fruit of the Spirit in Galatians 5:22-23.

What is the last quality? ______________________________

In today's text, imagine Christ acting out of exactly the opposite of self-control. Stick with me here until you grasp the meaning. When Christ saw the woman in such agony and faced with such hopelessness, I'm suggesting He literally cast off self-restraint and reacted! The difference between Jesus and us is that He doesn't sin even when He casts off self-control! Christ does not depart from the Spirit whether He responds or reacts.

Herein lies the most profound difference between the miracle in Nain and the previous miracle in Capernaum. In the second case, the only prerequisite was her pain. Unlike the centurion, she made no request. She exhibited no faith. In fact, we have no idea if the grieving mom even realized Christ existed. She was probably too enveloped in her own agony to notice. He awaited no conditions nor apparently had any intention of using the moment for instructional purposes.

Jesus ran into a woman in hopeless despair and just reacted with what came most naturally to Him: healing mercy. Oh, how I praise Him! I believe we possibly have a small glimpse into what Christ would do in every one of our despairing situations if a greater plan was not at stake. I believe what comes most naturally to Christ every time He encounters need is to instantly fix it. Is it possible He exercises great restraint to work any other way in the face of devastation? I think so.

A plan of profound importance exists that sometimes overrides the miracle we desperately desire. I am comforted to know that instantaneous healing and resurrection power comes even more naturally to our Christ than waiting and working through long but necessary processes. The biggest reason why I can trust in the sovereignty of God is because I am so utterly convinced of the sweetness of God.

How about you? Are you convinced God is sovereign? ❑ Yes ❑ No
Are you convinced God is kind, even sweet? ❑ Yes ❑ No
In the margin, describe how He could be both sovereign and sweet.

I believe we will see both these dimensions appearing side by side many times throughout our study. Back to the text! After touching the coffin and stunning the unsuspecting carriers, Christ said emphatically, "Young man, I say to you, get up!" (v. 14).

What I'd give to view this moment on videotape! Picture the expressions on the pallbearers' faces. This stranger had not only come close to touching the dead body, but also He began talking to it. They didn't have long to make a mental diagnosis before movement erupted on the tabletop. Imagine what they were doing down below as the entire weight shifted and the dead body sat straight up. Now take the scene one step further—imagine their faces when the dead man spoke. The second wonder in this scene is that they didn't drop him like a hot potato.

How amazing! Who had ever heard of such a thing? Actually, they had, which adds another interesting twist to this story. Just on the other side of the hill from Nain was a town called Shunem. Several centuries earlier something very dramatic happened there. Read it for yourself in 2 Kings 4:8-37. Please understand that Elisha was the patron saint of the entire region surrounding Nain. He was their claim to fame. The two events would undoubtedly be compared.

Imagine the discussion. What parallels did the villagers draw?

____

They missed the point, however, amid the similarities if they didn't notice at least one very important difference. Compare the amount of effort exercised by Elisha and Christ each as instruments of resurrection power (see 2 Kings 4:32-35 and Luke 7:14-15).

What difference do you see in the effort expended? ____________

____

No contest. A wide gulf of difference lay between Elisha the prophet and Jesus Christ, the omnipotent Son of God. With the same expediency of "there was light" in Genesis 1:3, there was life in Luke 7:15. Nothing gradual. No slight twitch causing them to wonder if they were seeing things. No gradual warmth as blood began pumping its way through thousands of capillaries. No pacing, waiting, or wondering. No warbled nonsense from a patient slowly regaining consciousness. No stiff muscles from a hard case of rigor mortis. Jesus said, "Get up!" and the dead man did. Instantaneously.

Christ's actions should have settled a debate before they could raise it. John the Baptist was rumored to be Elijah raised from the dead. Jesus proved to anyone who was listening that He was most assuredly not an updated version of Elijah's sidekick, Elisha.

As the curtain draws on the scene, two crowds became one and all were filled with awe, praising God. Their words? "A great prophet has appeared among us," they said. "God has come to help his people." Far more than a great prophet had appeared among them that day. God had come in human flesh to help His people.

If you have received Christ as Savior, in many ways this is your story, too—only yours is even better. Read Ephesians 2:1-7 and explain how.

____

____

DAY 3

A Bout with Doubt

Today's Treasure
" 'I tell you, among those born of women there is no one greater than John; yet the one who is least in the kingdom of God is greater than he' " (Luke 7:28).

Sometimes a lesson comes along that I wish you and I could simply discuss in my den over a cup of French-roast coffee. Today's lesson is one of those. In fact, if I don't stop reflecting on it and start writing, this study may never make it to print.

I love studying people. I also love studying biblical doctrine. But I am most edified when the two collide. Sometimes the two work together as naturally as a candle and a match. Other times they work together like a fire and a firecracker!

People who seem to live out the faith almost flawlessly inspire me; but I am also moved to meditation by those who grapple and wrestle with it. For most of us, the lives of the latter are those to whom we most readily relate. I find that rather than give me "permission" to doubt, their stories usually give me permission to move through my doubt to a place of spacious faith. May God use this lesson toward such an end.

Part One: Read Luke 7:18-28.
If you were writing a paper on this portion of Scripture, what title and subtitle would you give it?

________________:________________

Matthew's version of these events is almost identical to Luke's with the exception of one additional piece of information. Read Matthew 11:2.

Where was John the Baptist at the time?
❑ in exile ❑ in the wilderness ❑ at the Jordan
❑ in prison ❑ in the temple

According to Mark 6:17-18, why was he there?

____

How might John's location have influenced the question he sent his disciples to ask Christ?

____

I believe John knew the Word. He knew every prophecy about the Messiah. Virtually no one other than the Son of God Himself was more acquainted with Christ's job description in Isaiah 61:1-2. Take a second look at Luke 7:18.

Noting the context, to what do you think "all these things" referred?

____

What could be more convincing than a dead man sitting up and talking at the command of Jesus Christ? Yet John still sent his disciples to ask, "Are you the one who was to come, or should we expect someone else?" My heart is awash with compassion for a man who sat in prison two thousand years ago. Four walls closing surely must limit your vision. The facts to support Christ's messiahship were all there, and I'm pretty certain John knew it. Furthermore, the baptizer knew Jesus was the Messiah the moment he saw Him at the Jordan River, before Jesus met a single criterion.

I don't believe John's sudden bout with doubt had anything to do with public merit. It was a private matter. John had heard the wonders Christ had done for others. I think maybe his faith was shaken because he could have used a wonder for himself, and he didn't appear to be getting it. John knew with his head that Jesus was the Messiah. Sitting in that prison cell, I think he was having a little trouble knowing it with his heart.

I don't think any of us have trouble relating here. Have you known Christ long enough to witness His marvelous works? Have you heard testimonies of His intervening power? Even after such evidence, has your faith ever been greatly shaken because of something He didn't do for you personally?

Like John, have you ever found yourself waiting and waiting on Christ to come through on a certain matter while hearing all sorts of wondrous works He was doing elsewhere? Share your heart on this matter:

____

____

It hurts, doesn't it? We can be believers in Jesus for years, literally seeking Him, finding Him, and serving Him—then suddenly have a staggering bout with doubt. Overwhelmed with guilt and fear, we'll think, *How in the world could I be doubting after all this time?* It's a horrible feeling! I'd like to suggest, however, that these kinds of doubts are probably not coming from our heads. They're coming from our hearts. Our feelings. Our emotions. Our hurts.

We've got to know what we know even when we don't feel what we want to feel. Based on Christ's unparalleled assessment of John in verses 24-28, I am utterly convinced that John was experiencing heart-doubt. Not head-doubt.

What do you think Christ meant by "a reed swayed by the wind" (v. 24)?

____

John was not like "a reed swayed by the wind." Rather, he was a man of absolute conviction. That's exactly what *faith* means. *Pistis*, the Greek word translated *faith,* means "firm persuasion, conviction." For our purposes today, firm persuasion or conviction represents head-faith! Perhaps John had questions, but they weren't enough to sway the reed! Had John really harbored deeply-embedded questions about Christ's authenticity, I don't believe Jesus would have hesitated to rebuke him. He certainly didn't hesitate with some others. Christ was very gentle with John. He simply reminded John that He was fulfilling His job description to the "t" and not to "fall away" on account of Him.

I believe the root of John's question was why he, Christ's forerunner, was sitting in prison while Jesus was going about His business all over the countryside. Surely John was wondering how he was supposed to prepare the way from prison. If Jesus were meeting all the criteria of messiahship, He was supposed to be proclaiming freedom for the prisoners (see Luke 4:18). John knew a prisoner who could use a little freedom.

John's ministry had lasted only about a year. The baptizer could not have imagined that his purposes were so quickly fulfilled. John couldn't have foreseen that he was a shooting star leading the way in the night until the Dawn would rise.

Our discussion raises an important question: If a real difference exists between head-doubt and heart-doubt, is heart-doubt "no big deal"? When our emotions begin to override what our minds know is true, can we just surrender to our heart-doubts? I don't think so. Our heart-doubts can be very dangerous if we remain in them. But, if we wrestle through them with the Lord Jesus, when we get to the other side of our crisis, we will find ourselves spilled into a place of spacious faith!

Without question God has used every doubt of my heart to bring me to a more steadfast faith. When I finally reach the other side, usually God has settled that particular issue for good. I still think of my first real bout with doubt as a Christian adult. I shared the story in my first Bible study, *A Woman's Heart: God's Dwelling Place*. A friend lost a preschooler to leukemia. When this tragedy occurred, I had been a Christian for a long time. But when God didn't answer our prayers for healing, the "no" sent all of us reeling in doubt.

I knew with my head that God is real, He is God, and that He is good, but suddenly my heart questioned every one of those issues. I wrestled with God for many days. Guess what? I still don't know why He took that child home, but He settled an issue with me that I have not questioned since. He is sufficient. We can make it through anything. I still don't understand at times why we must, but I know we can.

How about you? Has God ever taken you through your doubts to a place of greater faith? ❑ Yes ❑ No If so, what resulted from your struggle?

____

Our challenge is to work through our doubts and not let them imprison us like John's were threatening to imprison him! Christ stated the biggest risk of doubt in verse 23.

Read the verse carefully. What risk is inferred?______________________

The original word for *blessed* is *makarios*. Revel in the definition: "Biblically, one is pronounced blessed when God is present and involved in his life. The hand of God is at work directing all his affairs for a divine purpose, and thus, in a sense, such a person lives *coram Deo*, before the face of God."[2] Luke 7:23 tells us these words apply to the person who doesn't fall away on account of Christ.

What does *falling away* mean? The word, *skandalon*, means "a cause of stumbling." Add the meanings of these two definitions and I believe we can accurately arrive at the following sum total in Luke 7:23: The hand of God is at work directing divine purpose, or blessing, in all the affairs of the one who doesn't let the perceived activity or inactivity of Christ trap him or make him stumble. It's a mouthful, but chew on it awhile!

In the margin write your own paraphrase of the above definition.

I don't think Luke 7:23 is talking about falling away from Christ. It's talking about falling over a stumbling block and into a trap. One of Satan's most effective devices for causing a devout believer to stumble is to trap him over a matter of faith. Satan even tries to use Christ, Himself, against us. The most effective faith-trap Satan could set for a Christian is to tempt her to doubt the goodness, rightness, or mightiness of Christ.

Christ held John in highest esteem even after being questioned (see v. 28). Remember, ours is a God of compassion. John was under a terrible strain and his martyrdom was imminent. Christ knew that! He could handle John's questions because He knew the heart and mind from which they came. Christ knew John was suffering, but He also knew that a critical plan was in motion that could not be disturbed.

After proclaiming that no one born of women was greater than John, what did Christ say about those of us in the kingdom of God (v. 28)?

____

Please understand that this statement in no way diminished John's calling or importance. Christ simply meant that a new era was unfolding in the kingdom calendar and to be a part of it would be greater than being a prophet under the old covenant. Thank your God again today that you live this side of Calvary!

Part Two: Read Luke 7:29-35.

God's way is always right. God's way was also right for John the Baptist, but he would not fully realize it until heaven. I don't believe the timing of John's incarceration was an accident. It immediately followed Christ's introduction into public ministry. John's task was to prepare the people for Jesus, and he fulfilled his job description faithfully. Now John's work was complete. For him to continue in ministry might actually cause some to miss the very salvation the forerunner came to announce.

What did John the Baptist say in John 3:30?

____

Sometimes we can understand the purpose of our callings without fully understanding God's means. John's imprisonment and the events to follow were part of preparing the way for Jesus Christ. I think you can be certain of one thing about John the Baptist: when he got to heaven, he wouldn't have traded his place in the kingdom plan for anything. Among billions of people who would live on this planet, he alone was chosen to prepare the way for the Messiah. How could such a calling not have been costly?

Christ doesn't play games. Look back at verses 32-35. Christ did not come to be popular. He came to be Savior. I think sometimes we also play songs and expect Christ to dance or sing dirges and expect Him to mourn.

Can you think of any ways we can act like the generation described?

____

Sometimes we measure Christ's activity based on how much He does our bidding. Our attitude is, "I'll believe as long as you do what I ask." How grateful we should be that Christ sticks to His plans no matter how we demand another way! His unwillingness to play our games has no doubt been our salvation in more ways than we realize.

What is birthed and grown from God's wisdom will always prove Him right. "'But wisdom is proved right by all her children'" (v. 35). Time will always tell that He is God. Believe it with your head even when you're struggling with your heart.

DAY 4

Loving Much

Today's Treasure
"Therefore, I tell you, her many sins have been forgiven—for she loved much. But he who has been forgiven little loves little" (Luke 7:47).

I'm about to teach one of my own lessons. I have been the sinful woman we study today. I am still so deeply moved by the infinite grace God has poured out on my life that my eyes burn with tears as I pen these words. I'm going to ask you to indulge me in a few moments of personal testimony to prepare for our lesson.

During the writing of *Breaking Free*, the enemy used every trick in the book to break me. He is our accuser (see Rev. 12:10) and a shameless opportunist (see Luke 4:13). He knew that *Breaking Free* necessitated very deep scrutiny of my history because the study is based on my journey to liberty. My whole life has forever been laid bare before God, but it had never been so vividly laid bare before me. At the taunting of the enemy, I found myself at one point so grieved over the "yuck" in my history that I could not imagine how God could possibly use me. I literally questioned my own calling.

During this painful time, I had a speaking engagement in Louisiana. Customarily someone from the host church delivers a devotional to the conference team before the conference begins. That day a woman who did not know me, had never heard me speak, had never read a single word I'd written, walked in the door and pulled up a chair in front of me. The entire group could hear her, but the devotional she delivered was for me.

She sat only inches away and never took her eyes off mine. With obvious anointing, she told the story we're about to study, then she said: "I don't know you, Beth. I have no idea why God sent me with such a message to give you, but He told me clearly to say these words to you: 'Tell her that her many sins have been forgiven—for she loved much.'" I cannot describe my feelings then or my feelings now.

This Scripture is the only one framed on my desk. It sits only inches from my computer. As I sit down at my desk to write commentary on God's Word, after the things I've done, I stare at the reminder of God's unreasonable grace lavished on me. And I'm reminded—I'm forgiven. Indeed, how could someone like me not love Him much?

Please read Luke 7:36-50 and complete the following:
What does Christ's willingness to have dinner with a Pharisee imply to you?

___

What caused the Pharisee to inwardly doubt whether Jesus was a prophet?

___

In the margin summarize in one sentence the parable told by Christ.

Our scene unfolds in the dining area of one of the more prestigious homes in the village. The Pharisee's home was large enough to accommodate Jesus and an undisclosed number of other guests (see v. 49). The smell of baked bread and roasting meat filled the home. The Pharisee's wife and any other women involved probably ate separately. They would not have considered this a slight since the men customarily practiced segregated fellowship in many social settings. Incidentally, their manly discussions often turned into passionate theological debates that they thoroughly enjoyed. Such conflict tends to make me nervous, so I would happily have stayed in the kitchen with the dessert and coffee.

Do you have difficulty picturing Christ in this scene? Do you imagine Him never fitting into a Pharisee's home? I think God desires to broaden our understanding and fine-tune some of our mental footage of Christ. The more I study His earthly life, the more I'm grasping that He could fit in anywhere ... and nowhere.

If my last statement was clearer than mud, what do you think it means? As you think about this question, don't forget Luke 5:16 and Luke 7:34.

___

Remember, Christ is void of all prejudice. He was no more likely to stereotype all Pharisees than He was to stereotype all poor, blind, or ill. Furthermore, He was just as anxious to save them from their sins. The obvious difference was how anxious any individual was to be saved.

Sometimes the blessing to the destitute or depraved is a greater awareness of sin and need. Before we are too harsh in our view of the Pharisees, we are wise to remember that their negative tendencies resemble anyone who values religion and ritual over relationship with the Savior. Interestingly, in the Gospels not once do we see a Pharisee who is confronted in the stronghold of legalism and self-righteousness ever admit to seeing it in himself. My point is that no one is likely to see herself as pharisaical without an honest, penetrating, and courageous look inside. In fact, our story line today never indicates that Christ's host received the message delivered to him through these events.

Someone else, however, got the message somewhere along the way. While the respectable women were eating in another room and the men were enjoying hearty fellowship at the table, in walked a woman who had lived a sinful life in that town. Let's attempt to grasp the magnitude of the situation. The original word for *sinful life* is *hamartolos,* which "frequently denotes a heinous and habitual sinner."[3]

Based on this definition, what might this woman have been like?

___

Compassion stirs my heart as I look at the phrase "in that town" (v. 37). A large metropolis was the exception in Christ's day. Most of the settlements resembled small towns rather than big cities. Any of us who have sinned habitually in a small town may grasp the added shame of publicity versus anonymity. A small community increases the risk of *your* feeling so shamed that you can hardly go out in public. Church communities in a large city can create the same kind of atmosphere.

Destructive cycles of sin are hard enough to deal with in private. The shame others heap on the "sinner" magnifies the hurt and often tightens the chains of bondage. I've had the joy of working with several people who were breaking free from habitual sin. Without exception, a primary obstacle was the judgment of others. They seemed better able to break free from the behavior than the disapproval. In today's text, the publicity of the woman's sinful life is obvious by how much the Pharisee knew about her.

Under these circumstances, what does her willingness to go to the Pharisee's house with her alabaster jar of perfume tell you about her?

___

I can't help but think that her desperation to be different and determination to live her life in gratitude, no matter what anyone else thought, made her gloriously vulnerable to new life in Jesus Christ. She did not ask for Christ to come outside. She walked right through the door into the middle of the festivities. Talk about killing a party! I imagine the party she killed on earth gave way to a much grander one in heaven. Her sudden intrusion probably caused every single recliner to recoil into its upright position. No doubt, all but One were horrified.

She brought an alabaster jar of perfume to anoint Christ's feet, but she could not even open the jar before she began to anoint His feet with her tears. From behind. Picture it clearly. The word used for her tears in verse 38 indicates that she was sobbing.

For some, this scene has already grown far too personal and demonstrative. You may not be at all comfortable with the outpouring of this woman's heart. Believe it or not, I feel just as much compassion for the person who is uncomfortable with this scene as I do the hurting woman. You see, this woman was no longer in bondage. She had been loosed. Anything that holds us back from pouring our lives and our hearts out upon Jesus is a bond. Some bonds may look like angry ropes. Others like pretty ribbons. But if they keep us from the One who frees us, they are bonds just the same.

The spotlight momentarily shifts to the Pharisee.

To whom does the Pharisee make his comments in verse 39? ___________

This phrase and Christ's impending response have great importance because they force us to realize that Christ holds us responsible for the things we say to ourselves. Ouch. Yes, He reads our minds—and sometimes our thoughts need a viewer rating.

I am learning so much in my journey with Christ Jesus—lessons I wish I had learned long ago. I am learning that my heart and mind are of greater importance to Him than my words and deeds. Our innermost places desperately need daily purification. Part of the process is recognizing and confessing the judgmental, impure, or critical thoughts before they can make their way to our mouths and our actions. God really can change our negative thought processes, attitudes, and motives. The process takes time and cooperation, however, because these thought patterns are just as much habitual sin as the transgressions of the woman of ill repute.

Don't overlook the fact that Christ's willingness to allow the woman to wash His feet caused the Pharisee to question whether or not Jesus was a prophet.

What does this tell you about his impression of a prophet?

____

Deuteronomy 18:18 is a clear prophecy about Jesus Christ. What does it say God will do with the prophet He'll raise up from among their brothers?

- ❑ **rain down fire from heaven**
- ❑ **put His words in his mouth**
- ❑ **pronounce judgment**

What does Christ say about His words in the following passages?

John 6:63 ____

John 17:8 ____

If Christ could speak only the words God put in His mouth, we can know the very heart of God by what Jesus says. Luke 7 does not just reveal the heart of a gentle Savior. It reveals the heart of God Himself, His Majesty, the *El Elyon*—toward a heinous and habitual sinner who dared to go against public opinion and grab onto His grace.

The Pharisee implied that Jesus obviously did not know what kind of woman she was. The original wording is quite interesting. The English words *what kind* in this verse are derived from two Greek words: *poios,* meaning "what," and *dapedon,* meaning "soil." The Pharisee's comment that Christ did not know where she came from literally meant what soil she came from. If I may be so bold, his attitude expressed a little more graphic meaning of the word: "He has no idea the dirt she comes from."

You know what, beloved? Dirt is dirt, and we've all got it no matter where we come from. I'm not sure Christ sees one kind of dirt as dirtier than another. One thing is for sure: His blood is able to bleach any stain left by any kind of dirt. Oh, thank You, Lord.

I'd like to share the *King James Version* of Christ's first response after He read the Pharisee's thoughts: "'Simon, I have somewhat to say unto thee'" (Luke 7:40). Lest you think I'm feeling pious in my deep compassion for the habitual sinner, please know I'm presently shuddering over the amount of times Christ has had somewhat to say unto me! Lord, have mercy on my soul!

I also love the *King James Version* response of the Pharisee: "Master, say on" (v. 40). Makes me grin. I wonder what he was expecting the Master to say on? I have a feeling it wasn't what Christ said. Christ told a parable of canceled debts and asked Simon to summarize which debtor loved the moneylender most. The answer was obvious, but Simon's words, "I suppose," revealed his reluctance to acknowledge it. After Simon pinpointed the one with the bigger debt canceled, Christ said, "'You have judged correctly'" (v. 43). Interestingly, Simon had been judging throughout the whole ordeal. It was just the first time he judged correctly.

Christ then brought the parable to life. According to the parallels Christ drew through the parable, both the Pharisee and the woman owed debts they could not pay. Her sins may have been regarded as 10 times greater, but at least she knew she was in debt.

Christ compared their responses to Him in verses 44 through 46. All three times Christ's description of the Pharisee's actions begins with the unsettling words, "You did not." How poignant. You see, one of the surest signs of an ancient or modern-day "Pharisee" is a life characterized far more by what he or she does not do than what he or she does. "No, Simon. You did not sleep around. You did not take bribes. You did not externalize your depravity. But as well, you did not give Me any water for My feet. You did not give Me a kiss. You did not put oil on My head. You did not see yourself as a sinner, and you did not receive My gift of grace, but she did."

He packs the punch into the living parable in verse 47: "'Therefore, I tell you, her many sins have been forgiven—for she loved much. But he who has been forgiven little loves little.'" Not because that's the way it has to be, but because that's the reality of our human tendency. We tend to have very little affection for that which doesn't seem to meet a need.

Two truths strike a chord in me as we conclude with Christ's confrontational statement:

He never downplayed nor minimized her sin. Human sympathy makes excuses like, "What you did wasn't that bad," or "after all you've been through, no wonder … " Christ never calls sin less than it is. The original word for *many* in Christ's description of her transgressions is *polutropos,* which means "in many ways, in diverse manners … diverse modes." In reality, Jesus knew sins in her life the Pharisee had yet to imagine. To picture Christ minimizing the woman's sinful past is to miss the entire point of the encounter. The point is that even though her sins had been many, heinous, and habitual, she had been forgiven (see v. 48), saved (see v. 50), and liberated to love lavishly (see v. 47).

Of all the commandments the Pharisee had kept, she rather than he observed the most important one. What was it, according to Mark 12:30?

The exquisite beauty of loving Christ is that it makes it impossible to keep only one commandment. The Word tells us that the person who truly loves God will pursue the obedient life (see John 14:21) and be far more likely to persevere in trials (see Jas. 1:12). No other commandment has the vital lifeline to all others that loving God does.

Christ never preached the annihilation of affection. He taught the redirection of affection. Human affection first directed to God and filtered through His hands returns to us far healthier and fit for others. That's one reason we are commanded to love Him first before we love others. Love that goes through Him first is filtered. Before we conclude today's lesson, give some thought to a few other ways the redirection of the woman's affections would have turned out to be her deliverance as she faced the future.

The curtain draws on the scene with Christ's pointed words: "'Your faith has saved you; go in peace'" (v. 50). Notice that her faith is in His grace; it was not that her love had saved her. She was saved by His love, not hers. His last words to her represent far more than the common Hebrew benediction, *shalom*. Christ's intention for this woman who had committed such sin and suffered such shame was a very literal peace. Perhaps, as it did for me, this lesson has caused you to picture yourself in her place. If you, too, have been in this scene with Jesus, perhaps you know the inner struggle of a sinful past. When I began the lesson, I shared my testimony of how Satan accused me. During that difficult period, not once did Christ say, "What you did wasn't that bad," or "After all you've been through, no wonder… " He simply sent a woman to deliver His Word—that I was forgiven. He whispered to my spirit, "Now, My child, be at peace." Oh, how I would love to be that woman to you today. Allow me to pull up my chair right in front of you, look you in the eye, and tell you what He told me to say: "Your many sins have been forgiven—for you love much." Go in peace.

DAY 5

His True Brothers and Sisters

Today's Treasure

"He replied, 'My mother and brothers are those who hear God's word and put it into practice' " (Luke 8:21).

One of my chief goals in this journey is to feel as if our feet have felt the warmth of the sand in every place where Jesus stood. I am asking God to give us the spiritual vision of an eyewitness. As Luke's eighth chapter unfolds, we have a fresh opportunity to adjust our mental images to include a few new people on the scene.

Read Luke 8:1-3 and list those who were traveling with Jesus.

Jesus actively summoned the twelve disciples to follow Him. Whether or not the others received a verbal invitation, a powerful force drew them. I believe, based on my own experience, that after all Christ had done for them, these women could not help but follow Christ and serve Him. You don't have to talk many captives who've been set free into serving Christ. Like Paul in 2 Corinthians 5:14, the love of Christ compels them.

Read Luke 8:4-21. Describe the sudden development in family dynamics.

___

Jesus was not rejecting as much as redefining His family. His statement reflected inclusion more than exclusion. In all likelihood, Christ's physical family came to take Him home to keep Him from appearing foolish. The verb tense used for their desire to see Jesus indicates quite an insistence. They surely weren't there to encourage Him. John tells us that "his own brothers did not believe in him" at this time (John 7:5).

Of course, we know that Mary certainly believed Jesus was the Son of God, but the pressure of family members can be quite forceful. Perhaps her other sons were intent on confronting Jesus, and she came along to act as a peacemaker. Sound familiar, moms? You don't have to be a mother to imagine how she felt in her present position.

List in the margin several things you imagine Mary felt.

As Christ redefined the family dynamics, He stated, "'My mother and brothers are those who hear God's word and put it into practice'" (Luke 8:21). He meant for His words to be revolutionary. They are as critical for us today as they were for those who heard them then. Please don't miss the profound importance of God's Word. Based on Luke 8:21, our kinship to Jesus Christ is directly revealed through what we do with the Word of God. What you are doing right now—studying God's Word—is not just a good idea. It is the very warmth and vitality of the family bloodline—proof that we are family to Jesus Christ.

Christ's priority is not how much we study the Word, enjoy attending Bible study, discuss Scripture in small groups, or finish our homework. His priority is for us to hear it and do it. Receive it internally. Express it externally. Both the verb tenses reflected in the words *hear* and *do* in verse 21 indicate continuous or repeated action.

The context of Christ's statement in Luke 8:21 is the parable of the sower. His redefinition of family was to be understood in the relation to His teaching on the Word. Thankfully, Christ did not leave His disciples to decipher the meaning of this parable.

What were Christ's disciples given that others were not (Luke 8:10)?

___

All of us love to know a wonderful secret, not only because we enjoy the information, but because we enjoy the trust a shared secret implies! The word for *secret* in Luke 8:10 is *musterion,* meaning "some sacred thing hidden or secret which is naturally unknown to human reason and is only known by the revelation of God." Beloved, I want you to understand that the deep things of God were not limited to Christ's first twelve disciples.

In John 8:31, who did Christ say were His disciples?

___

Take a moment to relish 1 Corinthians 2:9-13. How might our lives be different if we should become people with whom Christ could share the deep things of God?

____

____

Oh, friend, there is so much more to this journey. So much more to this divine relationship. So much more to the Word. We have scratched only the surface. Our lives with Christ were meant to be nothing less than the great adventure. Oh, God, make us people with whom You can share the deep things of Your heart.

The parable of the sower helps us to understand the obstacles that limit us and the elements that would free the Spirit to teach us the deep things of God. Glance back over Christ's interpretation of the parable in Luke 8:11-15.

Identify each of the following components in the parable:

The seed____

Those along the path ____

Those on the rock____

The seed that fell among thorns____

The seed on good soil ____

Before we study the differences in each of the above, let's address a critical common denominator. What relationship did all four have with the Word?
❑ They heard it. ❑ They believed it. ❑ They received it.

We cannot overemphasize the importance of applying and obeying the Word of God. You see, all four types of soil heard the Word, yet only one produced a harvest. It is not enough to hear the Word! We have just stumbled on my greatest burden for the body of Christ. How many people sit in church services where Scripture is never taught? They're not even hearing the Word of God! The thought should scare us half to death.

Furthermore, what masses of believers hear the Word but continue to live in defeat because they don't apply it? I was one of them. I desperately wanted to change. I was miserable in my captivity. I just didn't understand that the power to be transformed and liberated from the yoke of my past was in the authentic application of Scripture. Our obedience is not to make God feel like the boss. Trust me. He's the Boss and He knows it. Our obedience to apply the Word of God is so that we can live victorious lives that glorify our Father in heaven. Hearing it is simply not enough.

Now let's consider each of the types of soil the seed of God's Word fell upon:

Those along the path. Notice the activity of Satan in this example. Appropriately, he is pictured in the parable as a bird of the air.

What is Satan called in Ephesians 2:2? ______________________________

Luke 8:12 tells us Satan possesses the ability to come and take away the Word from a hearer's heart. The word for *take away* is *airo*, meaning "to take up and carry away." The image is one of an owl swooping down, snatching its prey in its claws, and soaring back victoriously to its perch. Scripture infers countless reasons Satan is so anxious to snatch the Word from us before we've internalized it. Contrary to the hopes of some, hell won't be an eternal party of depravity. No one will be glad they came. Eternity is a long time for regrets. Imagine the evil nature of one who seeks to keep people from being saved.

Those on the rock. The rocky soil represents the shallow hearers of the Word. These go a step further than those along the path. They do actually receive the Word. The Greek word for *receive* is *dechomai*, meaning "to take to oneself what is presented or brought by another." Perhaps you were troubled by the thought of Satan's ability to come and snatch the Word a person has heard. Understand that Satan can't take anything the believing hearer claims as hers. Once we've received the Word, it's out of his reach. He can try to distort our understanding of it, but he cannot steal it. As we'll soon see, however, we can give it up by our own volition.

The rocky soil didn't just receive the Word. It received the Word with joy! How eye-opening to realize that we can hear the Word and receive it joyfully, yet never let it penetrate the depths. Listen, some of the words of God are hard! I think He'd rather see us receive a Word, wrestle over it with tears, then let it take root forever, than jump up and down with ecstatic joy for only a while.

The shallow hearer believes … until the time of ______________ (v. 13).

What a terrible shame! We miss one of life's most awesome experiences if we don't get to see God's Word stand up under our trial. He wants to show us it works. He wants to show us He works! If we stop believing the moment we start being tested, we will never know the power and faithfulness of God. If you've developed a few deep roots of faith, you, just as I do, probably remember stages of superficiality and shallowness.

Share an example of something in your life which, in retrospect, you recognize was shallow, but at the time you were oblivious to the lack of maturity. (I wish I could be in your group for this question.)

____

____

Just think: in several years, if we cooperate with God and keep growing, we're probably going to shake our heads over a few things that characterize us now!

The seed that fell among thorns. We've seen hearers of the Word confront demonic thievery and life's adversity. As influential as these two can be, the thorns are probably a greater daily threat. These hearers are defeated by the distractions of the world: worries, riches, and pleasures. The word for *worries* is *merimna*, meaning "anxiety, care that brings disruption to the personality and the mind." We will deal with anxiety in a future lesson so we won't labor the point here. None, however, will argue it's a constant battle.

The word for *riches* is *ploutos*, meaning "material goods, … abundance." We don't have to be rich to be distracted by riches. You don't have to have much to want more. Working ourselves into the ground to afford more things is symptomatic of this distraction.

The word for *pleasures* is *hedone*, from which we get our term *hedonism*. Hedonism views "pleasure, gratification, and enjoyment" as the chief goals of life. Please take caution before you view all forms of pleasure as an enemy of the faithful believer. Few things frustrate me more than people who picture the Christian life as entirely sacrificial and for martyrs only. Walking with Christ is the greatest pleasure of my life. But even this sacred pleasure cannot be my goal. Knowing and pleasing Christ must be my goal. Distraction of all kinds is my biggest challenge in this pursuit.

For the sake of awareness, see if you can label any present distractions you are battling in any of the three categories:

worries	**riches**	**pleasures**
________________	________________	________________
________________	________________	________________

Now let's picture ourselves with every person or situation worrying us, every material good we're struggling to attain, and all the trappings of our pleasure-seeking heaped on top of us. It's enough to choke the life out of you, isn't it? That's exactly what Jesus meant. The distracted hearer chokes on her own worldly appetites. Luke 8:14 says she also doesn't mature, which is far more than unfortunate. It is a tragedy. The word *mature* comes from two Greek words: *telos,* meaning "end, goal, perfection," and *phero,* meaning "to bring, bear." The hearer of the Word who is distracted by the constant call of the world will never fulfill God's awesome plan for her life. You saw it described in your earlier reading today.

According to 1 Corinthians 2:9, what are distracted individuals missing?

____

The seed on good soil. The good soil represents the one who hears the Word and retains it. The word for *retain* is *katecho,* meaning "to hold fast, hold down, ... seize. To occupy a place." The picture drawn by this definition is not just receiving the Word in our hands, nor putting it in our mouths to see if it tastes good. Retaining the Word is chewing it up and swallowing it until it occupies a place in us, until it abides there. When God's Word is deliberately internalized, it will be authentically externalized. Why? Because it's no longer what we do—it's part of who we are.

Read Isaiah 55:10-12. What does verse 11 say God's Word will do?

____

God's Word will not return void. That's a fact. But I want it to accomplish and achieve in me, don't you? When this generation asks who Christ's brothers and sisters are, I want Him to point us out joyfully. For our kinship to be obvious, we've got to hear God's Word and do it. When He sends forth His Word, may He find fertile soil in each of us.

Then, when we've reached our lives' intended goals, we will go out in joy and be led forth in peace; the mountains and hills will burst into song before us, and all the trees of the field will clap their hands. Persevere, doer of the Word. A harvest is coming.

---

[1]Ronald F. Youngblood, ed., *Nelson's New Illustrated Bible Dictionary* (Nashville, TN: Thomas Nelson Publishers, 1995), 1221.
[2]Spiros Zodhiates, ed., *The Hebrew-Greek Key Study Bible* (Chattanooga, TN: AMG Publishers, 1996), 1647.
[3]Ibid., 1583.

10-12-05

Session 4

Introduction: This week we've traveled with Jesus all over Galilee "from one town and village to another" as He proclaimed the "good news of the kingdom of God" (Luke 8:1). Today we're going to stand on the shore of the Sea of Galilee and consider life on the other side. Christ did not limit His ministry to the religious communities. We will spotlight some important considerations for those who are willing to cross over with Jesus to "the other side of the lake" (Luke 8:22). When Christ summons us to the "other side"—when He chooses the route of the water—He wants to show us the deep.

Read Luke 8:22-27.

1. We'd better be sure Christ has __Called__ us to go and that __He__ is __going__ with us (v. 22).

2. We're likely to be __tossed__ by the elements, especially if we're __inexperienced__. (v. 23) (See Eph. 4:14.)

   The Greek word *nepios*, means "one who cannot speak; an infant, child, a baby without a definite limit of age."

3. We are wise to recognize the very real __danger__ (v. 23).

4. We may be endangered, but we cannot be __destroyed__ (v. 24).

5. We are accompanied by the One who has __dominion__ over __all__ __things__ (v. 24).

The scene concludes with two questions:

1. Christ's question: "__Where__ __is__ __your__ __faith__?"

2. The disciples' question: "__Who__ __is__ __this__?"

*Don't go as a Savior — Go as a servant
" " " a speactator — " " led by him
"Grow up" & know sound doctrine
Breathe of Faith "Knowing the truth" & Speak the word
Inhale faith / ExHale faith

Faith is to be guarded

WEEK 5

The Christ of God

Day 1
The Other Side

Day 2
Interwoven Wonders

Day 3
Extended Authority

Day 4
Baskets of Blessing

Day 5
Confessions of the Heart

At the conclusion of this week's study, we'll be at the halfway point of our journey. Can you believe it? Let me applaud you for applying the personal discipline this journey requires. God does not take your commitment lightly. His Word guarantees that you will inherit a blessing. He is changing you through the power of His Word. Not one moment you spend with Him is trivial. So tighten the straps on your sandals and take another deep swig of Living Water from your canteen. This week we have some exciting miles to trek. We'll watch Christ deal with everything from demons to the dead. We'll also stand close by as He entrusts some of His power and authority to the disciples. You and I will receive a brisk reminder that His original disciples were privy to some of the same blunders that plague us. On the heels of Peter's bright and shining moment, he'll receive a reprimand that will make him want to hide behind the nearest bush. Thank goodness, the disciples weren't perfect. Christ's willingness to use them anyway is hope for us!

Principal Questions:

Day 1: What "super-human" characteristics did the man have due to his demon possession?

Day 2: Can you describe the peculiar swing in emotions in the people at Jairus' house?

Day 3: According to Luke 9:1, what did Christ give the twelve to perform certain supernatural tasks?

Day 4: What do you think Christ might have been testing in His disciples?

Day 5: According to Matthew 16:21-23, what did Peter do after Christ announced His imminent suffering and death?

Enjoy Christ this week, Dear disciple. Allow His Truth to penetrate the inmost places of your heart and mind. Ask God to imprint His Name on every cell. That's your safety and your satisfaction.

DAY 1

The Other Side

Today's Treasure
"Jesus asked him, 'What is your name?' 'Legion,' he replied, because many demons had gone into him" (Luke 8:30).

Although I am most excited that you and I are taking this journey on paper, I hope you are also joining me for the group sessions whether by audiotape or videotape. Session 4 provides an introduction to today's Scriptures by focusing on events that occurred on the lake before Christ and His disciples reached the "other side." We will see several connections today.

Glance over Luke 8:22-25 and write a brief synopsis of what happened as Christ and His disciples crossed over to "the other side of the lake."

____

Describe the condition of the man Christ met on the shore (Luke 8:26-33).

____

What "super-human" characteristics did the man have due to his demon possession? Don't overlook things he "knew" as well as things he could do.

____

Why was his name Legion? ______________________________

You and I don't really have a clue what happens between the kingdom of God and the kingdom of darkness. If we did, it would freak us out. God has told us as much as we need to know. Let's begin to walk through this scene together. In Luke 8:22 you'll recall that Christ summoned His disciples to accompany Him to the other side of the lake.

In the video session, we pictured "the other side of the lake" somewhat as the godless side of the tracks. Satan is constantly at work in what we'd consider the religious world and certainly sin abounds; however, if you've ever been in a totally godless environment, it has a completely different feel. Perhaps the less the devil is hindered, the more his dominion seems obvious. In Charles Ryrie's *Basic Theology,* he writes: "Satan's aim is to create a system that rivals God's kingdom but which leaves Him out. It is to promote a counterfeit order."[1] This suggestion brings us to our first consideration today:

Our God is even God over the godless. Notice that the second Christ stepped His foot on their "turf," the demons knew He carried His authority with Him. You see, as hard as the demonic world tries to keep Him out, no one can keep Christ out of any place He is determined to go. The one place He will not force His presence is the human heart. The demons that met Christ at the shore that day were far more wicked than ignorant.

What posture did the demoniac assume when he saw Jesus (v. 28)?

____

____

While I certainly wouldn't confuse the demoniac's quick trip to his knees with worship, it definitely was a sign of the demon's acknowledgment that Christ was the Son of the Most High God. Our second consideration is food for thought rather than doctrine for digestion.

The demons may have anticipated Christ's coming. Even my most conservative commentaries entertained the idea that the storm which occurred on the way "to the other side" could have been an attempt by the kingdom of darkness to discourage Christ's arrival. We see a hint toward the possibility of this idea in the way Christ rebuked the wind and waters almost as if they were disobedient. Could they have been temporarily acting under the instruction of the god of the air (see Eph. 2:2) while the overruling Son of God was sleeping? Just food for thought, but it would help to explain why the demoniac literally met Christ on the shore, knowing for certain who He was.

The pure basics of human dignity are often targets of demonic assault. I'm sure you didn't overlook the most tragic segment in the scene. The demons had not only overtaken the man's mind, but also they had stolen every shred of his dignity. Absent were some of the basic rights any humanitarian feels a person should possess: clothes on his back and a roof over his head. Here in the United States, our law prohibits even criminals on death row from having those same human rights removed from them. Even though our law prohibits such indignities for its prisoners, you and I both have probably witnessed human indignities among our nation's own citizens. Let's face it, no government is powerful enough to police and enforce all human rights.

Briefly describe the most pronounced scene of human indignity you have ever witnessed:

____

I have been to "the other side of the lake" on more than a few occasions. I have seen people living in conditions no human being ought to experience … sometimes not far from the confines of my own community. Although I do not begin to know the answers to all the questions regarding human injustices, I do know that stealing dignity is Satan's agenda, not God's. For now, the Word of God tells us that the kingdom of darkness has been granted a certain amount of latitude. That's one reason why the world's most well-meaning, efficient governments cannot stamp out all infringements on "human rights." Something far more powerful than earthly government opposes their efforts. Interestingly, communism boasted the remedy to human injustices. In fact, it resulted in a greater destruction of human life and dignity than any other form of government. According to God's Word, when Christ returns and God's "kingdom come[s]" and His will is "done on earth as it is in heaven" (Matt. 6:10), it will be absent of all human indignities. Why? Because these kinds of affronts are products of Satan's rule, not Christ's. Even so, Lord Jesus, come quickly!

Before we proceed to the next point, take another look at verse 27. The demoniac didn't live in a house. Where did he live? ____________________

If you were writing this study, what would you have to say about this demoniac living in the tombs? How does that piece of information hit you?

____

____

I wonder how many people are living their lives "in the tombs"? Share an example how a person could figuratively live "in the tombs" today.

___

I know a woman who is still so oppressed by despair that decades after the loss of a loved one, she still lives "in the tombs." In no way do I minimize the horror of her loss, but I despise how the evil one has used it to minimize her life.

The demons know their time is limited. Compare Luke 8:28 to Matthew 8:29. What added insight does Matthew's version offer about what the demons knew?

___

According to Revelation 12:12, what does Satan know?

___

The devil hated to see the Word wrapped in flesh and dwelling among us because he knew his time allotment was getting shorter and shorter. I don't believe the plan for the Son of God to come to earth as the sacrificial Lamb was any secret. Remember, according to God's Word, Satan lived in heaven with all the other angels until pride resulted in his expulsion. I believe Satan knew what was going to happen. I just don't think he knew when. The demons controlling the man on the Gerasene shore also knew a day of reckoning had been appointed for them. Seeing Christ on a turf they had staked as their own did nothing but remind them their time was getting short. The story also has another implication.

Demons can enact supernatural strength. Matthew tells us that "they were so violent that no one could pass that way" (Matt. 8:28). Luke tells us that the demons enabled the man to break the chains that had been on his hands and feet (see Luke 8:29). I feel the need to stress something about supernatural power: not all of it comes from God! I have felt chills run down my spine when I've heard someone say: "But it had to be God! It was totally supernatural!" The Book of Revelation clearly teaches that at times Satan is able to display signs and wonders.

How was demonic power displayed in Acts 19:13-16?

___

How was human indignity also displayed?

___

Did you notice the presence of violence in both demonic encounters? While Satan certainly "masquerades as an angel of light" (2 Cor. 11:14), he also enjoys coming out of his shell. Violence is one of the most obvious fingerprints of Satan. Peter described Satan as "a roaring lion looking for someone to devour" (1 Pet. 5:8). As you attempt to grasp the seriousness of this familiar Scripture, picture the gory scene of a predator going after its prey. We don't even have to wonder if the constant surge in societal violence is his activity. How life has changed! In the past, it was certainly not uncommon for families to own guns, but the children didn't turn those guns on their parents—or even more unthinkable, parents on their children. Those unthinkable crimes are now commonplace. We can underscore two truths from this point:

- not all supernatural power comes from God, and
- while not all demonic activity appears violent, virtually all violence originates with the power of darkness.

Remember, ours is the Prince of peace. All conflict He ordains is for the ultimate purpose of peace under His righteous rule. Oh, for the government that will be on His shoulders (see Isa. 9:6-7)! I see the passage suggesting another consideration.

Solitary places can be used by God or Satan. Take another look at Luke 8:29. The man "had been driven by the demon into solitary places."

Contrast Mark 1:35 and Matthew 14:13 to Luke 8:29. What do these verses have in common? ________________________________

In Mark 6:30-32 who did Christ include in the need for a solitary place?

____

In the margin list a few ways we might know if our times of isolation are being used by God or by the enemy.

Only Christ can defeat demonic powers. Only by the name and power of Jesus can demons be defeated. Without Christ a "legion" of humans cannot take authority over a single demon. However, Jesus the One and Only can instantly take authority over legions of demons. The climactic point of the story reveals an almost laughable irony. The demons begged to be cast into the swine rather than into the abyss. (If you think I'm going to say a word about deviled ham, you're mistaken!)

Almost every definition of *abyss* I could find associated it with a watery pit or a depth with some kind of water. The demons were probably referring to the abyss mentioned in Revelation 20:2-3. Ironically, although Christ did not send the legion into the abyss, He most assuredly sent them (packing pork, I might add) into an abyss.

I realize I have a strange sense of humor, but I'm somewhat amused that "those tending the pigs … ran off and reported this in the town and countryside" (Luke 8:34). After all, they suddenly had a little time on their hands. Let's not assume they pitched the story like it was good news. Their stock market had just taken a considerable dive.

Oh, well. Bad news usually gathers a bigger audience than good news anyway. The villagers came out of the woodwork only to find the talk of the region sitting at Jesus' feet, dressed and in his right mind—an important testimonial for all who think Christians are basically lunatics. Satan is the one who hopes to breed lunacy.

The people allowed fear to eclipse the life-changing facts, and they ended up begging Jesus to leave. He could have healed them, saved them, taught them, sanctified them, and, for heaven's sake, delighted them. But all they wanted Him to do was to leave them.

Have you known of something happening in someone's life that should have endeared him or her to Christ, but instead, the person moved further away from God? If so, why do you think that happens?

____

Jesus left the Gerasenes, all right. But not without a vivid reminder of who He was and what He could do. Long after they recovered from the swine at sea incident, there would still be a man about town with a restored mind and real dignity who couldn't seem to hush. Christ told him, "Return home and tell how much God has done for you" (v. 39). How long do you think it had been since he had been home? Not back to the tombs, but home. Clothes on his back. Roof over his head. Soundness in his mind. A message on his tongue. So the man went and told all over town how much Jesus had done for him. All the demons in the air couldn't stop him, for his knees had bowed to a new Authority.

DAY 2

Interwoven Wonders

Today's Treasure
"Then the woman, seeing that she could not go unnoticed, came trembling and fell at his feet. In the presence of all the people, she told why she had touched him and how she had been instantly healed" (Luke 8:47).

I long to sit at Jesus' feet in heaven and hear Him describe personally what His earthly experience was like. I can't wait to hear all the missing details and what He was thinking when certain things happened. I think He will have plenty to say about His peculiar confinement to a human shell. We haven't a clue how constricting a wrack of flesh must have been to Him. In today's text we see Jesus in the center of the throngs, surrounded by serious need. Indeed, is there any other kind? Something rather unique takes place in our reading today. We'll witness two interwoven wonders.

Please read Luke 8:40-56. Why is Jairus' approach to Jesus refreshing, considering who Jairus was? ____________________

____

Let's take a mental stretch. We are told that Christ knew someone had touched Him because He felt the power "go out" from Him (v. 46). We can hardly imagine what He felt, but let's give it a try! Think of some human experience we could compare with this divine experience in an effort to relate a little more readily to the unknown through the known.

What analogy would you use to describe what Jesus felt?

____

Describe the peculiar swing in emotions in the people at Jairus' house.

____

Can you think of possible reasons why God purposely included the details that the child immediately stood up and was capable of eating?

____

I don't doubt that I must often seem juvenile to others in my approach to Jesus. For instance, sometimes I will literally expend mental energy trying to decide what I love the very most about Christ. Silly, isn't it? I'm having another juvenile moment right now: I am honestly trying to decide which of these two interwoven wonders is my favorite. For heaven's sake, I drive myself crazy. Let's just plow on into the Scriptures!

The scene back on the home turf provides the perfect contrast to the Gerasene departure. Jesus was as warmly embraced on one side of the lake as He was shoved away from the other. As strange as it seems, do you know what is even stranger? When the same pair of arms intermittently embrace and shove, embrace and shove. We've all experienced those kinds of arms, haven't we?

Notice how Luke 8:40 says the crowd welcomed Him because they were all expecting Him. I do dearly love surprise encounters with Jesus Christ, but I think He is pleased when we live our lives in expectancy. He delights in faith that fully expects Him to act. We may not know exactly when or how, but, oh, to live in certainty that Christ will show up in our circumstances as we seek Him and welcome Him!

Verse 41 introduces a major player who didn't come just to welcome Jesus. He came desperate for Jesus. In his must-read book, *Fresh Wind, Fresh Fire,* Jim Cymbala writes: "I discovered an astonishing truth: God is attracted to weakness. He can't resist those who humbly and honestly admit how desperately they need him."[2] Amen! I never fail to be moved during a church service when someone comes to the altar for prayer. I am uniquely touched, however, when someone who appears to "have it all together" admits that life has him out of control and he humbles himself for prayer. Oh, yes, I believe Christ is attracted to the open admission of pure desperation.

I'm sure you noted that Jairus was a ruler of the synagogue. What two things did he do when he approached Jesus?

1. ______________________ **2.** ______________________

Jairus reminds me of the centurion in Luke 7. He seemed to understand the concept of authority because of his authoritative position. Likewise, the ruler of the synagogue seemed to grasp that one Ruler existed before whom all others should bow. Not only was this Ruler worthy of respect, but also Jairus was rightly convinced that He was merciful in power. The events that follow weave two scenes together in such a way that I am compelled to offer thoughts involving both. The following observations strike me as I consider verses 40-56 as one unique segment of Scripture:

The depth of need. Neither Jairus nor the woman in the crowd had any small concern. Neither do many folks in our world. My precious mother, who is presently trying to help God with His job in heaven, really struggled when my speaking took on less levity and more depth. I'll be honest with you. She liked my ministry better when it was funnier. One good reason is because she was so hilarious, and any gift of wit I have came from her. The other reason is because she said that her generation considered such talk inappropriate and even depressing. I respected her feelings very much, but not to the point of disobedience to God. I assure you it was a hard test of my commitment to His will.

If you asked me what I have learned from my travels, among other things, I would tell you that I have learned that people are suffering out there. They often need more than a good, clean joke, as helpful as that can be. They need Jesus. And a whole lot of Him.

For both Jairus and the woman in the crowd, Jesus was literally their last hope. Who else could heal from the throes of death? And who else could cure what countless doctors had failed to cure, especially without pay? Indeed, Jesus was their only hope. I want you to spend a moment reflecting. Who do you know that is possibly down to his or her very last hope? Perhaps, like me, you even know several people.

In the margin identify them by their initials and briefly describe their otherwise "hopeless" situation.

Keep them in your peripheral vision throughout our entire lesson today. Next I want you to notice another detail of these two wonders.

The length of need. Don't you think it's interesting that the woman suffered her infirmity for the same length of time that Jairus' child had been alive? Ask anyone who has suffered with a chronic ailment how much focus it commands, and she'll tell you she struggles to focus on anything else. Ask any set of parents how much they focus on their one and only child and they'll likely tell you the same thing.

Please look up each of the following and record any reference to a length of time the person had been in his or her predicament:

Luke 8:27 ____________________ **Luke 8:43** ____________________

John 5:5 ____________________ **John 9:1** ____________________

Christ healed every one of these people. What one-sentence conclusion can you draw from these facts?

____

The depth of discernment. We read in verse 42 that the crowd pressed so closely to Christ, they were almost crushing Him. Yet, a woman behind Him only touched the edge of His cloak and He discerned the difference. Please keep in mind, she never even touched His skin. Amazing! Notice that when Christ asked, "Who touched me?" they all denied it. Odd, isn't it? The people were so close they were nearly crushing Him, but no one admitted to touching Him. Their response reminds me of children too afraid of getting into trouble to admit to something. Did they not realize He wanted few things more than for them to reach out to Him?

Look at the woman's response in verse 47 and fill in the following blank: "Then the woman, seeing that she could not go ____________________, came trembling and fell at his feet."

Beloved, no one goes unnoticed by Christ, least of all, a person acting on faith. The word *unnoticed* ought to conjure up in all of us an ability to relate.

When was the last time you either feared you were going unnoticed by God or hoped you were going unnoticed by God?

____

The fact is, we're never unnoticed. Sometimes we're happier about that than others. I love the fact that the woman in the crowd came trembling, even though she had exercised enough faith to draw forth the healing power of Jesus. It's good to know that the faithful still come trembling. In fact, their reverence is a critical part of their faith. The truly believing will most certainly also be the bowing.

For what possible reasons do you think Christ asked her to identify herself?

____

I think one reason might have been so she could enjoy the healing she had received. The *New International Version* doesn't record one phrase found in the *King James Version* of verse 48: "Daughter, *be of good comfort:* thy faith hath made thee whole; go in peace." In this way I believe Christ was saying: "Do not go forth as someone who feels they have stolen a gift! Be of good cheer! I freely give it to you!"

The breadth of power. Verse 42 tells us Jesus was on His way to heal the dying child when the woman in the crowd touched the edge of His cloak. Christ Himself described what happened: "Someone touched me; I know that power has gone out from me" (v. 46).

The word for *power* in the verse is one of my favorites. We've talked about it before: *dunamis* means "power, especially achieving power." You see, when the power went forth from Jesus Christ, it achieved! That's the nature of *dunamis*. We discussed in an earlier lesson that *ischus*, when used distinctively from *dunamis*, can represent more of the factuality of God's power. In other words, you might think of *ischus* as often meaning God's possessed power. *Dunamis* represents, among other things, that God is willing to apply the power He possesses.

The primary point I want to make is that Christ released enough power to heal a woman of a 12-year hemorrhage but still had plenty to raise Jairus' daughter from the dead! Let that sink in! I know you know it with your head, but I want you to receive it in your heart. Christ's power supply is limitless. He's not the Wizard of Oz with a limited number of wishes to grant. This is reality! And His resource of power and mercy is infinite. He can take you much farther than Kansas, Dorothy.

One night at Bible study I asked the entire group to come to their feet for a time of intercessory prayer. I then asked anyone with an "overwhelming need" that seemed absolutely "insurmountable" to sit down. I don't mind telling you, few people were left standing, and based on their tears, I don't think they were just being dramatic. I had anticipated having enough intercessors left standing to lay hands on all those who sat down. Boy, was I mistaken! For a split second I didn't know how to proceed, then the Spirit of God seemed to speak to my heart. What joy flooded my soul that very moment as God called upon me to come boldly before His throne and ask for a miracle for every single life because He had plenty of power to go around. That's exactly what I did. The testimonies written to me the next week were unforgettable. Virtually everyone witnessed some type of wonder that week.

Now hear this: Jesus has more than enough power! Does He seem to be on His way to another need, one that you perceive may be more important than yours? More a matter of life and death? No problem! Reach out and grab that hem! You are not going unnoticed—not even if He's on His way to raise the dead!

Right this moment, I'd like for you to write in the margin a few sentences of intercessory prayer for the person or people you recognized earlier as being at their last hope.

Now, beloved, what is your greatest need, the deepest desire of your heart? Write it. Two or three? Write them all—all over the page. Don't tell me how trivial they seem in comparison! Write them! After you've written, I want you to consider your list carefully. Now I want you to say out loud: Jesus, You have enough power.

Oh, friend, would you dare to believe that He is completely able? If He doesn't grant you what you ask in faith, it is never because He lacks the power. I believe it's because He wants to release an all-surpassing power and reveal an even greater glory through another answer. Will we laugh at the thought like the foolish mourners outside Jairus' home? Or, will we be invited into the house to behold a miracle?

DAY 3

Extended Authority

Today's Treasure
"When Jesus had called the Twelve together, he gave them power and authority to drive out all demons and to cure diseases, and he sent them out to preach the kingdom of God and to heal the sick" (Luke 9:1-2).

Thus far in Luke's Gospel the twelve have watched Christ at work and have witnessed His miracles, but they have not yet been empowered to exercise those wonders. The rules the disciples have known are about to change. Accompanying Jesus was never dull; I don't imagine the disciples expected to do anything but watch. They were about to receive a very special welcome to the wild world of Jesus Christ. Matthew is considerably wordier about this account, so we will interview him as well.

Please read Luke 9:1-9 and Matthew 10:1-16. List the names of all twelve disciples.

____

____

Christ gave the twelve ________________ and ________________ to perform certain supernatural tasks (Luke 9:1). What is the difference between these two words?

____

____

What were they to preach and to whom (Luke 9:2; Matt. 10:6)?

____

Read Luke 9:3 and Matthew 10:9. In the margin list as many reasons as you can why Christ may have given them this specific instruction.

What do you think Christ meant by *shrewd* and *innocent* (Matt. 10:16)?

____

Wouldn't you love to eavesdrop on the conversations between the disciples as they prepared to go out? Try to imagine yourself in one of their positions. What kinds of emotions do you think they experienced after Christ told them what He was equipping them to do?

Let's begin walking through these verses together, concept by concept. Consider …

The extension of power and authority. Christ had a very good reason for giving His disciples such power and authority at this time. They had seen Him perform all sorts of miracles so they knew the power and authority was authentic. Their faith had been fueled by fact. The time would come when Christ would depart from them and work through them rather than beside them. Christ very wisely gave the disciples power and authority while He was still on earth tutoring and policing them personally and visibly. They would be "in charge" of the kingdom message from an earthly standpoint long before they wanted to be.

The distinction of assignment. Think about the disciples' calling in Luke 6:13. An important distinction existed between their original call and the assignment in Luke 9. In Luke 9:10 we see that the apostles returned. In other words, Christ's instruction to go and minister was for a specific mission or task. They returned to await their next instruction. Their task was immediate, but their calling was permanent (with the exception of Judas). I believe the concepts of calling and task are often confused in the body of Christ. I know that I confused the concepts in the early years of my surrender to ministry.

When I was in my mid-20s, my wonderful ministry mentor, Marge Caldwell, helped me to see that God had equipped me with some of the speaking gifts. Once I began to exercise those gifts, I assumed that speaking was my calling. God soon made very clear that my calling was to surrender my life every single day to His will, to be His woman, and to do what He asked, whatever that was. I remember sensing Him speak to my heart through His Spirit, saying: "Beth, I do not want you surrendered to an assignment. I want you surrendered to Me." I realized that God did not want me "hung up" on the kind of assignment He would give me. In fact, I believe He didn't want it to matter to me one iota whether He asked me to teach the Word of God to a hundred people or to rock one baby in the church nursery. My calling was to be abandoned to Him.

Think of God's purposes in your life.
As best you know, what is your task? ______________________________

What is your calling? ______________________________

Do you see the difference? The twelve were called to be Christ's learners or pupils. They also were designated apostles, meaning they would be sent forth.

What would His pupils be sent forth to do? Whatever He told them. In our human need for the security of sameness, we tend to want one job assignment from God that we can do for the rest of our lives. He's far more creative than that!

You may ask, "Isn't it possible for God to assign a lifelong task such as preaching at one church for 40 years?" Absolutely! But we are wise not to make assumptions by surrendering to the assignment! Our calling is to surrender to God.

Brainstorm and list in the margin pitfalls you think we could avoid if we were more abandoned to God than to a particular kind of service.

How do you think you could know if God desired to redirect your assignment or mission?

____

____

Remember the meaning of *disciple*! Pupil, learner! We can't keep skipping class (our time with God in Scripture and prayer) and expect to know when He's scheduled a field trip! Part of the excitement of the wild world of Jesus is that we are challenged to keep learning, keep growing, keep listening, and when He commands, keep moving.

The motivation for giving. Like us, I'm not sure the disciples had a clue what they had been given. They had the privilege to be the closest earthly companions to the Son of God. They were chosen to witness the most remarkable phenomenon in all human history: the Word made flesh and dwelling among us. They broke bread with Him, laughed with Him, and talked Scripture with Him. They knew the sound of His breathing when He slept. They knew His favorite foods. They watched Him heal the sick, deliver the demon-possessed, and raise the dead. If they had never received another thing, they had been granted a privilege beyond all others. However, Christ didn't stop there. He also gave them power and authority.

Christ's words in Matthew 10:8 should inspire us to pour out our lives like drink offerings for the rest of our days. Look at the last statement in Matthew 10:8. The word for *freely* is *dorean,* meaning "freely, gratis, as a free gift." I think you might be very interested to see another way this same Greek word is translated into English.

Fill in the blank from John 15:25: "They hated me __________________."

The fill-in-the-blank words are translated from the same word, *dorean.* What does that tell you about the things we've received from Christ?

____

Unreasonable grace! Nothing is reasonable about the love of God or the gifts He so freely gives! Matthew 10:8 tells those who have received freely to also give freely. The word for *give* is *didomi,* meaning "to give of one's own accord and with good will."

Like me, I know you've received freely from God in ways you can't begin to count, but, presently, what are you most aware of freely being given?

____

Has that particular unreasonable grace caused you to freely give of yourself

recently? If so, how?____________________________________

The balance of receiving. Jesus told the disciples to depend entirely on those who would welcome them to provide for needs such as food and shelter. The concept of God's people assuming responsibility for the needs of those who serve them vocationally is delightfully consistent throughout the Word.

How do the following passages teach a similar concept?

Deuteronomy 10:8; 12:10-12,18-19 __________________________

____

1 Timothy 5:17-18 ______________________________________

We can express care for God's servants in all sorts of ways, not just wages. For instance, a tiny congregation meeting under a tree in Africa may have no money for their pastor, but they may be able to share a little food, some clothing, or a space in their dwelling. Remember, God commands us to help take care of needs, not greeds. Yes, a congregation may also choose to lavish love on their pastor, but I believe God demands that they meet his needs as much as possible.

When Christ established this concept of outsourcing care for His disciples, I think He had more in mind than physical issues. I believe He also wanted to develop the following two characteristics.

Describe how you think outsourcing their care would help develop:

Trust ____

Humility ____

The wisdom of awareness. Lastly, let's consider Christ's instruction to His disciples in Matthew 10:16. I believe this word is just as applicable for all Christ's modern disciples as for the original twelve. We, too, must "be as shrewd as snakes and as innocent as doves." The Greek word for *shrewd* is *phronimos,* meaning "prudent, sensible, practically wise in relationships with others." I had no idea when I entered ministry how prudent I would have to become about relationships.

Why do you think the twelve might have needed extra prudence in their "ministries"?

____

____

The Greek word for *innocent* is *akeraios,* meaning "without any mixture of deceit, without any defiling material." I don't care who we are or what we do, all of us meet challenges when momentarily, a lie would seem to serve us better than the truth. Look ahead to the verses that follow Christ's admonition about being shrewd and innocent.

Read Matthew 10:17-20. List temptations that could arise to cause the disciples to forfeit their innocence in the midst of those challenges.

____

Finally, let's look at the wisdom of possessing both biblical shrewdness and innocence because, between them, we will discover a vital balance. Second Corinthians 11:3 speaks specifically of Satan, but it also tells us what a snake without innocence can be like .

If our shrewdness was not balanced by innocence, which one could we become? ❑ **cunning** ❑ **disbelieving** ❑ **unreasonable**

What does Hosea 7:11 tell us that an innocent dove could be like without

biblical shrewdness or prudence?______________________________

Can you think of a reason why those who aren't very deceitful themselves might be easy to deceive? God doesn't want us to know we're being conned because we're master con artists ourselves. He doesn't want us to recognize deception because we know how to twist the truth. God deeply desires to develop godly integrity in each of us. He wants us to recognize the counterfeit because we're so familiar with the true article. He wants us to be smart without being suspicious—innocent without being naïve. The challenge is mammoth, so take it seriously. We, too, are sheep among wolves. I've been eaten alive a few times, and I have some "scars" to prove it. What I'd give to save you some!

It's dangerous out there. My best advice, dear sheep, is to stick to your Shepherd.

DAY 4

Baskets of Blessing

Today's Treasure
"They all ate and were satisfied, and the disciples picked up twelve basketfuls of broken pieces that were left over" (Luke 9:17).

I love the old hymn, "Great Is Thy Faithfulness." Indeed, "all I have needed, His hand hath provided." But God has gone far beyond what I needed. That's what stuns me. The same wonderful hymn also sings forth God's lavish overflow: "Strength for today and bright hope for tomorrow, Blessings all mine, with ten thousand beside!"[3] I will never comprehend how God could give us a blessing and, as the song says, then throw in an extra ten thousand beside. That's the overflow of today's lesson.

Our focus will fall like a picnic blanket on the countryside where throngs of people gather but only one packed a lunch.

Read Luke 9:10-17. If the story is familiar, ask God for a fresh insight.

Did you know that this is the only miracle recorded in all four Gospels? Christ performed so many signs and wonders that no single Gospel contains every reference, yet all four include the feeding of the five thousand—proof of this miracle's significance! Today we're going to interview all four writers simply because we can. We won't often have exactly this kind of opportunity.

Compare Luke 9:10 to Mark 6:30-32. Why did Christ desire to withdraw with His disciples? ____________________________________

Their rest time was interrupted by a restless crowd. Compare Luke 9:11 to Mark 6:34. Mark specified the reason such compassion surged from the heart of Christ. The people "were like sheep without a shepherd."

What did Christ see in them that made Him describe them this way?

____

The disciples showed concern for the crowd because it was late and the location was remote. I find it interesting that Christ pitched the challenge right back into the laps of the disciples. In the dialogue with Christ, John mentioned the two primary players among the disciples. Because so little is said about them in comparison to Peter, James, and John, let's give them notice. Read John 6:5-9. For our present purposes, treat these verses as if they contained the only pieces of information available on these two disciples. Think creatively! This is strictly conjecture for the purpose of helping us to explore the human dynamics.

What possible insight might these Scriptures suggest about Philip and Andrew? Consider their personalities or thinking processes.

Philip ____

Andrew ____

How much did the people eat (John 6:11)? (Choose one.)

- ❑ **all they had**
- ❑ **half the food**
- ❑ **as much as they wanted**
- ❑ **all the fish**

We know that Jesus "already had in mind what he was going to do" (John 6:6). I believe He planned every detail down to the exact end result. All four Gospel writers tell us 12 baskets of broken pieces were left over.

Even though we don't know exactly what Christ had in mind, offer your thoughts as to any significance to the number of baskets.

____

Now that you've had a chance to express your own thoughts about the passages, let's walk through this countryside together. Any of us who have ever been exhausted by an intense time of ministry can deeply appreciate the opening scene in Luke 9:10. We are told "the apostles returned." Recall your previous lesson.

What had they been doing? ____

I love Mark's version of Christ's reception. Take another look at Mark 6:30-32. Picture it: He's surrounded by the twelve disciples who are probably so excited, they are all talking at once. What an endearing scene! They are so happy to see Him … and He them! What affection floods this setting! We can assume He omnisciently knew everything they had done and taught, yet I love how He celebrated their news with the excitement of someone at a surprise party. Sometimes I'll be busy telling God every detail of something exciting that happened, a thousand words a minute, when suddenly I will stop and say, "But I guess You already knew that." Every single time I sense Him saying: "Don't let that stop you, child! Tell on!" And I do.

Beloved, do you feel free to talk to Him with the excitement of a friend? Elaborate on your answer.

____

____

Christ not only sees our excitement, He sees our exhaustion. I love the way the *King James Version* says it: "They had no leisure so much as to eat" (v. 31). He saw their need for leisure over a refreshing meal. His invitation to them is so warm and intimate that my affection for Him swells every time I read it: "'Come with me by yourselves to a quiet place and get some rest'" (v. 31). I can't pass up the opportunity to point out that the original word for *rest* in this verse is *anapauo*. *Pauo* means "to cease, give rest." Guess what *ana* means? "Again"! We don't need this kind of rest just once. We need it again and again. We not only have Christ's permission to rest when we're exhausted, but also He beckons us: "Come to me, weary one, and rest again!"

Wouldn't you know it? In the middle of their private getaway, the public showed up. Christ's response to the crowd touches me: "He welcomed them" (Luke 9:11); "They were like sheep without a shepherd" (Mark 6:34). Desperate, vulnerable, without direction, without protection, and He had compassion on them. According to Matthew, we are pretty safe to picture at least ten thousand people gathering all over the countryside. When was the last time you were in a group of ten thousand people? Can you imagine how overwhelming the sight would have been to anyone less than God Incarnate? Yet, His Word tells us He "healed those who needed healing" (Luke 9:11). The day wore on, and the sun rested again on a western hill. About that time, some interesting things began to happen. Consider the following observations with me.

Christ sometimes provokes a question so that He can be the answer. I love how John's version tells us Christ prompted the question, "'Where shall we buy bread for these people to eat?'" (John 6:5). Verse 6 tells us, "He asked this only to test him."

What do you think Christ might have been testing in His disciples?

____

Again I'm reminded of the meaning of *disciple*: learner, pupil. I think Christ might have been testing His disciples to surface what they had learned, or, like me, what they had yet to learn!

What kind of miracles had the disciples seen and even done by this time?

____

Yet they couldn't imagine how they were going to feed all these hungry people. I think Jesus may have been testing them to see if they were beginning to think in a "faith mode." Their response proved they still practiced fragmented faith. While they had seen Christ cast out demons and heal the sick, it had not yet occurred to them He could feed the masses. They still had much to learn about Christ's complete jurisdiction.

Christ can meet our spiritual needs, our emotional needs, and our physical needs. He is both deeply spiritual and entirely practical. He can also apply a miracle to absolutely any situation. Christ was teaching them to see Him, His power, and His authority in every area of life. Boy, am I convicted! How about you?

Have you begun thinking in a pretty consistent faith mode, or can you still see evidences of fragmented faith? Give your answer in the form of a personal example.

____

____

Christ wants us to be open to what He can do through us. I'm sure you didn't miss the way He tossed the responsibility for feeding the crowd right into His disciples' laps. "'You give them something to eat'" (Luke 9:13). Mind you, they had received power and authority to heal the sick and cast out demons, yet they looked helplessly at two fish and five loaves as the totality of their resources.

Again I believe Christ was saying, "Think bigger, boys!" This time, not only about what He could do, but also what they could do in His Name. Where the disciples were concerned, I believe this event was all about stretching their thinking. Look again and you'll see that His words are entirely absent of rebuke. Don't miss the fact that He used the disciples to distribute the meal. He wanted them to feel the weight of the baskets and see the hands of those reaching to be fed. Real power in real forms in real life.

Christ can perform astounding wonders when we bring Him all we have. Matthew 14:17 records the disciples saying, "We have here only five loaves of bread and two fish." Christ then responded in verse 18, "'Bring them here to me.'" Beloved, I want you to hear something loud and clear: no matter what your "only" is, when you bring all of your "only" to Jesus, it's huge! When we bring Him everything we have, He multiplies it beyond our wildest imagination. On the other hand, we can surrender Him "some" of our lot and it can dwindle to virtually nothing. I know of no other way to say it: Christ is into "whole" and "all," not "half" and "some."

When was the last time you saw Him take the equivalent of a few fish and loaves and multiply them before your eyes?

____

Christ saved a basket-load of leftovers for each disciple. When all had eaten and were satisfied, the disciples picked up leftovers to fill 12 baskets. I just can't make myself think that was a coincidence. I'm no mathematician, but the numbers work for me. Twelve baskets. Twelve disciples. I'm a simple woman. The disciples could have used some rest that day. After the slightest breather, they had a responsibility thrown in their laps and a basket thrown in their hands. All it took was everything a willing boy offered and the blessing of Jesus. Next thing you know, the masses were happy as hound dogs in sunshine, and the disciples were standing there with a basketful of leftovers each. That's what happens when you take part in God's provision.

At the age of 20, my older daughter was asked to speak to a group of teenage girls in Oklahoma. She is the shier of my two children and is very resistant to any sort of spotlight. With horror on her face, she told me she was certain God was telling her to say yes. I cannot express to you how far outside her comfort zone this was at the time.

The butterflies never left her stomach from the time of the invitation until the day of the conference. What emotion flooded my heart as I put her on that plane to go forth and speak—instead of the other way around. Contrary to her worst fears, she lived through it! And the young women received a sound message from the Word … even if the voice was a little shaky here and there.

The next morning she called me with such a tender heart, her voice cracking and said, "Mom, I just had my time with the Lord … and He was so … sweet."

I realized she was having trouble articulating what she was feeling, but I knew exactly what she was talking about and said: "Oh, my precious child, you have just experienced that which would be worth selling all your earthly possessions to gain and yet it's a gift of grace: divine approval. The smiling nod of God. Nothing like it."

With the slightest whisper, my very humble, gentle child said, "Yes."

Think bigger, boys!
You've yet to find
I've got all the power
All of the time

Think bigger, boys!
While it is day
Watch what I do
Do what I say

Think bigger, boys!
See every scene
With Me in the middle
Reigning as King

Think bigger, boys!
For one day you'll see
Me in my glory
Then you'll say to
Me…

We should've thought
bigger.

I'm fighting back tears at the thought. You see, this act of obedience was terribly hard for her. She felt ill-equipped, though she was not. She could have provided a list of other students she considered better choices. But she didn't. In effect she said, "All I have is this pitiful handful of fish and loaves," and Jesus said, "Bring them to me." When all was said and done, she wasn't sure what the girls had received, but God had given her bread from His Word and she had distributed it the best she knew how.

Amanda was glad to have survived ... but imagine her surprise when she didn't just survive. The next morning as she sat before the Lord, He handed her a basket full of leftovers. Blessings all hers ... with ten thousand beside. She had been willing to be a disciple. A learner. A novice. He would not have dreamed of leaving her emptyhanded. You either, my friend. It's not His style.

Strength for today and bright hope for tomorrow. Blessings all theirs ... with 12 baskets beside. Great is His faithfulness.

DAY 5

Confessions of the Heart

Today's Treasure
" 'But what about you?' he asked. 'Who do you say I am?' Peter answered, 'The Christ of God' " (Luke 9:20).

Today we come to one of the most crucial points in Christ's earthly ministry. We see a chain of critically important conversations that are best understood when linked together. We will need all the space we can get today, so I'll limit my introductory statements to these. Please begin with prayer for insight that will take you further with God than my commentary. No doubt, I will leave much lacking. Our reading will take place in four segments today.

Part One: Peter's Confession. Scripture points out that Christ was praying privately, yet we know His disciples were in His company. I think we can probably conclude that He wasn't praying with them, but He certainly may have been praying about them.

Please read Luke 9:18-21 and Matthew 16:13-19. Take particular notice of the context of this interchange. What had Christ been doing when He stopped and asked His disciples who the crowds were saying He was?

____

Glance ahead for just a moment to Luke 9:22. Considering the question He asked in Luke 9:18 and the prediction He was about to make, try to imagine what kinds of things Jesus might have been praying about.

Write your thoughts below:

____

____

In all probability, Herod's determination to know Christ's identity as recorded in Luke 9:9 may have helped heighten the talk among the crowds. We need not doubt that all who knew about Christ were trying to figure out who He was. Considering the events that were imminent on Christ's earthly timetable, it was not critical for the crowds to know Christ's full identity at that time, but it was of utmost importance that the disciples know. They would desperately need to know who He was even when they couldn't understand what He was doing. "'Who do you say I am?'"

Peter stepped up to the plate: "The Christ of God" (Luke 9:20). The Christos. The Anointed One. The Messiah. Matthew's Gospel records the divine approval of Christ over Peter's inspired response: "'Blessed are you, Simon son of Jonah, for this was not revealed to you by man, but by my Father in heaven'" (Matt. 16:17). Do you realize, my dear sister, that if you know the true identity of Jesus Christ, no preacher or teacher revealed it to you? The Father of all creation, the God who sits on the throne of the universe pursued you in the midst of millions and chose to reveal His Son to you. Remember that the next time you feel insignificant.

On several occasions we will see Peter act somewhat as a spokesman for the disciples. I don't think we're to conclude that he was the only one of the twelve who knew Christ was the Lord's Messiah. He was no doubt a leader among them, however, and he did not hesitate to answer the question. Christ's response to him is awesome and the play on words is amazing. "'I tell you that you are Peter, and on this rock I will build my church'" (Matt. 16:18). The name *Peter* is the original word *petros,* meaning "a stone, … a large stone, a piece or fragment of a rock such as a man might throw." His name might more literally be translated as "stone-man." Isn't that an awesome name?

After reconfirming Peter's Christ-given name, Jesus then said, "'On this rock I will build my church.'" Stay with me here! In this use of the word *rock*, the word switches to *petra*, meaning "a projecting rock, cliff … Distinguished from the masculine *petros* in that *petra* is a mass of rock while *petros* is a detached stone or boulder, a stone that might be thrown or easily moved … Used metaphorically of Christ and the testimony concerning Him which is an unchangeable, immovable testimony."

To nail down the concept, what do each of the following words mean in Matthew 16:18?

"Peter": Greek word ________________, meaning______________________

"rock": Greek word ________________, meaning ______________________

When He referred to the rock upon which He would build His church, I believe Christ was talking about the unchangeable, immovable testimony of Jesus Christ that Peter had just delivered. Based on the definitions above, I believe Christ was saying: "Peter, the testimony of my identity is the immovable rock upon which I will build my church. A cliff on which all of eternity hangs. You, my Stone-man, are a chip off this immovable rock whom I will greatly empower." Peter was a chip off the unshakable block of Jesus Christ—one Christ would throw from place to place to give the testimony about the Rock from which he was hewn. How beautifully Isaiah 51:1 speaks advice that would have applied to Peter and certainly applies to us!

In your own words, what does it say? ______________________________

____

Notice that Christ said specifically that the gates of hades will not overcome His church. The thought often occurs to me that Satan can do nothing to overcome the church, the body of believers in Christ, from the outside. No amount of perversity, depravity, or even persecution will ever be allowed to overcome the church. Satan can't tear us down from the outside; that's why he seeks to do an inside job: division, bitterness among believers, infighting, denominational elitism. Local church bodies don't die because of the world's influence; they die from internal diseases. Let's be on the lookout for inside jobs. Keep Satan out and the very gates of hades cannot prevail against us.

Part Two: Christ's Prediction. Read Luke 9:22-23. Does a fresh look at these verses astonish you as much as it does me? Christ didn't talk in parables here! No veiled truths. No innuendoes. Not a single mixed message.

Record each fact Christ told the disciples to expect:

___

___

The clarity with which Jesus told His disciples what to expect will make their desertion all the more complex when the time comes. I am awed again by Christ's very literal awareness of every detail that He would face. "'The Son of Man must suffer many things … and he must be killed.'" The Greek word for *must* is *dei,* meaning "inevitable in the nature of things."

Based on your own understanding, why was His suffering and death inevitable in the nature of things?

___

Part Three: Peter's Reaction. We don't have to wonder if the disciples were horrified at Christ's future suffering and death. I think they were so caught up in the "bad news," they missed the good news of the glorious resurrection. Once again Peter takes the lead, but this time his mouth gets him into trouble. Boy, can I relate!

What did Peter do (Matt. 16:21-23)? ___

___

For all practical purposes, Peter took aside the Christ, the Son of the living God, and shook his finger in His face. Try to picture Peter in the midst of the disciples right after Christ had announced His future, saying something like: "Jesus, can I see You just a minute right over here? Excuse me, Brothers. We'll be right back." Then he commenced his rebuke. In my opinion, the Stone-man was pretty fortunate he didn't get "thrown" into the nearest lake! Several thoughts surface as I look at this interchange:

1. One minute we can be so "on target" and the next minute so "off"! Amen? Without a doubt, some of my better moments preceded my worst disasters.

How about you? Any comments?

___

I keep looking at those words: "This shall never happen to you!" I wonder, based on Christ's response to Peter, if in his heart he might have been thinking more readily: *This shall never happen to me! I've given up everything and followed You! You can't die on us here! We've got a kingdom to build!* He didn't understand that Christ's suffering and death were the means by which He would indeed secure the kingdom.

Peter understood Christ's identity: the Christ, the Son of the living God. But he didn't understand Christ's destiny: the cross, the grave, the right hand of God. He might have been wiser to have asked a question like, "Why must You die?" than to rebuke.

However, Peter was not cast away—nor are we in our moments of outlandish foolishness. Glory to God! Christ did not retract Peter's calling, but He certainly told him a thing or two.

2. All Satan needs to have momentary victory over a disciple is for us to have in mind the things of men. Satan doesn't have to get us thinking blatantly satanic thoughts to have victory over us. All he needs is to get us looking at life from man's perspective rather than God's. If we surrender our minds to the things of God, we are safe! We don't have to constantly look out for our own best interests, because He's constantly looking out for them. What Peter didn't understand is that what may have seemed best in the short run would have been disastrous in the long run. Had Jesus saved His disciples the anxiety of His betrayal, His capture, His trials, and His death, He wouldn't have saved them at all. Without the cross, man had no chance.

I don't know that we will ever walk so long with Christ on this earth that we will at some time perpetually have in mind the things of God rather than the things of man. If we don't make the deliberate choice to have in mind the things of God when faced with our biggest challenges, most of us will probably default, like a computer, back to our natural mental instinct—the things of man.

What is your biggest challenge presently?__________________________

____

Are you making the deliberate choice to "have in mind the things of God"?
❑ Yes ❑ No

We all find ourselves vacillating at times. When we're struggling, how can we stir in our thinking the things of God rather than the things of man?

____

____

Peter's example demonstrates our vacillation between having in mind the things of God and the things of man. In comparing the Gospels of Luke and Matthew, all these events appear to have happened in a solitary scene. One moment Peter made a statement that Christ said could only have been revealed to him by the Father. The next thing we know he's made a statement Christ attributed to the devil. One minute a rock—the next minute a stumbling block. Whew! What a frightening thought! How on guard we must be!

Part Four: Christ's Invitation. In light of Peter's performance and subsequent rebuke, we see an amazing response from our Lord.

Read Matthew 16:24-28 and Luke 9:23-27. Write down three words that you think characterize this invitation:

____________________ ____________________ ____________________

You probably cited a word like *radical*. Indeed it is. I'd like for us to focus on Luke's version of this invitation, but before we do, please don't miss the fact that Peter was still invited to "follow" after his horrible faux pas. I am intrigued that Peter actually heard the invitation to follow three times before Christ ascended to the right hand of the Father: Matthew 4:19, this passage, and John 21:19. Almost as if he were getting a crash course in Follow 101, Follow 202, and Follow 303. The first one was to follow Him as a disciple. The second one was to follow Him with a cross. The third one was to follow Him to death. Not coincidentally, tradition teaches that Peter indeed ended up following Christ to the death … on a cross.

I will be addressing the concept of taking up our crosses in week 8, but for now, what do you think Christ meant by cross-bearing?

____

____

Developing the mind-set of one who is continually taking up his cross and following Christ is the heart of "having in mind the things of God" rather than man. Don't forget that the issue which prompted this discourse was that of identifying Christ. When we surrender to carrying our crosses and following Him, we identify with Him.

Let's look at two other concepts in Christ's invitation before we conclude:

1. Denying self. Those who accept this invitation are called to deny themselves. In context I don't believe Christ was talking about the things we typically consider self-denial. The issue here wasn't fasting from food, nor was it denying self a single extra. It wasn't about self-loathing, for Christ commanded us to love our neighbor as ourselves. Once again, recalling the original concept of Christ's identity, I believe the primary issue involved in this kind of self-denial is denying our right to be our own authority.

Today I believe we came to the sobering realization that what we might think is our own authority—having in mind the things of men—could easily be transferred to Satan's authority. I've learned the hard way that denying my right to be my own boss is what keeps me from getting slaughtered by Satan in warfare. Let's face it: this "be-your-own-boss" stuff is nothing but a myth.

2. Taking up the cross daily. The key to true "follow-ship" with Christ is the daily recommitment to His cross. One reason I am drawn to Luke's version of this invitation over Matthew's is because he includes an all-important word.

Please fill in the blank: "If anyone would come after me, he must deny himself and take up his cross ____________________ and follow me."

In my opinion, Dr. Luke wrote the prescription for the victorious life, and he wrote it for all of us who would desire to become Christ's disciple: live life one surrendered day at a time. Eyes to the East. Hands to the cross. Feet to the path.

[1] Charles C. Ryrie, *Basic Theology* (Wheaton, IL: Victor Books, 1986), 152.

[2] Jim Cymbala, *Fresh Wind, Fresh Fire* (Grand Rapids: Zondervan Publishing House, 1997) 19.

[3] Thomas O. Chisholm, "Great Is Thy Faithfulness." © 1923 Hope Publishing Company, Carol Stream, IL, 60188. All rights reserved. Used by permission.

VIDEO RESPONSE SHEET GROUP SESSION 5

Session 5

Introduction: Our fifth week of study offered us far deeper insight into Christ's relationship with His twelve disciples. On day 5 Christ asked a critical question: "Who do you say I am?" (Luke 9:20). The Scriptures reveal that, eight days later, three of them received an even more dramatic glimpse into who He was. Our focus today will center on the transfiguration of Christ.

Read Luke 9:28-36.

We can apply the study of this phenomenal event to our own relationship with Christ in several ways:

1. Christ seeks to readjust our vision of Him.

   The more we are willing to receive, the more He is willing to reveal to us.

   God is the fullness of all security and mystery. He meets all of our emotional needs as well as our mental needs.

2. To readjust our vision, Christ may choose to rearrange our surroundings (v. 28).

3. No matter how our earthly perception is readjusted, the immortal reality still greatly exceeds any mortal revelation (vv. 29-32).

4. Our meeting places with Christ are not locations where we build tabernacles and stay (v. 33).

   The original Greek word for *good* is *kalos,* meaning "constitutionally good without necessarily being beneficial; expresses beauty as a harmonious completeness, balance, proportion."

5. Christ ordinarily reveals Himself to us in private so He can reveal Himself through us in public. Look ahead to verse 37.

6. When our spiritual vision is being readjusted, our hearing is as vital as our sight (v. 35).

7. Our vision of Christ is under appropriate readjustment as we come to see Jesus alone (v. 36).

8. Consider redefining a "mountaintop experience." Any place we see Christ transfigured can turn out to be the greatest mountaintop experience of our lives.

? What are God's purpose for your life?

What is your God given calling?

WEEK 6

The Necessity

Day 1
Everything Is Possible

Day 2
The Road to Greatness

Day 3
The Seventy-Two

Day 4
The Heart of a Neighbor

Day 5
A True Tale of Two Sisters

I love the portion of the journey waiting just ahead! Because our subject matter is biographical rather than topical, God is dealing with our hearts and minds on countless issues each week, isn't He? We're simply going wherever Jesus goes. And does He ever go! Have I told you lately how much fun I'm having on this trip with you? Together we get to be disciples #13 and #14. If we really assimilate and apply what we will encounter in this week's study, our discipleship will be completely transformed. God will challenge us to overcome unbelief, pride, and any misplaced motivation for serving Him. Christ has just as much to say to us this week as He said to those who stood face-to-face with Him in each encounter. We won't have to look for creative ways to apply these encounters to our lives. These sandals will instantly fit if we're willing to wear them. They will also keep our feet from slipping as we walk the ministry miles ahead. Let's ask God to help us be completely willing to relate.

Principal Questions:

Day 1: To what part of the father's request did Christ take exception in Mark 9:23?

Day 2: What two events had taken place in Luke 9:28-43 that may have provided a breeding ground for the greatness question in Luke 9:46?

Day 3: What did Christ establish as the primary cause for joy for the seventy-two?

Day 4: Based on the account in Luke 10:25-37, and using one sentence, how would you define *neighbor*?

Day 5: Which one did Jesus love: Mary or Martha? What does that tell you?

Let's not hesitate for a single moment. Day 1 may be just in time for a situation you're presently facing. Get completely involved with Jesus.

DAY 1

Everything Is Possible

Today's Treasure
"'If you can?' said Jesus. 'Everything is possible for him who believes'" (Mark 9:23).

We have hit the halfway point in our journey. Aren't you something? You have done a fabulous job! We have more than a few Galilean miles behind us, but Christ's most critical miles still lie ahead. Let's take a moment to refresh our commitment. Let's stay with this journey until all we can see is Christ's feet over our heads as He ascends into the heavens. Pause and ask God to help you stay focused until we've walked every mile.

I so hope you are participating in the video sessions or have access to the audiotapes. Today's text immediately follows the transfiguration of Christ, which we studied in video session 5. If you were unable to join us for the study of the transfiguration, please precede today's reading with Luke 9:28-36 so you'll know what has just taken place. Today's events are recorded in Luke 9:37-45. Read these verses carefully, then read Mark's more detailed version of the same events in Mark 9:14-32. Complete the following based on both Gospels:

As Christ, Peter, James, and John came down from the mountain, what were the other disciples doing?

❑ fishing ❑ sleeping ❑ attempting to cast out a demon

Describe the emotions you think may have been behind Christ's statement in Luke 9:41 and Mark 9:19.

____

What effects did the demon possession have on this particular boy?

____

To what part of the father's request did Christ take exception in Mark 9:23?

____

Luke's Gospel doesn't include the disciples' request to know why they couldn't cast out the demon. Both Matthew and Mark include their inquiry.

What was Christ's explanation in each version?

Mark 9:29 ______________________________

Matthew 17:20 ______________________________

You may be thinking: *Another lesson about faith! Didn't we just have two lessons on faith in week 5?* Absolutely! And we'll have many more because our whole lives are about faith! Where His children are concerned, faith is everything, for "without faith it is impossible to please God" (Heb. 11:6). This series is about two things: Christ and our faith. One is heavenward; the other is earthward. God uses our faith to demonstrate on earth what He has already accomplished through Christ in heaven.

Let's sketch the opening scene. Luke's Gospel sets the time frame as "the next day," while Matthew and Mark imply the time immediately following the transfiguration. This might indicate that the transfiguration happened during the night. When Christ and the three returned from the mountain, the other disciples were engaged in an argument with the teachers of the law. At first glance, the dispute seems to have little bearing on the events surrounding the demon-possessed boy, yet God purposely wanted us to know about it. I'd like to suggest that the argument may have greatly affected the disciples' failure. This statement ushers in our first point:

We are often empowered to do far more than we exercise. In Luke 9:1 we read that Jesus gave the disciples "power and authority to drive out all demons." Do you think He had taken it back? They still possessed the power but were unable to exercise it for some reason. What in the world happened to disable them? Let's explore a few possibilities.

1. Their most positive influences were absent. Keep in mind that not only was Christ out of sight, but also the three leaders among them. In moments like these, we learn where our confidence is. However unintentionally, is it in the presence of other believers with stronger faith? If we have boldness when certain empowered believers are close by but lose it in their absence, could it be that we've been sipping out of their power shake of faith instead of filling our own?

I'm not taking anything away from the power of the Spirit we sense when many believers gather together. However, we don't ordinarily operate, day in and day out, in that kind of corporate atmosphere. Furthermore, we'll never discover what God has empowered us to do personally if we're dependent on the presence of our leadership. We'll never discover our strengths in the power of God if we keep drawing off another's.

2. Not only were their positive influences absent, but also some of their strongest negative influences were present. Nothing compares to trying to do your job when surrounded by people who would rather debate than eat! The presence of the teachers of the law must have been terribly intimidating to these comparatively uneducated men. You and I aren't always surrounded by faith-encouragers either.

Our entire life is a faith-walk. We can't afford to wait for all the right atmospheric conditions to act on the power of God. I think God is teaching us that the worst conditions can provide the best atmosphere to act in faith. He doesn't want our confidence regulated by our "audience." In fact, if faith-discouragers can shake our confidence badly enough to disable us, our confidence may be in ourselves instead of God. God's strength is unaffected by His audience.

When was the last time your confidence was shaken and you were unable to do what God had empowered you to do?

____

I remember a recent time when a critical letter from a seminary graduate shook my confidence. As I read the letter, my confidence drained like someone had pulled a plug. I started thinking: *She's right! What in the world do I think I'm doing? I have no formal theological education.* I looked over some mistakes she pointed out and thought: *I'm so stupid! I shouldn't even be doing this!*

God nearly snatched me baldheaded. He reminded me during the following days that I was exactly right: I shouldn't be doing this at all. This ministry is God's. If my confidence is in myself, I'm in big trouble. God also assured me that I will always make mistakes, but they will serve as reminders to my readers never to think more highly of this teacher than they ought. Only One can be taken at His every word. What counts most to God is that our hearts are right. He will forever be more interested in our fellowship than our scholarship. I believe the presence of those more educated than the disciples may have undermined their ability to exercise the right and might God had given them.

Prayer is the critical element of faith. I asked why the disciples could not cast out the demon. Matthew's Gospel says it was their little faith. Mark's Gospel says it was their lack of prayer. Do these two answers represent a discrepancy?

Hardly! Their little faith was the result of their lack of prayer. You see, without prayer, we return to our own ability rather than to God. The disciples were arguing with the teachers of the law when they should have been rehearsing the greatness and power of God through prayer and asking Him to demonstrate His authority. True prayer, not just mindless, halfhearted petitions, is what digs the well God wants to fill with faith.

Can you think of a time in your life when you were really trying to exercise faith but aside from intense prayer? ❑ Yes ❑ No If so, explain.

____

____

Christ strongly reproves faithlessness. Christ responded strongly to the disciples' failure to exercise the power He gave them. All three synoptic Gospels record Him saying: "'O unbelieving generation, how long shall I stay with you? How long shall I put up with you?'" (Mark 9:19). I believe His phrase concerning how long He would stay with them inferred the shortness of time He had left in His earthly tenure. I sense Him saying: "How long are you going to take to get this together, Boys? I won't be visible in your presence much longer!"

Look back at the adjectives Christ used to describe the generation. The first word is *unbelieving*. *Little faith* in Matthew 17:20 is *apistian*—unbelief. After three-and-a-half decades of knowing Christ, I am only beginning to realize the magnitude of the sin of unbelief. The word *unbelieving* means "not worthy of confidence, untrustworthy."

The definition implies that when we are faithless, we are concluding by our attitude and actions that Christ is not worthy of our confidence and that He is … I can hardly bring myself to write the word … untrustworthy. The disciples' unbelief was their willingness to let the temperature of their faith rise and fall according to the surrounding dynamics rather than His steadfast Word.

The Bible Knowledge Commentary offers a thought-provoking statement on the subject: "**O unbelieving generation** emphasizes the characteristic cause of all spiritual failure —lack of faith in God"[1]

Name some example of "spiritual failure." Then describe how it could be connected to a lack of faith in God (i.e.: idolatry, adultery, crippling fear).

____

____

The disciples weren't the only ones in the scene having a faith crisis. Let's spend the remainder of the lesson focusing on the faith of the boy's father. Read again the exchange in Mark 9:20-27 as Christ turns His attention to this tormented pair. Only the son was possessed by a demon; we don't even have to wonder if his father was suffering. Try to imagine what he had been through.

In the space below, describe what you imagine the father of this boy had suffered, using as many adjectives as apply.

____

____

In my opinion, Mark 9:22-23 describes one of the most important spiritual conflicts represented in the entire Word of God. I am nearly overwhelmed with compassion for the father in this scene. Unfortunately, like many people, he was far more familiar with the power of the devil than the power of the Son of God.

Even in our churches, many are learning more about the power of the devil than the omnipotence of the living God! Like the father in today's scenario, many do not understand that surrounding dynamics like the length and depth of defeat have absolutely no bearing on Christ's ability to perform a miracle. Hear it again: no bearing. Let's consider the dynamics of length and depth in today's text. Both are expressed in verse 21.

How long had the boy been in this state? _______________

Describe the depth of defeat noted in the verse.

____

Christ did not ask how long the boy had been in his present state because the answer had a bearing on His ability to free him. He asked the question for the purpose of framing a miracle against the backdrop of hopelessness. The father stated the hopelessness of the boy's state, then made a statement that probably provokes a host of emotions in each of us: "But if You can do anything, take pity on and help us" (v. 22). I'd like to break down the phrase into several pieces, then consider Christ's response.

"But ..." This one little word suggests the tiniest mustard seed of faith in the father—a seed Christ compassionately watered. I am continually moved by Christ's willingness, not just to meet us halfway, but, like the father of the prodigal, to run the entire distance once we take the first step in His direction. The Word of God is filled with accounts of hopeless situations followed by the wonderful little word: "but ..."! The word itself has no power, but it whispers an openness to the possibility of change. Because of His great compassion, sometimes that little whisper is all the invitation Christ Jesus needs to show His power.

Fill in the following statement based on your experience with God:

____

but ____.

"if you can" Christ took exception to the father's use of the word *if*. When the action is consistent with the Word of God, the question is never if He *can*. It may be if He *wills*, but never if He *can*. The father was actually saying, "If You have enough power or ability ... " Oh, He has enough all right.

What do the following verses say about God's power or ability?

Genesis 18:14 ____

2 Kings 3:18 ____

Long-term defeat in the lives of those with access to Christ is often wrapped up in a continued "if You can" mentality. Are we still praying "If You can" prayers?

In at least one way, you and I can't claim the ignorance of the father in this story. We assume he didn't know Christ personally. Notice that Jesus didn't reprove the father the same way He reproved the disciples. Like them, you and I know Christ Jesus as far more than a teacher rumored to possess supernatural power. We call Him *Lord*. Consider the irony of addressing Him as Master of the universe, then asking Him to come to our aid—if He can.

"do anything" Contrast the two words for a moment: *anything* (v. 22) and *everything* (v. 23). Dear one, Christ can't just do *anything*. Christ can do *everything!* I may have to shout hallelujah! Stop wondering if Christ can do anything in your situation and start believing Him to do everything glorious!

Immediately the father exclaimed, "I do believe; help me overcome my unbelief!" (v. 24). I can't describe the encouragement this father's honesty has given me through the years. Look closely at his two statements. First he cried out enthusiastically, "I do believe!" Then he confessed his unbelief. I believe the father changed his tune because he was looking straight into the face of Truth. The closer we get to Jesus, the more difficult it is to stretch the truth. The wonderful part of the father's exclamation is his realization that, although he lacked faith, he wanted to believe! Then he did exactly what he should have: he asked for help to overcome his unbelief. I can't count the times I've imitated this father's actions. In my earlier days with God, I viewed faith as my willingness to make a believing statement with my mouth rather than face the questions of my heart.

How would Romans 10:10 suggest that I had the "cart before the horse"?

____

It's time for a dramatic change of approach. If we don't have bold faith, let's start asking boldly for the faith we lack. Imagine the love of a God who says: "It's true that without faith it is impossible to please Me, but I am so anxious to reward you with blessing, I'm even willing to supply the faith you lack. Ask Me, My Child! Ask Me for what you lack! I am the only One who can help you overcome your unbelief!"

DAY 2
The Road to Greatness

Today's Treasure
"For He who is least among you all—he is the greatest" (Luke 9:48).

I'm not sure the devil himself is the hindrance to us that our own egos are. We're going to stare that hindrance in the face. We may want to find a pair of steel-toed shoes because the Holy Spirit is probably going to step on our toes today.

I used to view the sense of conviction as a negative feeling until I began to realize that I've never been freed from a sin without first experiencing conviction. Praise God for the conviction of the Holy Spirit! Without it, we would never be changed! Let's tell Him we're willing to take a deep look inside today in hopes that we'll see something all together different tomorrow. Without further delay, please read Luke 9:43-56.

Before I offer my commentary on these segments of Scripture, I want you to think it through for yourself. The last thing I want to do is spoon-feed anyone. How I would cheat you! My role is to offer you an appetizer of God's Word, to invite you to "taste and see that the Lord is good" (Ps. 34:8), and to pray you'll go to Him yourself for a feast.

Put on your thinking cap and look back at three snapshots of the disciples captured in each of the following references. Write a sentence describing their activity or participation in each snapshot.

Luke 9:46-48 ______________________________

____

Luke 9:49-50 ______________________________

____

Luke 9:51-56 ______________________________

____

What attitudes in the disciples cast all three snapshots in a similar light?

____

Forgive me if this seems harsh, but we can be so full of ourselves at times, can't we? We are not so unlike Christ's original disciples. Let's look at each segment individually, then we'll draw some conclusions based on the attitudes propelling all three.

The Greatness Question (Luke 9:46-48). We don't have to look far to find breeding ground for argument for those who made the choice to sift the circumstances through the sieve of the flesh.

What two events had just taken place in Luke 9:28-43? ______________

____

How might these two simultaneous events have provided a breeding ground for comparisons and discussions of greatness?

____

____

Notice that Christ knew their thoughts. We may never have argued with someone openly about our greatness, but Christ knows our thoughts in which similar attitudes swirl. I am convinced that if Christ sent today's church a checklist of commendations and criticisms like those in Revelation 2–3, one of the things He would have "against" us would be staggering spiritual ambition. Our society thrives on ambition, and if we're not extremely discerning, we will bring our ambitions into the church. Our biggest hindrance to greatness may be the desire to be great. Don't miss the contrast of Christ and His disciples at this point in His earthly tenure.

What was the basic timetable according to Luke 9:51?

- ❑ **time for the feast of weeks**
- ❑ **time for the cross**
- ❑ **time for Jesus to declare His messiahship**

Fill in the blank based on the same Scripture: "Jesus ________________ set out for Jerusalem." What do you think that word means?

____

What was awaiting Christ according to Luke 9:22,44?

____

Christ was most assuredly on the road to greatness. His journey would ultimately take Him to His Father's right hand. Yet, the road to greatness would take Him through betrayal, rejection, suffering, and ultimately death. Even so, Scripture tells us that "he stedfastly set his face to go to Jerusalem" (v. 51, KJV).

What do the following Scriptures say about Christ's road to greatness?

Philippians 2:6-11 ________________________________

____

Hebrews 12:2-3 ________________________________

____

Hebrews 2:9-10 ________________________________

____

Don't be confused by the idea that the Author of our salvation became perfect through suffering. Christ was always perfect in terms of sinlessness. The word *perfect* in this verse is *teleioo,* meaning "to complete, make perfect by reaching the intended goal." Christ reached the goal (our salvation and His exaltation) through suffering. His road to greatness was a rocky one. A painful one. He knew it in advance, and yet He set His face resolutely toward the goal and accomplished it. Simply put, we were worth it to Him.

No matter how resistant we may be to the call, our road to true greatness is also the highway of humility. At times, it, too, will involve suffering, rejection, betrayal, and, yes, even death—to self. The question becomes, "Is He worth it to us?"

Without a doubt, one of the primary works God has sought to accomplish in me is to help me get over myself. The process has been excruciating and will no doubt be life-long, but I have never been more thankful for any work in my life. I know no other way to say it: God finally got me to a place where I made myself sick. Oh, I still get plenty of glances at my self-centeredness, but never without a good wave of nausea. God and I now have a term for it in our prayer time. Don't expect something deeply intellectual or theological. We just call it my "self-stuff." Almost every day I ask God to help me address any active "self-stuff" and nail it to the cross. I literally name anything He brings to mind and look it straight in the face even if it makes me cry.

The following terms fall under the category of "self-stuff": Give them a good look. Place a check by the items you struggle with most.

❑ **self-exaltation**	❑ **self-protection**	❑ **self-righteousness**
❑ **self-will**	❑ **self-loathing**	❑ **self-worship**
❑ **self-serving**	❑ **self-promotion**	❑ **self-indulgence**
❑ **self-absorption**	❑ **self-delusion**	❑ **self-pity**
❑ **self-sufficiency**	❑ **others** ______________________	

Is that some stuff, or what? If you think of others, by all means, add them to the list. Self, self, self! May it be enough to make a "self" sick! Here's the big lie: Satan has convinced us that laying down our self-stuff is some huge sacrifice. Oh, beloved, what deception! Our self-stuff is what makes us most miserable! What an albatross our self-absorption is.

What does Matthew 16:24-25 say about those who deny their self-stuff?

____

We will discover the life planned for us even before the foundation of the world. Our own 1 Corinthian 2:9s! Precious one, abundant life is on the other side of our self-stuff!

I cannot stress strongly enough that getting over the self-stuff is a daily challenge. As long as we inhabit this tent of flesh, it will rise up in us. We must choose to "deny [ourselves] and take up [our] cross daily" (Luke 9:23). The challenge demands total honesty before God. Remember, conviction is never for the sake of condemnation but for liberation! Oh, God, so deal with self in each of us that when You read our thoughts as You did the disciples in Luke 9:47, You will find stronger and stronger evidences of Your own. Let this mind be in us that was also in Christ Jesus (see Phil. 2:5, KJV)!

The Exclusivity Question (Luke 9:49-50). Take another look at the second snapshot in today's photo album of arrogance in Luke 9:49-50. Based on the context and Scripture's highlight on the attitude of the disciples, I don't believe John was concerned simply about the validity of the other man's actions. You see, Scripture tells us that this man actually was driving out demons in Christ's name.

Contrast Acts 19:13-16. What might have been the difference?

____

Remember, the twelve apostles were chosen from among a much greater number of disciples. Soon we will see Christ send out 72 that He will empower with immense authority. Many others believed and, if God saw fit, their faith could have enabled them to exercise a certain amount of authority in Christ's name.

What is a way to recognize authenticity in an individual (Luke 6:43-44)?
❑ **his words** ❑ **his actions** ❑ **his fruit** ❑ **his power**

The man described in Luke 9:49 was bearing good fruit! I don't think John had a problem with the man's results. He had a problem with his rivalry. John took issue with the fact that the man wasn't one of them.

Don't you think Christ sometimes looks at us and says, "Who do you think you are?" Few things probably raise Christ's ire like our versions of "Tick, tock, the game's locked, and nobody else can play." We make the outrageous assumption that if someone else is not like us or among us, he or she isn't one of us.

I remember the moment I realized God was changing my thinking and sickening my stomach over similar attitudes. We were having a women's banquet at my church and I went to the sign-up table to buy my ticket. One of the ladies at the registration table said, "We'll be sure and seat you with good people, Beth!" I turned around and said: "You don't have to do that. I'll enjoy whoever I sit by." I couldn't get it out of my mind for days. I was not offended by her. How could I have been? I thought like that for years! I was offended by our pitifully selfish sin nature. I knew that moment that I never wanted God to let me get away with elitist attitudes again.

Can you think of a time when God opened your eyes to a similar attitude? If so, in the margin briefly describe the situation.

The Judgment Question (Luke 9:51-56). Take a look over the third snapshot in the album. Reread verses 51-56. James and John remind me of two little boys holding their pop-guns, jumping up and down pleading: "Let me shoot! Let me! Let me!" The difference is, this was no game. They were eagerly asking for permission to be agents of massive, irreversible destruction. Nothing is more permanent or terrifying than the destruction of the lost. We ought to be scared to death to wish such a thing on anyone. Eternity is a long time. Even when punishment comes to the terribly wicked, we are wise to remember with deep sobriety, humility, and thankfulness that only grace saves us from a like sentence.

What insight do each of the following references shed on this subject?

Ezekiel 33:10-11 ____________________

Jonah 4:1-3,10-11 ____________________

Lamentations 3:22 ____________________

Matthew 7:1-2 ____________________

We know this world is filled with wickedness. As Christ's present-day disciples, we will no doubt be offended when people reject the Savior as the Samaritan village did that day. God's desire, however, is for us to pray for His mercy, His Spirit's conviction, and their repentance rather than their judgment. Christ said even of those who hammered the nails into His flesh, "Father, forgive them, for they do not know what they are doing" (Luke 23:34). Oh, thank You, Jesus! If not for Your mercy, I would surely be destroyed.

God is indeed the Righteous Judge. When Christ returns, those who rejected Him will literally cry to the mountains, "'Fall on us!' and to the hills, 'Cover us!'" (Luke 23:30).

Judgment is coming, but may the thought of it cause us to weep, plead, and pray. Never boast or feel satisfaction … for by grace we have been saved (see Eph. 2:8). Only one thing stands between us and the lost: a blood-stained cross.

Dear one, I know I've seemed harsh today, but even when I wanted to cry, God would not seem to ease up. Please know this message was written with such love. I have been the worst of transgressors in so many ways. No matter how common these attitudes are, they are terribly offensive to Christ. May we humble ourselves before Him, repent, and daily choose to lay down the albatross of our own egos.

Oh, God, give us a longing—not for the sin of this world to be judged—but for the sinners of this world to be forgiven.

DAY 3

The Seventy-Two

Today's Treasure
"At that time Jesus, full of joy through the Holy Spirit, said, 'I praise you, Father, Lord of heaven and earth, because you have hidden these things from the wise and learned, and revealed them to little children'" (Luke 10:21).

Part of what I love about God's Word is that it reaches us in every way. I don't have an emotion that God hasn't quickened through His Word. I have laughed and cried. I've been offended. Amazed. Shocked. Frightened. Delighted. Changed. I absolutely love it. I appreciate even the uncomfortable feelings God's Word raises in me because they are proof the Word is working. If you happen to still be "face-to-the-carpet" after our previous lesson, then prepare to get up off of that floor and dance today. Read Luke 10:1-24 and complete the following:

How would you explain to a new believer why Christ says ask the Lord to send out workers rather than sending them out at His own initiative?

____

____

Carefully search Luke 10:1-24 and document the activity or implied roles of each of the three Members of the Trinity:

God the Father ______________________________________

____

God the Son ______________________________________

____

God the Holy Spirit __________________________________

____

Korazin, Bethsaida, and Capernaum were cities considered to be religious in which Christ openly ministered. Tyre and Sidon were considered to be godless cities.

What do you think Christ meant when He said that judgment would "be more bearable for Tyre and Sidon" than the others (v. 14)?

____

In the margin describe how you would apply Christ's warning to our religious world today.

The 72 were joyful because the demons were subject to them. What did Christ establish as their primary cause for joy?
❑ names written in heaven ❑ power to heal diseases

These verses are so full of "teachables," I hardly know where to start and what to prioritize! Because sending out the 72 bears a marked resemblance to the sending out of the twelve in Luke 9:1-9, we will focus on the additional dimensions rather than use our time with repetition. Let's highlight the following elements in this passage:

The "two by two." The original language calls this phrase *ana duo*. I love the fact that Christ sanctions companionship in the work of the gospel! The point is not the magic number of "two" as opposed to three or four. The point is togetherness.

The following Scriptures suggest reasons why two is better than one. Note each reason by the corresponding reference.

Ecclesiastes 4:9-12 ____

Deuteronomy 19:15 ____

Exceptions exist when we are called to stand alone, but the "rule" of our lives in Christ is far more often the fellowship, protection, accountability, and double dividends of joint service. I can hardly describe the joy my coworkers in the gospel bring me. My best friend and I met each other by serving together in "Mothers Day Out" over 20 years ago. God called us to work *ana duo* and we've been a duo ever since! We haven't worked side-by-side in ministry for years, but God used those initial years to make us and our Christ a cord of three strands … not quickly broken.

How about you? Do you happen to have a few three-cord relationships in the gospel (not limited to vocational ministry)? If so, briefly identify them.

____

The transfer of rejection. Jesus taught another great truth in Luke 10:1-24.

Take another good look at verse 16. What do you think Christ was saying?

____

This concept represents something else I love so much about Christ. In many ways, He says to those who belong to Him and seek to do His will: "Don't take rejection personally. Let Me take it for you."

How is this "transfer" of sorts obvious in a comparison between Acts 9:1 and Acts 9:4-5?

___

Beloved, can you accept that Christ takes very personally the unfair things that happen to you? Consider a few reasons we are wise to let Christ assume our rejections.

• Only Christ can handle rejection without being personally incapacitated or hindered by it. Who can begin to estimate the mileage Satan gets from rejection? We have an overwhelming tendency to take it personally. From a bit of rejection Satan can get anything from a mile of discouragement to a thousand miles of despair. Christ says to us: "Let Me take it personally for you. It can hurt Me, but it can't hinder Me."

Paraphrase Psalm 35:1. ___

___

• Only Christ can properly handle rejection. We are often powerless to do anything about it. Our attempts often make the situation worse. We don't fully understand what lies at the heart of rejection. We cannot judge another person's heart or motive.

On what does God base His judgment of a situation? (Rom. 2:2)
❏ appearances ❏ rumors ❏ truth ❏ history

Occasionally I love to hear Keith say, "Elizabeth, let me worry about that." In essence, Christ says the same thing to us. If we suffer rejection, let Him worry about it. Let Him take it personally so we don't have to. Now take one last look at Luke 10:16.

Who takes it personally for Christ? ___

The ecstatic joy of effectiveness. The 72 returned, rejoicing with something that resembled amazement. In verse 17 they essentially said: "Wow! It happened just like You said it would. Even the demons were subject to us in Your name! What a rush!"

Sandwiched between expressions of jubilation, Christ took a quick moment to remind them they had plenty of motivation to rejoice because their names were written in heaven. Though we see Him celebrate their victories, we also see Him teach them to base their joy on something far more reliable than accomplishments and abilities. He wants us to understand that the greatest cause we have for joy is not what we do, but who we are. We are children of the eternal *El Elyon*. Our names are recorded in heaven.

Why would we be very wise to find our joy in who we are because of Him, rather than what we can do because of Him?

___

Christ's moment of redirection in verse 20 is sandwiched between two awesome moments of celebration in verses 18-19 and 21. Let's look at the expression of His delightful response, then we'll look at the two primary catalysts for His joy in this segment.

Take a close look at verse 21 and fill in the blank:

"At that time Jesus, _________________________ through the Holy Spirit."

Here's a place where the original is so much fun. In English we equate the joy of the disciples in verse 17 with Christ's joy in verse 21. After all, joy is joy, right? Not in Greek! Luke used two different words. In verse 17, the word for *joy* is *chara,* meaning essentially what you'd assume: "rejoicing" and "gladness." To our delight, the word switches in verse 21 to a far more intense original word. The word is *agalliao,* meaning "to exult, leap for joy, to show one's joy by leaping and skipping, denoting excessive or ecstatic joy and delight." In the Septuagint of the psalms, it was "often spoken of rejoicing with song and dance."

Someone may ask, "Do you expect me to believe Christ jumped up and down with ecstatic joy?" I don't have one bit of trouble believing it!

Could the word simply mean He rejoiced in His heart? Possibly, but the essence of the word *agalliao* is when *chara* gets physical! You may apply it either way, but I prefer to jump up and down with Jesus. Perhaps no one could celebrate the greatness of God with more demonstration than David, and he was called "a man after God's own heart." With all my heart, I believe Christ Jesus was and is demonstrative.

How did God demonstrate His love according to Romans 5:8?

____

Seems to me Christ and His Father can be pretty dramatic in their demonstration of affection. What would cause Jesus to leap with ecstatic joy in this scene (whether physically or internally)? At least two catalysts for colossal joy appear in these verses:

• ***Satan's defeat.*** "I saw Satan fall like lightening from heaven" (v. 18). Beloved, take a good look at Revelation 12:10-12. Sometime before Adam and Eve inhabited the garden of Eden, Satan was cast out of heaven for pride, rebellion, and his desire to usurp the Most High (see also Ezek. 28:16-17; Isa. 14:12-13). At the risk of oversimplification, he has attempted to get back at God ever since by targeting those He loves.

We who are in Christ possess the power through His Word and His Spirit to avoid being defeated by the evil one. Problem is, we don't always exercise that power. In today's segment, the disciples exercised the authority He had given them, and Christ was ecstatic! At the end of the contest recorded in verses 1-16, the scoreboard read: Believers 72, Satan 0. That was a score Jesus could have spilled His popcorn over! Forgive me if my parallels are offensive at times, but it's a mystery to me how a football game can provoke more cheering than the defeat of the devil by the power of God.

When was the last time you got excited over the defeat of the devil?

____

• ***The servants' victory.*** "I praise You, Father, Lord of heaven and earth, because you have hidden these things from the wise and learned, and revealed them to little children" (v. 21). The God of heaven revealed Truth and the small of earth received it. The result? The all-surpassing power of God shined through simple "jars of clay" (2 Cor. 4:7). I'm about to jump up and down over it myself! You see, the wise and learned of this world are often too sophisticated to throw caution to the wind and believe they're capable of doing something they've never done—never even thought possible. If we stay in our neat little perimeters of safe sophistication where we walk by sight and not by faith, we'll never have room to leap and skip with Jesus in ecstatic joy.

Oh, beloved, give Him a chance to leap and dance over you! Dare to do what He's calling you to do! And don't always be so reasonable. I have a feeling there's one thing Christ likes better than leaping and skipping and dancing over you. How about with you? When you hear that victory music playing, get up out of that chair and shake a leg!

DAY 4

The Heart of a Neighbor

Today's Treasure
"But a Samaritan, as he traveled, came where the man was; and when he saw him, he took pity on him" (Luke 10:33).

Today we share the consummate human-interest drama. Simple enough to capture a preschooler's imagination. Complex enough to challenge a brilliant scholar. Morally excellent enough to convict the surest saint. This is the story of the good Samaritan.

Read Luke 10:25-37. Take it slowly. Picture every moment of it as if you were an eyewitness hiding behind a boulder on the Jericho road.

Why do you think the expert in the law felt the need to justify himself?

____

In the margin, list each of the "players" in this scene, even the less obvious. Use your imagination to describe what you think each of them might have been like or may have been feeling.

Based on this account, define *neighbor* using one sentence.______________

____

Let's concentrate first on Christ's over-confident opponent in the match of the minds. Scripture describes him as an expert in the law. His job was to interpret the law of Moses the way modern lawyers interpret the U.S. Constitution. Scribes made a career of answering questions like the one he asked in this scene. He considered himself such an expert that he intended to make Jesus look foolish. The problem is, you can't find a subject on which Christ isn't the ultimate expert. The expert in the law didn't know that Christ knew the drill better than he did.

Jesus responded with a question that means little to us but was very familiar to the lawyer. He asked, "How do you read it?" The question was used constantly among scribes and lawyers. One would ask the other his interpretation on a certain matter. Before he would give his answer, he would say, "How do you read it?" The one who asked the question ended up having to "go first."

Of course, you and I know what the scribe didn't know. Christ, the fullness of the Godhead bodily, not only wrote the law, He came to fulfill it. The resident expert in the law was way over his head when he threw a pop quiz at the Author of the book.

The expert, being forced to "go first," delivered the correct answer according to Old Testament law. In your own words, what was his answer?

____

The conversation could have stopped at Christ's retort, "Do this and you will live" (v. 28). Instead, the lawyer had to ask one more question, "And who is my neighbor?" (v. 29).

Do you hear a change in tone? The man wanted to justify himself—to show himself righteous—but why? Who said he wasn't? Christ didn't say a single condemning word to him. Jesus simply told him his answer was correct and to go live his answer.

The man couldn't let the matter go. In Christ's presence, the lawyer felt condemned by his own words. He knew God intended for His people to help those in need. The lawyer attempted to justify himself by splitting hairs with his definition of a neighbor.

God demands compassionate action no matter how we try to hide in loopholes of terminology. The lawyer's immediate defense mechanism was to try to start an argument. Not an unfamiliar tactic, is it? We've all been experts at that one! Let's agree for the sake of positive results to do an exercise we might compare to stomach crunches—painful.

Identify a time when you used reason to justify an action but knew deep inside it was not the heart of God.

____

Not a good feeling, is it? I know from experience! That feeling was probably magnified tenfold as the lawyer stood face-to-face with the embodiment of God's mercy.

Jesus answered the question, "Who is my neighbor?" with one of the most repeated stories in the New Testament. The crime scene was a spot on a 15-mile road between Jerusalem and Jericho. The road was so treacherous it became known as Adummim or The Pass of Blood. As many as twelve thousand priests lived in Jericho, commuting to Jerusalem when they were chosen by lot for temple service.[2]

Earlier I asked you to write a brief character sketch of each "player." In some ways, we've probably played them all. We've each injured someone in some way and then walked away. Perhaps we've even robbed them of dignity or self-respect. No doubt we've each been injured by someone and felt they left us half-dead. Let's spend a few minutes focusing on the next two players: the priest and the Levite.

Christ's terminology suggests they were each on their way home to Jericho from Jerusalem. He described each as going down the road; it was quite a sharp descent in terrain. The irony in the unwillingness of the priest and Levite to help would have been more obvious to the lawyer than to us. He would have quickly understood that they were on their way home from the most important life work they would ever do: performing their brief tenure of service in the temple. We would expect that at no time would they have been more humbled, grateful, or willing to meet someone's needs. That's not what happened. In fact, we are told that both the priest and the Levite passed by on the other side.

What are a few ways we pass by on the other side today?

____

____

How does the law in Exodus 23:4-5 make the actions of the priest and Levite even more incriminating?

___

We don't want to draw the wrong conclusions. Christ certainly wasn't indicating that all priests and Levites would leave an injured man to die.

In your opinion, why did Christ use these two types of religious leaders?

___

We who have been raised in church and steeped so long in religion must be very cautious that our legalistic religious practices are not masking a bad case of *sklerokardia*. That's Greek for "hard heart." The lawyer approached Jesus with a test and ended up taking a pop quiz of his own. Often the tests of our hearts will be similar. They usually involve our behaviors and reactions to one another. How we deal with people may be a truer test of the heart than how we relate to things.

Look at a conversation with a different lawyer in Matthew 22:34-40. What did Christ say about these two commandments in verse 40?

___

Read Exodus 20:1-17. How many of the Ten Commandments concern matters of relationship either with God or others?
❑ two ❑ five ❑ seven ❑ ten

What did Christ mean when He said that the essence of the entire law hung on the two commandments prioritized in Matthew 22:37-39?

___

God's law was always far more about relationship than ritual! That's how Jesus could offer Himself as the fulfillment of the entire law. The ultimate point of obedience to the law was never about human goodness.

Let's spend the remainder of our time on the third passerby in the scene. Our common name for this parable would have been an oxymoron to many Jews of that era. Most would have believed there was no such thing as a good Samaritan. They were considered little more than mongrels. Half-breed dogs. That's precisely why Christ interjected the Samaritan into the play.

What do you think was His point in using the Samaritan as the example?

___

Scripture tells us the Samaritan saw the man and took pity on him. I love the inference in the original language. The Greek word for *took pity* is *splagchnizomai*, meaning "to feel deeply or viscerally, … have compassion, pity." Think about this carefully. You would think at least the priest and the Levite would have done the right thing because of their positions, even if they felt the wrong thing. In sharp contrast, the Samaritan came upon the scene with no obligation whatsoever, and everything within him was deeply moved with compassion. He didn't just do what was right. He felt it.

Here's the shocker: the traveler left half-dead was almost certainly a Jew. The route was used almost entirely by Jews, and virtually all of Christ's parables centered on the experiences of Jewish people. I love the way one commentary explains it: "Jesus introduced a Samaritan as the only one on that lonely, dangerous Jericho road willing to befriend a helpless Jew. The very man from whom no needy Jew could expect the least relief, was the one who gave it."[3]

When in your experience has the least expected person come to the rescue?

____

What a rich discussion for small group. If you can't think of an example right now but one occurs to you later, come back and fill it in! Even today, God stages the screenplay of the good Samaritan in countless ways.

The Samaritan had the perfect opportunity to exact a little revenge on behalf of his people, but he didn't. Why? Because sometimes good at its best is when the law of the heart eclipses the law of the land. Stepping across a boundary to help is sometimes our first introduction to the commonality of humanity on the other side. Offering help in a time of need can be the first step to overcoming God-dishonoring prejudice.

Who did Jesus say was our neighbor? ______________________

I am reminded of an Old Testament verse that describes a neighbor at Passover. Turn to Exodus 12 and read verses 1 through 4. It will be worth the trip.

What was a family to do if they were too small for a whole lamb?

____

From Jesus' parable we can see that our neighbor is the person with a need—the broken one. In terms of Exodus 12, our neighbor is one with whom we can share the Lamb. As a people passed over by the angel of death, we are called to share the Lamb.

DAY 5

A True Tale of Two Sisters

Today's Treasure
" 'Martha, Martha,' the Lord answered, 'you are worried and upset about many things, but only one thing is needed. Mary has chosen what is better' " (Luke 10:41-42).

I'm already grinning and we haven't even started. I love women. I have a great appreciation for men, too, but I don't share their psyche. I get a huge kick out of women. We're just so … woman-y. You girls know exactly what I mean. With the exception of my best buddy who lives out-of-state, most of my closest friends work or volunteer at Living Proof Ministries. One reason I'm so crazy about them is because we are so hilariously different. I guess we represent almost every conceivable dimension of womanhood.

Among all of us, we're in the throes of young motherhood, menopause, and memory pause. We've got a healthy population of Marys and Marthas. Marys never get to drive or plan our luncheons. Marthas never get to lead prayer time—except when we're hungry. They tend to give the quickest blessing. I hope you have such a group in your life. They are a blast! Fight isolation and independence. It's no fun.

Mary would want us to stop here and meditate on all the relationships we share in Christ, but I hear Martha chiding: "Get busy! There's homework to do!" Since I'm more intimidated by Martha than Mary, we better get busy and read Luke 10:38-42.

Let's start by capturing their personalities while having a little fun. While I was in Israel taping the video for this series, I learned that many believe Mary's and Martha's tombs are identifiable in Bethany. Supposedly their names are actually on them. I wanted so badly to go look for the tombs, then suddenly it occurred to me their names would be in Hebrew. Another "duh moment" with Beth Moore.

Based on your reading and your imagination, write a brief obituary for Mary and Martha. Conclude with the words inscribed on their tombstones.

Martha ______________________________

____

Mary ______________________________

____

What I'd give to be in small group with you! I have very little doubt you got the idea. This segment of Scripture is absolutely priceless. Much to laugh about, much to think about, much to convict us and coax us to change. Before we get to the heart of our lesson, let's allow John 11:5 to help us establish a critical fact.

Which one did Jesus love: Mary or Martha? ______________________________

What does that tell you? ______________________________

____

Today's lesson is not a contrast between *good* and *bad*. It's a contrast between *good* and *better*. Martha was a good woman. Jesus loved her very much, apron and all. Her joy and satisfaction, however, were sacrificed on the altar of self-appointed service. In the classic *My Utmost For His Highest*, Oswald Chambers wrote: "The great enemy of the life of faith in God is not sin, but the good which is not good enough. The good is always the enemy of the best."[4]

What do you think Chambers meant by that? ______________________________

____

Following our contrast between *good* and *best*, let's explore some applications together.

***1. Martha opened her home but Mary opened her heart* (v. *38-39*).** Don't miss the fact that Martha opened her home to Jesus. Not Lazarus, the head of the house. Nor

Mary, the depth of the house. It was the hands of the house that invited Jesus in. Otherwise, Mary wouldn't have had a set of feet at which to sit nor would Lazarus have had a friend with which to recline. Martha's hospitality brought Him there. If only Martha had understood that Christ wanted her heart more than He wanted her home. I have a missionary friend who preaches a service every Sunday under a certain tree in Nigeria. Martha's well-equipped home was nice, but any old shade tree would do.

Sometimes we think like Martha regarding our church buildings. We're so interested in a well-equipped building, we overlook the absolute priority of intimacy with God.

Here's a place where we who are not Marthas must fall under a little conviction. Although I force myself to keep an orderly home, I am so far from a "Martha" that I rarely ever open it to others. I have a very public ministry and I view my home as my sanctuary with my family. Not a bad idea, but I fear I've taken it too far. Although our home is open constantly to our daughters' friends, I almost never have anyone over for a bite to eat, a few moments of prayer, or a look at the Word. I save those things for the office. Ouch! I have an idea God is saying to some of us un-Marthas, "It's best to open your heart, but it's also good to open your home."

What about you? Which side are you falling on with this point?
❑ Martha—hospitality plus ❑ Mary—hospitality, what's that?

2. ***Distraction is the noble person's biggest hindrance to listening (v. 39-40).*** Martha wasn't stopping her ears and refusing to listen. She simply "was distracted." In this way, we've all been Marthas! How many times have we reached the car after a church service only to realize that we missed half the message due to a distraction?

What tends to distract you?______________________________________

____

Now imagine that the church service was meeting in your den while you were preparing lunch! Talk about distracting? Listen, I have to turn off every television and radio in the house and make my family go outside just to read a recipe. Even then, I read it aloud and if anyone interrupts me, I have to start over. In Luke 10:40, the Greek word for *distracted* is *perispao,* meaning "to draw different ways at the same time, hence to distract with cares and responsibilities." Can we relate? You see, our culture may be entirely different, but women have had the same challenges since the beginning of time.

3. ***Sometimes ministry can be the biggest distraction to the pursuit of true intimacy with God (v. 40).*** "Martha was distracted by all the *preparations* that had to be made." You may faint when you see the Greek word for *preparations*. The word is *diakonia.* It means "service, attendance, ministry." We are more familiar with the word *diakonos,* meaning *servant*. God's Word is saying that if we're not careful, even our need-meeting, well-meaning ministries can distract us from what is most important. My dad would tell you that he served his church tirelessly, doing all sorts of good for many years, while remaining unchanged by a heart-to-heart relationship with Jesus Christ.

I've heard the words many times, "If Satan can't make us bad, he'll make us busy." Actually, he can't make us anything, but he gets a lot of cooperation. I am reminded of our previous lesson on the good Samaritan. How wise of our God to place these two accounts back-to-back in Scripture. Day 4 gave us an incriminating look at servants of God who ministered in the temple but refused to help a dying man. Today's lesson gives us a look at a servant far too busy helping to hear from the heart of God.

How would you balance the two lessons into one rule of thumb?

____

4. *Martha forgot to keep the "pre" in preparation (v. 40).* Let's not overlook a very important little phrase. "Martha was distracted by all the preparations that *had to be made.*" Understand that these preparations were not frivolous. They were important! By doing them, Martha served Christ very appropriately and enhanced the atmosphere in which He taught. Very likely she served a meal and made sure all the arrangements were made for His comfort and the exercise of His own ministry.

I wish to make absolutely no inappropriate comparison to Jesus' ministry. But if I'm going to stay in someone's home when I travel and speak, I want to stay with a Martha! You could starve to death at Mary's, and you might even have to sleep out under that shade tree where you taught! Martha's preparations were important. They just weren't limited to the "pre." The issue is that she continued all her duties when the time came to sit at Christ's feet and listen.

I speak at many conferences during which the event's leadership either never makes it into the sanctuary or, when they do, they never lose that harried and distracted look. Recently I spoke at a conference where the leadership was the most participatory, involved group during Bible study. When I inquired later, they said, "Oh, we worked really hard in advance to get everything finished so we could relax when the time came." They made all the preparations, but when the time came, the men of the church and several hired caterers served while they attended. What wisdom we find in keeping the "pre" in preparation!

You see, their preparations were critical. What if they hadn't planned for all those women? What if they hadn't taken registration and the overflow of people were never seated? What if they had made no arrangements for an adequate sound system for the praise team or a microphone for the speaker? I don't believe God would have been honored by the lack of preparation. But God was doubly honored because they prepared in advance, yet didn't miss the most important part by immersing themselves in further preparations. What if I didn't prepare for a message and justified myself by misusing Mary's example—simply waiting for the Spirit to move me at the microphone? Again, God would not be honored by the lack of preparation. We simply need to do everything we can to keep the "pre" in preparation. How does this point relate to your life?

How can you keep the "pre" in preparation so you don't miss out on the best part of what God has planned for you?

____

____

5. *Those distracted by service are often those who miss how much Jesus cares (v. 40).* Martha came to Christ and asked, "Lord, don't you care?" I have a feeling if someone had asked Mary at the end of the day if Christ cared about her, she would have answered affirmatively without hesitation. Mind you, John 11:5 has already assured us Jesus loved both of them very much. I don't think it's unreasonable to assume that at times Mary probably sensed His love and care more readily than Martha. Why? I believe John 15:9 holds the key.

In this verse what did Christ tell us to do? ______________________

____

Beloved, the more we cultivate a keener awareness of Christ's presence, the more we will abide or remain in the sense of His love. Christ's love for us never changes. However, our sense of His loving care changes dramatically from time to time. I think we'd all agree the difference is not hardship. I may sense the loving care of God more readily when I'm going through difficulty than when I'm not. I believe the determining factor is our willingness to abide in Him or seek to practice a relationship in which we develop a keener awareness of His presence.

Sometimes we are so shocked when a seasoned servant of God confesses that she is struggling with her belief and awareness of God's loving care. We might think: *You of all people! You are such a wonderful servant of God. How can you doubt for a moment how much He cares for you?* Could it be that somehow service has distracted from the abundant, life-giving intimacy? Do you often wonder if Christ cares how others are neglecting you or not helping you? Do you give Him ample opportunities to lavish you with the love He always feels for you?

What explanation could Philippians 4:6-7 offer for the fact that Martha had more worries and upsets than Mary?

____

6. ***Many things are important but only one thing is necessary* (v. 42).** In our fight for right priorities, many things vie for the top of the heap, but only one is necessary. Ultimately, our relationship with Christ is the one thing we cannot do without.

Christ's message is not that we should neglect family and responsibilities to pray and to study the Bible. If that were true, the man in our previous lesson would have died. His message is that many things are important, but one thing is necessary: Him. Incidentally, Mary turned out to be one of the greatest servants of all, lavishing Christ with her most expensive offerings (see John 12).

As we conclude, look at three simple words from Luke 10:42: "Mary has chosen." That's how it will always be. A choice. Right priorities will never choose us. Even the worst of times or the hardest of lessons will not enforce them. They are a choice—in the midst of many other good ones. The word *chosen* comes from the Greek word *eklego,* meaning "to choose, select, choose for oneself." We can't choose what is necessary for anyone else, but we can certainly set an example. The remainder of the definition reads: "not necessarily implying the rejection of what is not chosen, but giving favor to the chosen subject, keeping in view a relationship to be established between the one choosing and the object chosen. It involves preference and selection from among many choices."

That's what I love most about Mary and Martha. Their story started us laughing, but ended with us really thinking. Shall we allow *good* to become the enemy of our *best?* The choice is ours.

---

[1]*The Bible Knowledge Commentary, New Testament,* edited by John F. Walvoord and Roy B. Zuck (Wheaton: Victor, 1983), 144.

[2]Herbert Lockyer, *All the Parables of the Bible* (Grand Rapids, MI: Zondervan Publishing House, 1963), 261-262.

[3]Ibid., 262.

[4]Oswald Chambers, *My Utmost for His Highest* (Grand Rapids, MI: Discovery House Publishers, 1935), 146.

tools of faith

Video Response Sheet **Group Session 6**

Session 6

Introduction: No matter how long we've known Christ or how much we've prayed, we still seem to cycle back to the sobering reality that we know very little about prayer. We find ourselves in the same position as Christ's closest companions who wisely came to Him and said, "Lord, teach us to pray."

Why we are not prayer experts:

- Prayer is about relationships. And relationships are subject to change.
- Prayer is the basis of a relationship we share with Someone we cannot fully know or understand. No matter how *high* we think, God's ways are still higher.
- The return on prayer will fluctuate and even leave us baffled at times.

What can we do?

When we are baffled and none of the old rules seem to "work," ask Jesus again and again to teach us how to pray!

Read Luke 11:1-13.

Concepts of Prayer

1. The place (v. 1). As often as possible try to choose an environment conducive to the practice of prayer.
2. The position (v. 2). At the very inception of every prayer, remember your position: God is your Father and you are His child.
3. The perspective (v. 2). The One we address in prayer is King. He occupies the throne of heaven and His name is hallowed.
4. The priority (v. 2). God seeks to mature us in prayer to the point that we understand the ultimate goal in every situation: For his will to be accomplished on the soil of earth just as it is on the floor of heaven.
5. The petition (v. 3). God desires for us to develop a day-by-day mentality in prayer.
6. The pardon (v. 4). God graciously forces the issue of forgiveness by giving us a serious incentive to forgive others.
7. The preparation (v. 4). Prepare for the day's temptations by directing approaching the seriousness of the matter with God in advance. proactive approach to prayer
8. The persistence (vv. 5-13). As long as you keep the prayer burden, keep praying!

Boldness w/o shame

Holy Spirit is the greatest gift we can be given

Agape - best interest love Philo - take up his interest

- I'm not letting you go to you bless me. {Know his will}

The great adventure → Life

I need more of you Lord.

ABBA

II Corinthians

When in your experience has the least expected person came to your aid?

WEEK 7

The Infinite Treasure

Day 1
Someone Stronger

Day 2
His Treasure, Your Treasure

Day 3
Keep Your Lamps Burning

Day 4
How Often Have I Longed?

Day 5
When God Runs

Week 7? Can you believe we've made it this far? I realize countless things are vying for your attention and that the Evil One has performed no few feats to distract you. I am so thankful you're hanging in there. Keep resisting the temptation to put aside your study—even with the intention of returning to it "later." "Later" has a strange way of getting later and later, doesn't it? Here's a little fresh motivation: Deuteronomy 29:29 says that the truths God reveals to you are yours forever! You are allowing God to inscribe His Word on the tablets of your heart. Scripture is literally becoming part of you. That's what Christ meant when He instructed us to let His Word "abide" in us (John 15:7). The same Scripture also tells us that His abiding Word transforms our prayer lives. Beloved, the intense study of God's Word has mammoth affects. You may be the last to notice them in yourself, but I assure you, Scripture never returns void! God has a specific purpose for this study in your life. Let Him have His awesome way.

Principal Questions:
Day 1: What do you think is represented by "a strong man" and "someone stronger"?
Day 2: Of what did Jesus say we do not need to be afraid?
Day 3: What are the descriptions of a *faithful servant* implied in Luke 12:35-48?
Day 4: What dimension of Christ is illuminated in Luke 13:34?
Day 5: In Luke 15 what common theme do all three parables share?

Christ's approach grows pretty radical in week 7. I think we're ready for the challenge. The look at our Father God in day 5 will remind us again how worthy He is when our callings are costly.

DAY 1

Someone Stronger

Today's Treasure
"But when someone stronger attacks and overpowers him, he takes away the armor in which the man trusted and divides up the spoils" (Luke 11:22).

When Satan wants to trip someone up, often his most powerful weapon is to distort the Word of God. In 1 Timothy 4:1 "the Spirit clearly says that … some will abandon the faith and follow deceiving spirits and things taught by demons." Now isn't that a frightening thought? Demons teaching Bible doctrines.

Satan loves to distort the comparison between his kingdom and the kingdom of God. On their best day Satan and his legions can't come close to the power of God. God alone is omnipotent. God alone is matchless in power. May today's lesson dispel any areas of false doctrine we have unwittingly learned from the world's most unreliable source.

Read Luke 11:14-28. Of what was Jesus indirectly accused in verse 15?

____

Christ responded to the accusation by making three primary points.

Write in one sentence what you believe to be Christ's primary point in each of the following verses in Luke 11:

Verses 17-20: ____

____

Verses 21-22: ____

____

Verses 24-26: ____

____

Let's explore each of them together.

A Divided Kingdom (Luke 11:17-20). Do you wonder how in the world some could have made such a ludicrous accusation? In essence Christ responded: "Think this through with Me. If I were part of the kingdom of darkness, why would I work against Myself by driving out demons?" He then made a statement that may have turned the religious leaders inside out: "But if I drive out demons by the finger of God, then the kingdom of God has come to you" (v. 20).

Christ's brief discourse implies that two origins of supernatural power exist: the kingdom of God and the kingdom of Satan. The obvious assumption was that if His power didn't originate with Satan, it obviously came from God. If Christ was performing all those signs and wonders through the power of God, what was the revolutionary implication? The kingdom of God had come to them. In other words, they were staring the Messiah in the face (see Luke 7:20,22).

The phrase "the finger of God" is used only a few other times in Scripture. One of them is found in Exodus 8:16-19.

Can you see any similarities between the conclusions implied in the Exodus passage and Luke 11:15-20? ❑ Yes ❑ No If so, what are they?

____

I love the reference to the finger of God. Every time I read it I have the thought that God is so powerful, all He has to do is point and His intended work is accomplished. Allow me to say with a grin that I know a few things I wish God would point at today, don't you? We have to trust that God not only knows what to point at but also when.

Before we go to Christ's second response, I would be remiss if I failed to emphasize the implications of division in Christ's words. Satan knows he can hinder God's kingdom by provoking division among Christ's people. Satan's most effective approach is an inside job. We desperately need to make unity in the body of Christ an ongoing pursuit.

A Strong Man (Luke 11:21-22). Keep in mind that the context of Christ's present discourse is a comparison between the kingdom of God and the kingdom of darkness.

Who do you think is represented by each of the following?

"a strong man": ____

"someone stronger": ____

How does Ephesians 6:12-13 imply a similar principle?

____

Assuming the strong man in Luke 11:21 is Satan, we can make a few important observations. The first one seems obvious, but it needs emphasizing: Satan is strong. The original word is *ischuros,* meaning "strong, mighty, powerful. Figuratively, meaning strong in influence and authority."

When was the last time you were reminded how influential the devil is?

____

We are wise neither to overestimate nor underestimate Satan's power. He is no match for God, but we are no match for him. As you read in Ephesians 6:12-13, we can take our stand against Satan only when we are strong in God's might. Second, we observe that not only is Satan strong according to Luke 11:21, but also he is "fully armed."

Name a few weapons you believe to be in Satan's arsenal.

____

____

I have personally encountered the weapons of shame, secrecy, and deception. Based on this short parable, a third observation is that Satan guards his own house.

Just as God is possessive over His holy house, you can be sure Satan is possessive over his unholy house. Second Corinthians 4:4 describes just one way he attempts to guard his house or protect his interests. Paul said Satan "has blinded the minds of unbelievers, so that they cannot see the light of the gospel."

Luke 11:21 would be pretty frightening without the verse that follows. Let's concentrate now on Luke 11:22 and make a few observations about Christ.

First, let's restate the obvious: ***Satan may be strong, but Christ is "someone stronger."*** Count on it. We may be at war with a very powerful enemy, but we who are in Christ are at peace with a far more powerful God.

A second observation is cause for celebration: ***Christ will attack and overcome Satan.*** The Scripture doesn't say *but* if someone stronger attacks and overpowers him; it says *when*! Satan is a defeated foe. The defeating blows actually came through a hammer on the nails of the cross. Christ finished the work when He willingly gave His life for our sins. God is busily biding His time until His kingdom calendar has been accomplished and all who will accept His offer are redeemed. Then one day, God's finger is going to point right at the strong man and he's going to wish he'd never existed.

A third implication concerning our Someone stronger is: ***He's going to take away Satan's armor.*** I believe the representation of the armor is anything Satan "wears" to keep from being defeated.

Lastly, we're told that ***Christ is going to divide up the spoils.*** Do you know what this means to us? Jesus Christ is going to steal back what Satan has stolen from us! Do you want to hear some even better news? Not all the spoils have to wait until we're in heaven!

I can readily cite a personal example. Even though Satan stole so many things from me through my childhood victimization, I am finally ready to say that God has given me back more than my enemy took. The spoils or plunder that finally tipped the scale has come to me in the form of response letters to *Breaking Free: Making Liberty in Christ a Reality in Life,* the Bible study. I believe I can now say that the grace gift of seeing others helped through the power of the Holy Spirit has begun to outweigh the horrible repercussions.

God doesn't love me any more than He loves you. Can you think of ways God has already divided with you some of the spoils of Satan's defeat?

____

I love the line from the song of Moses. God had just delivered them from Egypt. Moses declared: "The Lord is a warrior; the Lord is his name" (Ex. 15:3)!

A Vacant Place (Luke 11:24-26). We'll draw our final points from Christ's third response to the accusation that His power originated with the prince of demons. Reread this crucial segment of Scripture. One of my goals is to draw applications that are most appropriate for the types of individuals who read Bible studies like these. My assumption is that most of us are not demon-possessed, so I will opt for a conceptual rather than a direct application of these verses.

Mark the following statements T (true) or F (false) based on inferences made by these three verses:

____ Demons never again bother those from whom they've departed.

____ People who clean up their lives and get themselves in order are not vulnerable to attack.

____ A person's first encounter with the devil will always be the worst.

I hope you marked each of those statements false. Let's make three statements that are indeed true, then briefly discuss the false statements:

1. Demons seem to be more at home where they've previously dwelled.
2. Those of us who are believers in Christ cannot be demon-possessed, but we can certainly be demon-oppressed.
3. I tend to believe Satan would rather return to a previous job on an individual than find a new one.

Satan is a lot of things, but creative is not often one of them. He ordinarily sticks to what has worked in the past. I've experienced this personally when he has attempted to return to an area in my life where he held a previous stronghold—even though he's already been forced to leave.

Have you experienced something similar? Briefly explain.

____

Lives swept clean and put in order are vulnerable to demonic defeat. Beloved, listen carefully. We were created by God to be inhabited by His Spirit. We were not created to be empty. The vacuum in every human life does not yearn to be fixed. It yearns to be filled. God can deliver us from a terribly oppressive stronghold and we can truly clean up our lives and put them in order, but if we don't fill the void with Him, we are terribly susceptible to a relapse.

My Sunday School class has what we call V.I.P.'s.—*Victors In Process.* Every quarter, members who need extra prayer and accountability come before our class for special notice. Throughout the quarter, they can hardly get through the door without lots of hugs and direct questions about how they are doing. We also give reports of their progress to the entire class. Presently one of our V.I.P.'s is a beautiful young woman recovering from a fierce cocaine addiction. How wise she is to realize that she can't just "get clean." If she's going to be safe, she's got to fill the cavernous void left by the cocaine with the satisfying, liberating filling of the Holy Spirit.

A second round of the same demonic stronghold can be more powerful than the first. What a frightening prospect for someone who isn't sealed by the Holy Spirit (see Eph.1:14; 4:30)! Most of us are at higher risk of oppression than possession, but the principle still applies: once we've been delivered from a stronghold, if we make ourselves vulnerable to it again, our second encounter may be far worse.

What reasons can you think of which explain the above principle? ______

____

I can think of a few: Satan hates to lose. If he was defeated once, given the opportunity, he'll try harder the next time. Furthermore, a second onslaught can cause such discouragement and feelings of hopelessness that the victim is weaker than ever. And, finally, the empty space—if left uninhabited by Christ—leaves the victim with a voracious appetite. The greatest tragedy is that all the defeat was unnecessary. Yes, Satan is strong, but Christ is far stronger! We'll repeat this concept until it's engraved in our cranium: victory is not determined as much by what we've been delivered from as by what we've been delivered to. The only safe house for every former captive is our Someone stronger. When Satan comes prowling, may we "be found in him" (Phil. 3:9).

DAY 2

His Treasure, Your Treasure

Today's Treasure
"How much more valuable you are than birds!" (Luke 12:24).

I want to give you a word of warning. Very soon we will arrive at one of the most difficult challenges I face when writing a Bible study. We will have to bypass some wonderful segments of Scripture and prioritize others. As I outlined the Gospel of Luke, I knew we would never be able to study it verse by verse in 10 weeks. God has revealed several important criteria to help me determine where we spend our time in this study.

Our specific goal is to capture a more accurate picture of Christ in His first advent. When forced to choose between segments of Scripture, I've tried to discern which one helps us to know the most about "the Word ... made flesh" (John 1:14, KJV).

When making choices between certain segments of Scripture, I also keep in mind the types of people who most likely will participate in a Bible study of this nature. I consider the present challenges in the world surrounding us and pray that God will lead me to the messages we need most desperately. When the segments meet the first two criteria but we still have too much to cover, I throw myself upon the leadership of the Holy Spirit and pray like mad that He will lead me to the correct Scriptures.

From the beginning, I felt that the mid-portion of the Gospel (where most of the parables are located) was the wisest place to bridge and accelerate. Keep in mind that we are accelerating now so that we can slow down later. We will bridge 10 chapters of Luke in weeks 7 and 8, so that we can spend the entirety of weeks 9 and 10 on Luke's climactic conclusion. With this in mind, please read Luke 12:1-34 and complete the following:

What was "'the yeast of the Pharisees'" (v. 1)? ______________________
How would you define this word?

____

Of what did Jesus say we do not need to be afraid?

____

Instead, we are wise to fear ______________________________

Comment on Christ's statement from verse 20 in which He said, "'Who will get what you have prepared for yourself?'"

____

In what specific way did Christ call us to be different from the pagan?

____

Where is your treasure? ______________________________

I hope you gave that last question a little thought. I did. Today's lesson is about value—what God values and what we value. Luke 12:34 reveals that you can find someone's heart if you discover what he or she truly values. One of the best ways to become more acquainted with the heart of God is to search the Scriptures and study the things He values most. The next question may seem very obvious and basic, but too much hinges on it to make any false assumptions.

In terms of earthly things, what does God appear to most value according to Luke 12:24? ____

For just a moment, take a look at all the things around you. Glance over at the pile of bills. Or, your "to do" list. All the needed repairs. Everything that represents a problem to you. Everything of value to you. Take a quick mental inventory of every important thing that concerns or challenges you right now. Then fix your eyes on this phrase until it burns into your soul: "how much more valuable you are."

Check any of the following that are of value to you. Mark through any that don't apply to you.

❑ **work**	❑ **children**	❑ **relationship with God**
❑ **home**	❑ **marriage**	❑ **health**
❑ **church**	❑ **friends**	❑ **health of loved ones**
❑ **integrity**	❑ **success**	❑ **cause of some kind**

No matter how much value everything you checked represents, you are more valuable to God. These aren't just feel-good words. I pray that today's lesson will display them as fact. A good friend, who is a speaker and a Bible-based counselor, has said, "We act out what we believe, not what we know." Our actions, our lifestyles, and our decisions are all reflections of our belief systems. We may say otherwise, and, intellectually, we may know better, but we will live out what we truly believe.

I'd like to build the remainder of this lesson on one precept: if we truly believe what God says about our value to Him, our lives will be dramatically altered. Based on today's segment of Scripture, I want to suggest five ways such a belief makes a difference.

1. Believing our great value to God frees us from much hypocrisy. Christ opened the bold declarations in Luke 12 with a warning against hypocrisy. The primary meaning of the word is *pretending*. Please give special attention to His specific audience. Although He was surrounded by crowds of unbelievers and religious leaders, "Jesus began to speak first to his disciples" (Luke 12:1). Why did He address this word to His followers?

True disciples, those who follow Christ and lead others to do likewise, face great temptation to be hypocritical. Christ warned, "Be on your guard" (v. 1). In other words, if we're going to live free of hypocrisy, we must proactively guard against it. The bottom line of hypocrisy is the need for people to think more highly of us than we really are. Let's face it. It's easier to act than to clean up our act.

How might our willingness to really believe our great value to God affect authenticity and transparency?

____

____

In addition to your thoughts, I'll add one of my own. Hypocrisy has so much to prove. Ironically, it seeks to prove what is not even true. When we accept our real value to God, we don't have anything to prove. We can be "real" about where we've been, where we are, and where we want to be. We don't have to keep things "concealed" or "hidden" (v. 2). We can be real because we are of great value to the only True Judge.

2. Believing our great value to God frees us from unnecessary fear. Christ's words in Luke 12:4 come like a shock wave to our systems: "'I tell you, my friends, do not be afraid of those who kill the body and after that can do no more.'"

Why do we have such difficulty grasping His point of view? Because we are far more convinced of the "here and now" than the "after that." What a shock to realize that our "after that" is the only reason here and now even exists! Eternity is a far greater reality than this short breath of time. In essence, Christ said: "Don't fear people who can kill you now but can do nothing to you after that. The only healthy fear is of the One who controls forever." But if we are in His fold and are called His friends, Christ's word to us is this: don't be afraid; you are worth more.

Record every way these verses imply our value to God.

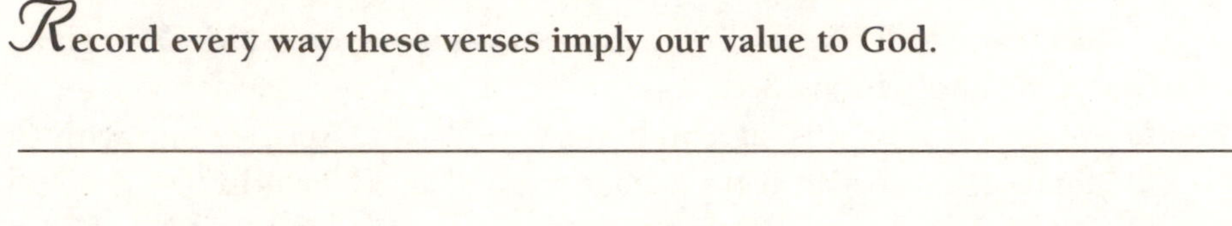

Keith and I keep a bird feeder on the back porch. I sit at the window and watch the sparrows scatter the seed and flutter their wings. They are not beautiful like the jays, red birds, or hummingbirds that grace our yard. Rather, they are plain and ordinary; but I love knowing that God never forgets a single one of them. When fear seeks to assail me, I go to the window and am reminded once again—if He cares for them, He most assuredly cherishes me. After this short breath is a long after that.

3. Believing our great value to God frees us to acknowledge Him shamelessly. Please don't miss the critical issue of willingly acknowledging Christ as Lord before others. I don't think Christ is talking about a one-time public profession of faith, although I certainly see its importance. I believe He's talking about our being unashamed of Him and openly acknowledging His lordship over us at any appropriate time.

Take a good look at verse 8. Christ Jesus can hardly wait to acknowledge us before the very "angels of God"! Even after all our frailties and failures! (Check out Jude 24.) If He is unashamed of us, in all our imperfections, how can we be ashamed of Him, our Redeemer and our Deliverer? Don't duck your head in shame under your coffee table. Listen, Satan is the breeder of all shame. At one time or another, all of us have faced the temptation to shrink away from openly acknowledging Christ.

Describe a time when you were really uncomfortable with an opportunity to publicly acknowledge Him as Lord. Don't worry! Everyone's got one.

I've learned one of the best ways to get over our attacks of shame. Do it over and over until it loses its intimidation! The more we practice, the easier it gets! Tell Him if you're afraid and all the reasons why; then ask for the power of the Holy Spirit to come upon you and make you a powerful witness (see Acts 1:8). He will! Then one day, He'll acknowledge you before the angels!

4. Believing our great value to God frees us from the need for riches. In verse 15, Christ also warns us to "be on our guard against all kinds of greed." His next statement is even more awesome.

Write the remainder of the verse:________________________________

____

Aren't you thankful it doesn't? However, once again I'm reminded of my friend's statement. We act out what we believe, not what we know. If we believe our value to God and believe our life does not consist in the abundance of our possessions, why do we have such an abundance of possessions?

Perhaps we know Luke 12:15 with our heads, but we really don't believe it with our hearts. Two sights offer me stunning reminders of the abundance of our possessions in the United States. First of all, my travels to third-world countries make me nauseated with my own abundance of possessions. Secondly, I see one storage company after another popping up on every corner. Storage is big business in the United States! We Americans have so much, we can't even keep it all in our spacious houses. We pay businesses to keep it for us.

Colossians 3:5 calls greed "____________________." Explain briefly how that is true.

____

In what ways can we guard against greed?

____

____

James 1:17 tells us our Father is the Giver of all good gifts. Throughout all of eternity, we will be lavished in the limitless wealth of the CEO of the universe. Until then, we show ourselves to be sons and daughters of the One True God when we give, give, and give. Let's keep shoving that abundance out the door to help others in need, and God will lay up treasures for us in His own divine storage lot.

5. Believing our great value to God frees us from much worry. Read again verses 22-34. You've got to be kidding. "Life is more than food" (v. 23)? I need a needlepoint of that for my kitchen! The issue of food, however, is not the point. The point is worry. I'm not sure many things compare to the challenge of ceasing to worry.

Why do you think worry is so difficult to control? ____________________

____

I'd love to hear your answers. I guess if I were limited to only one, it would be because we have so many prime opportunities to worry! We're never going to overcome worry by eliminating reasons to worry. Rest assured, life isn't going to suddenly fix itself. We will always have plenty of opportunities for an anxiety attack. God wills that we overcome worry even when overwhelmed by reasons to worry.

How many reasons for worry do you have right now? In the margin list just a few.

Christ summed up the futility of worry in verses 25 and 26. Simply put, worry is useless. Luke 12:25 has helped me with a much greater issue than my own life. It has helped me with the lives of my children. I am prone to worry somewhat about myself but endlessly over them. All our worry in the name of love can accomplish absolutely nothing. But all our praying in the name of Jesus could entreat God to accomplish anything. When will we learn to turn our worry effort into prayer?

Christ's remedy for worry is to be like the ravens and lilies—trust God to do His job. The prescription for worry is trust. Trust comes to those who take God at His Word. Re-visit your reasons to worry, and write the word *TRUST* in big, bold letters on top of your list. Then seek Him and seek His kingdom with everything you've got … and all the right things will be given to you as well (see Matt. 6:33).

As we conclude, please feast your eyes on verse 32: "Do not be afraid, little flock, for your Father has been pleased to give you the kingdom." What tender words. Do you hear the love? Do you sense the care? With one glance in the nearest mirror, you can see a reflection of the heart of God. For where His treasure is, His heart is also.

> "For you are a people holy to the Lord your God. The Lord your God has chosen you out of all the peoples on the face of the earth to be His people, His treasured possession" (Deut. 7:6).

DAY 3
Keep Your Lamps Burning

Today's Treasure
"Be dressed and ready for service and keep your lamps burning, like men waiting for their master to return from a wedding banquet" (Luke 12:35-36).

Many years ago, a stray dog took up residence on the Moore's front porch. The last thing we needed was another pet, so I made Michael promise he wouldn't feed her or get attached. He wasn't obedient. And am I ever glad. That dog is one of the most cherished members of the Moore household!

A neighborhood boy asked Michael what breed of dog Sunny was. He answered proudly, "A guard dog!" Sunny sits on the front porch each night until every family member is safely inside. If I'm out of town, she sits at the edge of the yard and watches for my car to turn the corner. If a bird flies by while we're outside, she chases it and barks furiously, saving us from any "fowl" play. Sunny isn't playful and silly like our other pets. Being the Moore's guard dog is serious business. Today's lesson indicates we could take a few lessons from Sunny! Read Luke 12:35-48, then complete the following.

In the margin, list all the descriptions of a faithful servant you can find in the passage.

Christ employed easily understood examples to teach something not so easily understood. We need to avoid dogmatic interpretations of those parables that aren't crystal clear. A common, easily understood example to an ancient Middle Easterner may not be common to us. We're also not always certain when Christ used hyperbole or of when we can draw very literal parallels.

Keeping these things in mind, record the responses each of the following servants received from their master upon his return:

The "'watching'" servants (v. 37): ______________________

____

The "'faithful and wise manager'" (v. 42): ______________________

The unwise servant (v. 45-46): ______________________

The "'servant who knows his master's will and does not get ready'" (v. 47):

____

The servant "'who does not know [his master's will] and does things

deserving punishment'" (v. 48): ______________________

Christ summed up the point of the parable in the last sentence of verse 48. How would you state the point in your own words?

____

____

Pretty harrowing verses, aren't they? Remember—our goal is to develop a more accurate picture of Christ. The Gospel portrait does not fit a simple category. Christ is multifaceted like the most brilliant diamond. The common denominator of every dimension is perfection. I hope God will use this study to shine light on the points of this perfect Diamond. Take a moment to reflect on our study. Even flip through and briefly review.

In the margin list several dimensions of His personality you've identified.

Certainly we've seen Christ's deep compassion. His overflowing mercy. His lavish love. We've also seen Him cut straight to the heart of many matters, mincing few words. Now we're beginning to see the throngs grow dramatically. Few seem to possess pure motives. Many simply want to see signs and wonders. Others have an entirely different motive.

What is the mood and motive of those described in Luke 11:53-54?

____

The temperature is rising. If you listen carefully, you'll also hear the temperature rising in the tone of Christ's message. I see at least two clear dimensions of Christ's personality today: His justice and His derision of irresponsibility. I believe we'll see these two dimensions illuminated as we apply the concepts illustrated by these passages:

1. Christ wants His people to be ready and waiting. No matter whether you're a pretribulationalist, a post-tribulationalist, an amillennialist, a dispensationalist, or have no clue what any of those mean, Christ is coming back. Every eye will see Him. Some things about God's ways make me grin ... like the way He knows our tendency to play amateur prophet. He puts all of us in our date-setting places by basically saying, "The only thing I'll tell you about My next visit is that you won't be expecting Me." The urgency is to be ready at all times.

Why do you think Christ told us to "keep your lamps burning" (v. 35)?

____

Our modern-day version of keeping our lamps burning is leaving a light on at night for someone out late. One of the shocks of the empty nest is no longer having someone to "wait up for" at night. Those of us who have older children have experienced the late-night difficulty of falling into a deep sleep before they get home. We can doze perhaps, but we don't fully sleep until they're safe inside. Even though waiting up is exhausting, it's a reminder of close family relationships and responsibility.

At this particular season in my life, my heart is encouraged to know that we have Someone for whom to "leave the light on." Five years ago a precious friend of mine lost her only son, a young adult. Last week she lost her husband. I have ached for her aloneness. I am so grateful that those of us in Christ always have Someone for whom we can wait expectantly at all times. Christ calls on us to be watching for Him when He returns (v. 37). Not inactively, mind you, but as servants (v. 35). Luke 12:37 tells us: "'it will be *good* for those servants whose master finds them watching when he comes.'"

Christ's deepest desire is that we live our lives in such close involvement with Him that all we lack is seeing Him face-to-face. Oh, that God would create in each of us such an acute awareness and belief of His ever-Presence that we won't be caught off guard! That our faith will simply be made sight! That we'll be gloriously shocked but unashamed! I think the apostle Paul lived this way.

How is this mind-set implied by Paul's last words in 2 Timothy 4:6-8?

____

God, create in us a longing for Your appearing so our lamps will be ever burning. I can't imagine what Christ meant when He said that those He finds ready and waiting will recline at a table and He will wait on them (v. 37). My mind can't fathom such a thing. *Blessed Lord, what wondrous love is this? Need we any further reward than the sight of You?*

For those with a knowledge of God, the cost of wickedness during the wait is astronomical. I'm not sure we ever hear stronger words out of the mouth of Christ than these in verse 46: "'He will cut him to pieces and assign him a place with the unbelievers.'" I believe Christ was most likely talking to people like those He described in Luke 11:52.

How did He describe them? ____________________________

____

These are people who were given knowledge, but they did not enter in. They had knowledge but no faith in the Truth. The example of many of the Pharisees provides an ongoing reminder that we can have heads full of knowledge and souls full of death. Please note the behavior of the servant in Luke 12:45. Much may be represented in the picture of him beating his menservants and maidservants. I believe Christ addressed His remarks primarily to the religious leaders. Take a look back at Luke 11:46.

What had the experts in the law done? ______________________________

____

I'd like to suggest that the picture of the head servant beating the menservants and maidservants while the master was away could easily represent spiritual abuse. Leaders, do you realize that God will hold us responsible for any spiritual abuse? Really think this concept through.

Give a few examples of what you think might constitute spiritual abuse.

____

I can think of many examples, but one instantly raises its ugly head in my mind—the preacher who beats and bangs hellfire and damnation on his pulpit, piously condemning his flock for all manner of evil, while abusing his wife and children at home. I wish I could tell you that I've only heard such a testimony once or twice. Let me stress that I still believe the far greater population of Christians resists that kind of hypocrisy, but spiritual abuse of this nature exists far more than we want to believe.

Another form of spiritual abuse is using Scripture or the name of God to manipulate others. I have very little doubt we will be called to account for the times we have used God's name to get what we want. Christ despises all forms of human oppression. A huge penalty awaits those who possess a knowledge of God yet persist in meanness and self-indulgence. Forgive me if my temperature on this matter is showing. If not for the authentic examples of godliness, I would despair over all the abuse I've seen in the religious community.

2. ***The future punishment of the unfaithful will be fair.*** Let's conclude with a look at the last sentence in our focal passage today: "'From everyone who has been given much, much will be demanded; and from the one who has been entrusted with much, much more will be asked'" (v. 48). That's fair. But that's serious.

What in Luke 12:45-48 indicates fairness in the judgment?

____

How does Revelation 20:11-13 make the same strong implication?

____

Beloved, I believe that at times Christ laughed until He cried. I believe He very likely played practical jokes and told hilarious stories. Jesus obviously had an extremely magnetic personality. The conclusion of John's Gospel tells us He said and did far more than could ever be recorded. I believe the secret things of God untold by His Word and revealed in heaven will be awesome and wonderful beyond description. The secrets He is keeping are the great and glorious, but He was careful not to hold back on a single warning. Those with access to Scripture will not be able to reach eternity and say to God, "Why didn't You warn us?"

I have been given so much. I must accept the fact that much is also required.

How about you? In what ways have you been given much?

Here is our joy and security in the midst of much required: Christ is never the author of spiritual abuse. Every single thing required of us will be amply rewarded far beyond our imagination. Until then, keep the porch light burning. Your Master will return.

DAY 4

How Often Have I Longed?

Today's Treasure
"O, Jerusalem, Jerusalem, you who kill the prophets and stone those sent to you, how often I have longed to gather your children together, as a hen gathers her chicks under her wings, but you were not willing!" (Luke 13:34).

Today is one of those days I warned you about. We're going to have to bridge some material we would have loved to study. I am convinced that God is leading us to center our thoughts today on the last segment of Luke 13, but I want you to begin by reading the entire chapter. If you sense God wanting to speak to you through one of the other portions of the chapter, stop and listen! He sure doesn't need me to teach you! Some of your most meaningful moments with God in this journey will be those strategic detours He chooses to take you on personally. By all means, go with Him.

After you've read all of Luke 13, please draw special attention to our focal passages for today: verses 31 through 35. In our previous lesson, we compared the multidimensional facets of Christ's character and personality to a diamond. In today's lesson, the light of God's Word is illuminating a very different dimension of Christ.

Meditate on verse 34 and describe what you see in Christ.

Some Pharisees came to Jesus to deliver a warning that Herod wanted to kill Him. Their warning may or may not have been sincere. The surrounding Scriptures offer more to suggest their insincerity than their sincerity.

If their concern was not Christ's safety, what might their motive have been?

To be fair, we should also remember that at least a small number of believers and supporters existed among the Pharisees. Regardless of the motive for their warning, they could have saved their breath.

How would you describe Christ's response?

I love Christ's last five words in the *New International Version* of Luke 13:32: "'I will reach my goal.'" Not if all the conditions are right. Not if you cooperate. Not if I'm still alive. "'I *will* reach my goal.'" Beloved, find security in the fact that nothing is haphazard about the activity of God. He has a goal and He has a definitive plan to be executed precisely according to His will. You no doubt noticed Christ's symbolic phraseology.

Fill in the blanks according to verses 32 and 33: "'I will drive out demons and heal people ________________ and __________________, and on the _____________________ I will reach my goal.' In any case, I must keep going ________________ and ________________ and the ___________________."

In a sense, Christ's phraseology has the style of a parable. When He said *today* and *tomorrow,* followed by *the third day* and *the next day,* He spoke not in the immediate sense but in a future tense. Because of our hindsight advantage, we hear the unmistakable hint of the three days beginning with the cross and ending with His glorious resurrection. I love not only the prophetic tone of His words but also the practical tone. In essence, Christ said: "I have a goal. I have work to do today toward that goal. I have work to do tomorrow toward that goal. But very soon that goal will be accomplished."

Perhaps Christ's use of the words *today, tomorrow,* and *the third day* suggest three segments of time in our lives as well. *Today* is our now. *The third day* could represent our then, or the fulfillment of God's goals for our lives through our heavenly completion. *Tomorrow* could represent every moment in between now and then.

Christ's return message to Herod emphasized that nothing could dissuade Him from completing His goal. Neither Herod nor any other power posed a threat to the plan. They would be used only as puppets to fulfill it. When we live our lives according to God's will, I don't think any Herod in the world can thwart our efforts at reaching God's goal either. Not a Herod of sickness nor a Herod of crisis. Not even a Herod that seems to hand us over to death. When our lives are surrendered to the authority of Jesus Christ, our Herods may be used only as puppets to bring about the will of God, but they pose no threat to the plan. I want you to see a very intriguing example.

Read Revelation 11:1-14. Sum up the events in a few sentences.

____

____

____

____

What happens to the two witnesses is a perfect example of the principle we've discussed. I'd like to give this principle a name. Let's call it *immunity*. For our purposes today, let's define *immunity* as a shelter from all evil imposition on God's plan. I chose the two witnesses as an example because the account is so dramatic; the elements of immunity are easy to identify.

From whom do the two witnesses derive their power (Rev. 11:3)?

____

What happens when they are opposed (v. 5)?

____

How are they killed (v. 7)? ______________________

Now carefully read the first part of verse 7. How do you explain why the two witnesses are immune to any threat to their calling for a length of time, then are killed by the beast?

____

If I presented the question clearly, hopefully you responded that they were not allowed to be killed until they had finished their testimony. Also note that their deaths were by no means a tragic end to their story. God raised them from the dead and made a mockery of their enemy.

Although the prophecy of the two witnesses is far more dramatic than will likely be the story of our lives, they illustrate a principle I believe God applies to us as well. When we live under the umbrella of God's authority and seek to obey His commands, the enemy may oppose us and even oppress us, but he cannot thwart the fulfillment of God's plan for our lives. Any permission he receives to oppose us will only be issued for the greater victory of God. Death cannot come to the obedient children of God until they have finished their testimony. When we surrender our wills to the will of our Father, we find a place of blessed immunity. Strengthened by His power and shielded by His protection, we will reach our goal.

Look back at Luke 13:31-35 and notice the words of Christ immediately following His response to Herod's threat. To our great advantage, Christ draws a vivid word picture of that blessed place of immunity in these very verses.

What did Christ long to do (v. 34)? ______________________

____

Why didn't He do it? ______________________

For the remainder of our lesson, we'll discuss the answers to those two questions. First, Scripture tells us that Christ longed to gather the children of Israel in His arms "'as a hen gathers her chicks under her wings.'" What could more tenderly portray the nurturing, protecting love of Christ? Yes, God's righteous right hand must bring judgment and justice. Sin demands it. But His tender loving heart longs to hold us in His arms and protect us from eternal harm. The cross of Calvary is how He accomplished both works for those who would find immunity from judgment by trusting in His sacrifice.

Now is a perfect time to learn the meaning of a powerful word. Read Romans 12:17-21.

We are told not to take revenge "but leave room for God's____________."

The original word for *wrath* means "utter abhorrence to sin but longing mixed with grief for those who live in it." Let this sink in your mind until it is absorbed into your heart: even in God's wrath, He is merciful. Yes, He will judge those who refuse to receive the blessed immunity of the cross, but the word does not draw a picture of a God delighting in judgment but rather grieving over the loss.

The heart of God is beautifully illustrated in His Son as He cries out, "'O Jerusalem, Jerusalem, you who kill the prophets and stone those sent to you, how often I have longed to gather your children together, as a hen gathers her chicks under her wings.'" The Old Testament paints a similar portrait in Psalm 91:1-4. These words fall like a down comforter from heaven.

How do they describe a sort of immunity? ____________________

____

The Hebrew word for *shelter* means a "covering, hiding place, protection, secret (place)" *(Strong's)*. The implication of the verse is that a place of safety or a certain level of immunity from evil onslaughts exists for those who choose to dwell there. The concept of *dwelling* in Psalm 91:1 is virtually synonymous with the concept of *obeying* or *remaining* in John 15:10.

How do we abide or remain in Christ and His love?

____

Obedience to our Father's commands is the key to immunity from the enemy. Obedience is what positions us in the shadow of the Almighty; any evil that comes against us will have to go through God first. Christ lived for one purpose: to do the will of the One who sent Him (see John 6:38). Because He was entirely surrendered to the will of His Father, Herod's threat had no power over Him. When the time came, the rulers and the chief priests could be used only as puppets by God in His pursuit of greater glory.

Likewise, the two witnesses of Revelation live to do the will of God. Though they have much opposition, they possess God-given power to defeat it. When the time comes for their deaths, the beast is used simply as a puppet by God in His pursuit of greater glory.

I am convinced the same is true for us. Our place of immunity from the obstruction of God's plan for our lives is gained through obedience to His will.

This point answers the second question posed earlier: Christ longed to gather the children of Israel into His arms like a hen gathers her chicks under her wings, but He did not. Why? Because they weren't willing. They chose their own will over Christ's, forfeiting the shelter of His wings. The result was desolation and defeat (see Luke 13:35; 19:43).

The same unwillingness can have similar results today. As believers in Christ, two different forms of immunity apply to us. All who personally receive the grace gift of God have immunity from eternal judgment. We stand in the shadow of the cross. The judgment that should have come to us came to Christ instead.

A second kind of immunity does not come automatically upon our salvation. It results when we surrender our will to the Father's will and our obedience to His Word. When we bow to His authority, we become immune to defeat and all threats to the plan of God for our personal lives. I don't mean we're immune from trouble, tribulation, or even a certain amount of oppression, but they won't be able to defeat us. We will possess and practice the God-given power to overcome them and the plan will be uninterrupted.

I know these principles because I've experienced them. I have complete assurance of my salvation. I am convinced that the cross has immunized me against all judgment for sin. However, in my lifetime I have without a doubt been temporarily defeated by the enemy and done things that were not part of God's plan for my life. By surrendering to my own will in certain seasons, I stepped outside the shelter of the Most High and, although he could not have me, the enemy certainly had a field day with me. I am a living, breathing grace-filled Plan B. But I'm a Plan B who has learned some painful lessons that have changed my practices. I presently jump out of bed with one primary plan of attack for the day: ducking under the sheltering wing of the Most High so the enemy will have to get through Him to get to me. As we conclude today's lesson, I want you to read Psalm 17:7-9.

Personalize these verses as if every word were written just to you. Use the space below to turn the verses into your own words of faith and gratitude to the God who invites you to a blessed place of immunity.

____

____

____

Christ Jesus longs to draw us under the shelter of His wings—so close to His side that we can hear His tender heartbeat. He yearns to lavish us with His possessive, protective love. To cover us from so many unnecessary harms.

There is a secret place. Go, beloved, and hide.

DAY 5

When God Runs

Today's Treasure

"While he was still a long way off, his father saw him and was filled with compassion for him; he ran to his son, threw his arms around him and kissed him" (Luke 15:20).

Perhaps the most mind-boggling doctrine in the Word of God is that the Creator and Sustainer of the universe who dwells in unapproachable light—pursues us. Fallen humans. How can it be? I will never comprehend why, but His Word assures us it is true. Beloved, God pursues you. He rides the clouds like a chariot and chases after you. He has chosen you not out of obligation but out of love. His is a love that will not let you go. May God's Word offer us a timely reminder.

Today we approach a chapter of Scripture much like we did on day 4. Please read all of Luke 15, giving particular attention to our focal passages in verses 11 through 32. After you have completed your reading, please complete the following:

What prompted the three parables in this chapter?

____

What common theme do all three parables share?

____

I cannot think of a more pointed summation of this chapter of Scripture than Christ's words in Luke 19:10. Please write it in the space below.

____

____

Christ didn't come to save the pious and perfect. He came to seek and to save the lost. At times I've descended from the place of appropriate repentance where I was sorry for my sins to the place of inappropriate self-loathing where I was sorry Christ was "forced" (as if He could be) to save me. I'd find myself wishing I had been a nicer sinner. More pleasant to save. Emotion washes over me today as I remember again: Christ came for sinners like me. He wanted to save me. Our Savior came to seek and to save the lost. The hopeless. The foolish. The weak. The depraved. In His own words: "'It is not the healthy who need a doctor, but the sick. I have not come to call the righteous, but sinners to repentance'" (Luke 5:31-32).

I have no idea how many times I've read and even taught the story of the prodigal son, yet it still brings me to tears. I am such a product of this kind of father love. Perhaps you are, too. If not, you may more readily identify with the older brother, and God's Word will speak riches to you. This parable offers a priceless inheritance to everyone. Rather than attempt to exhaust the entire segment and apply every applicable point, I'd rather center unhurriedly on just a few. Notice them with me.

1. A son sick of home. As the curtain rises, the younger son asks his father for his share of the estate. Although his father was not obligated to give it to him, he did. The wise father knew that his son was unwise, but sometimes allowing a persistent young adult to do what is unwise leads to wisdom, albeit down a painful road. The son set off for a distant country. This was no mistreated son, and his was not a dysfunctional home.

What kinds of things motivate a person to leave a healthy, loving, and even wealthy environment? Offer your thoughts.

____

Perhaps we prodigals distance ourselves from the good in an attempt to keep it from haunting us in the bad. Sometimes in our rebellion we foolishly long for a searing of conscience, having no idea it would be a fate worse than death. In the distant land the son squandered his wealth in wild living. The word *prodigal* comes from the definition of the Greek word for *wild. Asotos* means "profligately, riotously, prodigally." A very important element surfaces in the definition of *asotia,* the feminine noun from *asotos.* It describes the prodigal as "having no hope of safety."

List the results of the prodigal's riotous living recorded in Luke 15:14-16.

____

____

Consider the words *having no hope of safety* in terms of our previous lesson. Do you remember all we learned about the place of immunity on day 4? Keep in mind that the father represents God and the younger son represents every prodigal.

Why wasn't the condition described in Psalm 91:1-4 true of him?

___

When the prodigal chose to step out from under the umbrella of his father's authority, he forfeited the protection of the umbrella as well. He did not lose his father's love, but he lost his father's shield. How many of us have been right there with him? The devil is so sly. He tempts us to think that God is somehow out to cheat us.

Check any of the following that you have ever been tempted to think.

- ❑ **God just wants to imprison me and take away all my fun.**
- ❑ **I'll spend eternity doing what God wants. I want to do what I want while I'm here on earth!**
- ❑ **God just wants to make a robot out of me.**

As we begin to grow up in Him and in His Word, we understand that nothing could be further from the truth. Our freedom, our abundant life, our dignity, our dreams come true—are all found in the glorious will of God. We finally learn that under God's umbrella, we are free to sing in the rain. Outside God's umbrella, we nearly drown in the flood.

2. *A prodigal life in a spiral.* At first, it's so exciting, it's intoxicating. Soon it's dizzying effects spiral downward and truth gives way to consequences.

In the margin draw a downward spiral. Label it with each point you can identify on the prodigal's descent.

Now go back to each point of descent the prodigal experienced and list some of the feelings or emotions you think might have been associated with each one. Keep in mind that he was a young man who was reared well. Imagine his feelings and responses based on his upbringing. In ways I'm not sure we Gentiles can understand, this Hebrew son hit rockbottom. He came from a home where pigs were considered unclean animals. I assure you his father did not bring home the bacon, and his mother didn't fry it up in the pan. Yet not only was he forced to take a job feeding swine, but also he longed to eat their food!

How many times could he have run home before he hit bottom?

___

One of the most wonderful things God has taught me from my past is that we don't always have to hit the bottom. When tempted to wander, we can turn back to Him early. God's most effective method for teaching me this principle is the memory of excruciating consequences from the past. I'd have to lose my mind before wanting to go back to some of the places I've been.

I've watched God take a young woman I love very much and restore her to the right road after a prodigal detour. She has cried out to me, "When will all these painful repercussions end?"

I have answered her, "Not until the very idea of straying causes you such painful flashbacks that you're hardly ever tempted to depart His will again." God wants to whisper to our hearts, "Are you sure you want to go back there again?" and hear us say, "No way do I want that kind of pain!"

Can you see ways in which allowing painful consequences could be part of the concept in Hebrews 12:5-11? ❑ Yes ❑ No If so, explain.

____

____

God is far too faithful to allow the prodigal life to be cost-free. In fact, consider that if we can sin freely, we may have a far more serious problem. If we can remain outside the umbrella of God's authority for an extended period of time without feeling the negative effects of it, we may not be saved. The Holy Spirit never falls down on His job. To feel no conviction of sin for a length of time is a serious sign that the Holy Spirit may not reside in us. To experience no chastisement is to suggest we may not be "sons." We can quench the Spirit, but we cannot disable Him. Now let's focus on the prodigal's "about face."

3. *A homesick son.* The words in verse 17, "'When he came to his senses,'" introduce a turnaround. Few things force us to look up like being all the way down. The son realized that, considering where he came from, the way he was living didn't make sense.

The same is true for you and me. When we accept Christ, we are brought into a family of "more than conquerors" (Rom. 8:37). To live in defeat simply doesn't make sense! To be beaten down by the harsh elements of life when we could be shielded from so much is insane. Under the umbrella of God's authority we are not immune to some hard winds and getting our faces wet in the furiously pelting rain, but we cannot be defeated by them. May we quickly come to our senses when living any other way!

Luke 15:17 tells us that the son considered the abundance of his father's hired hands and realized the insanity of starving to death. He waited to go home until his desperation exceeded his pride. That the prodigal planned what he would say hints at the difficulty of his return. He literally practiced what he would say when he got home.

Briefly describe his approach. ______________________________

____

4. *A father homesick for his son.* Don't miss a single description of this father: "While he was still a long way off, his father saw him" (v. 20). The prodigal's father was looking for his son in the distance. I imagine that every day since his son's departure, his father studied the horizon in search of his son's silhouette.

I wonder if the son was pacing. And pacing. And pacing. He could see his home in the distance, but perhaps he could not bring himself to walk that last mile. He looked at his father's vast estate and glanced down at his own poor estate. His clothes were worn and filthy. Dirt was embedded under every nail. His hair was probably long and matted or shorn to the skin to defend against lice. All at once, he probably became aware of his own foul smell. He was destitute. Degraded.

But … "'his father saw him and was filled with compassion for him'" (v. 20). The word for *compassion* in this verse means "to feel deeply or viscerally, to yearn, have compassion, pity." Just as the starving son had longed for food, his father had yearned for him. His was a kind of yearning so deep that no amount of work could assuage it. Family members could not replace it. A yearning no distraction could soothe. Oh, friend, can you glimpse the heart of God? Do you realize that when you run from Him, He yearns for you every minute and cannot be distracted from His thoughts of you?

In Psalm 139:7-12 read the expressions of one who considered running from God's presence. How does the psalmist describe God?

____

____

When God sees our poor estate and the ravaging effects of our foolish decisions, He doesn't just sit back and say, "She got what she deserved." He is filled with compassion and longs to bring us back home. Yes, we face consequences, but those consequences are a loving summons back to the Father.

In one of the most moving moments in all of Scripture, Luke 15:20 records that the father "'ran to his son.'" Scripture often employs anthropomorphisms—descriptions of God as if He had a human body. We sometimes read that God walked (in the midst of His people) or that He rode (on the clouds like chariots), but this is the only time in the entire Word of God when He is described as running.

What makes God run? A prodigal child turning his face toward home! How can we resist Him? How can we not reciprocate such lavish love?

When was the last time you saw an older man, the father of adult children, run? Would you picture it now? Can you hear his heart pounding in his chest? Can you hear him catching his breath? Nothing could keep him from his son.

When he reached the son, what did the father do (v. 20)?

____

The son tried his best to give the speech he planned but to no avail. In all his talk of unworthiness, he didn't realize he was unworthy even before he left. He was a son not because he earned the right to be, but because he was born of his father. He could exceed the realm of his father's shield, but he could not exceed the reach of his father's love. "'Quick! Bring the best robe and put it on him. Put a ring on his finger and sandals on his feet. Bring the fattened calf and kill it. Let's have a feast and celebrate. For this son of mine was dead and is alive again; he was lost and is found'" (v. 22-24).

Herbert Lockyer's expression of this scene overwhelms me. May his words touch you too:

> The prodigal was not able to express all the plea he had prepared to present on meeting his father. His kisses smothered the lips of the prodigal, who was back home, and that was all that mattered. The original implies that the father "covered him with kisses." Often he had looked out along the road for this moment, and now his outgushing pity and unrestrained, overflowing manifestation of tender fatherly embrace were proofs of his unextinguished love for his lost son. How suggestive this is of God's welcome for the penitent sinner! Once enfolded in His fatherly arms, there is no casting up of sins. God 'kisses the past into forgetfulness.'[1]

Merciful Savior! Graceful God! You have kissed this prodigal's past into forgetfulness! Though mockers may accuse me, though gossipers may make sport of me, though brothers may jealously despise me, I will celebrate! Let all hear music and dancing! For I once was dead and now I'm alive again. I once was lost and now I am found.

[1]Herbert Lockyer, *All the Parables of the Bible* (Grand Rapids, MI: Zondervan Publishing House, 1963), 287.

VIDEO RESPONSE SHEET GROUP SESSION 7

Session 7

Introduction: In today's session we'll depart from our established norm. In sessions 1 through 6, our subject matter has "looked back" over the material we covered previously in our member book. Today we'll be looking ahead. One of our most important goals in this series is to develop a more accurate impression of what Christ was like when the Word was made flesh and dwelled among us (see John 1:14).

- We begin by correcting a common misperception: We have often mistaken Christ's meekness for __________ and misunderstood ____________________ to mean passionless.

Three Portraits of a Passionate Christ

(Because Jesus is the same yesterday, today, and forever, we will consider each of these points in present rather than past tense.)

Portrait One: Christ is passionate about His people's _________ (see Luke 19:28-40). Don't miss the few unpleasant faces in the portrait (painted in v. 39). Two observations based on the confrontation between Christ and the indignant Pharisees:

- The praises of God can reveal the ________ of ________.
- The __________ of Christ are our greatest cause for praise. However, some of Christ's most magnificent triumphs are the least _________________ to man. See Matthew 27:51 in terms of Colossians 2:13-15.

Portrait Two: Christ is passionate about His people's _________ (see Luke 19:41-44). The original Greek word for *wept* in this verse is *klaio*, meaning "to weep, to wail, implying not only the shedding of tears, but also _______ _________ ___________ of _________." Two observations based on Christ's lamentation over Jerusalem:

- The cause of Christ's deepest grief is when He stands before us, holding out exactly _______ we _________, and we refuse it.
- Our refusal makes us ______________ to a full-scale __________.

Portrait Three: Christ is passionate about His __________ __________ (see Luke 19:45-48).
In addition, see John 2:17. "Zeal for your house will consume me." The original Greek word for *zeal* is *zelos* from *zeo*, meaning "to be _____ or __________." The word can also mean "_____________."

Conclusion: We are a people of _________, created in the image of God.

WEEK 8

The Answer

Day 1
Causing Others to Sin

Day 2
Where Are the Nine?

Day 3
Lacking One Thing

Day 4
A Wee Little Man

Day 5
Signs of His Coming

One of my favorite things about God's Word is that it is gloriously inexhaustible. While I am somewhat frustrated that we don't have the space to pour over every single Scripture in the Gospel of Luke, I am reminded that we would still fall short of the definitive study of Christ's life. Colossians 2:3 says that in Christ "are hidden all the treasures of wisdom and knowledge." We'll never "out search" the treasures He's willing to reveal. May our present treasure hunt simply cause you to search for more. The week of study awaiting us is a bit confrontational. I hope we are beginning to think that's OK. I can't think of a single radical change in my life that didn't find its catalyst in a radical confrontation by God. We can find much encouragement in trusting that our God never confronts to condemn. Rather, He confronts to complete what is lacking. In the midst of some pretty straight talk from God, we also will share a few reprieving grins. We've got some tree climbing to do this week with a certain wee little man. Keep looking forward to it when the moments get heavy.

Principal Questions:

Day 1: How did Christ picture the seriousness of causing another person to sin?
Day 2: What evidence do you see of "spot counting" in Luke 18:9-14?
Day 3: What critical difference separates believing Christ to be good and believing Christ to be God?
Day 4: What insight about Zacchaeus' wealth do you see in Proverbs 15:27 and 28:25?
Day 5: According to Luke 12:40, why would forecasting a time of Christ's return be a waste of time?

By the way, has anyone reminded you lately that Christ is coming back? It's a fact. And one we'll study together briefly before our present week concludes. Let's get started.

D A Y 1

Causing Others to Sin

We are highlighting certain segments of Scripture over others in weeks 7 and 8 in an effort to speed through the main section of parables in Luke. Our goal is to slow down for Christ's final days on earth in weeks 9 and 10. Today's focal passages from the Book of Luke will be comparatively short in length, but I can hardly overemphasize their importance. Please read Luke 17:1-5 and complete the following:

Today's Treasure
"Jesus said to his disciples: 'Things that cause people to sin are bound to come, but woe to that person through whom they come' " (Luke 17:1).

Whom was Christ addressing? ______________________________

Why do you think "'things that cause people to sin are bound to come'" (v. 1)?

____

How did Christ picture the seriousness of causing another person to sin?

____

What is Christ's apparent stand on the issue of forgiveness?

____

What did the apostles ask for at the conclusion of this brief teaching (v. 5)?

____

Let's state a serious fact based on Luke 17—events or situations can actually cause people to sin. Before we attempt to interpret Christ's statements, let's make sure we understand what He didn't mean. Christ didn't mean that in some cases people have no choice but to sin. He didn't absolve the one who sins from the responsibility to repent. He did mean that conditions can exist and things can happen which so greatly increase the tendency toward sin that a terrible woe is due the responsible party.

What are these *offenses* or "'things that cause people to sin'"? I am confident you'll find the original word to be intriguing. The Greek word is *skandalon*. The idea of our English word *scandal* is present in the meaning of the Greek word. *Skandalon* is "the trigger of a trap on which the bait is placed, and which, when touched by the animal, springs and causes it to close causing entrapment … . *Skandalon* always denotes an enticement to conduct which could ruin the person in question."

Review the definition carefully, then read Luke 17:1. In this verse, to whom would the "woe" be directed?

____

If you grasp the concept, you responded that the woe would apply to the one who actually set the trap or figuratively speaking "became" the trigger of a trap. Woe to the person who baits another person into entrapment.

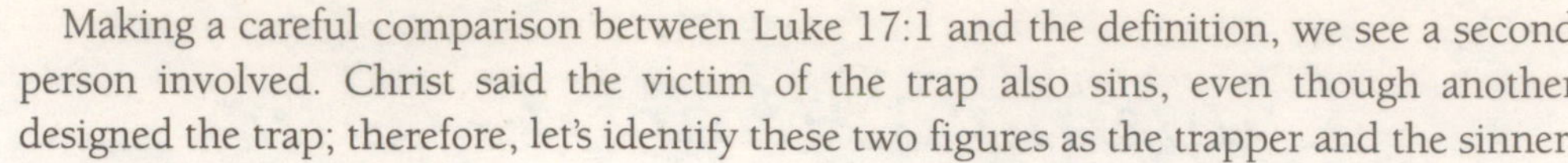

Making a careful comparison between Luke 17:1 and the definition, we see a second person involved. Christ said the victim of the trap also sins, even though another designed the trap; therefore, let's identify these two figures as the trapper and the sinner.

As you look once again at the definition of *skandalon*, what was the initial point of sin for the sinner? Check the best answer:

❑ trusting the trapper ❑ taking the bait ❑ noticing the bait

If I'm presenting the concepts clearly, you responded that the point of sin was taking the bait. Without a doubt, I have experienced entrapment, but to be liberated I must not shift all responsibility to the trapper. Unfortunately, all too often I took the bait. To live consistently outside a trap, I must recognize my own responsibility in at least three ways. I am responsible for:

1. Repenting of the sin of taking the bait.
2. Learning why I took the bait.
3. Asking God to mend and fortify the weak places in the fabric of my heart, soul, and mind so I will not continue life as a victim.

A critical part of my freedom has been asking God to help me search my heart, soul, and mind for vulnerabilities to foolish decisions. Why might this step be so important?

Taking responsibility in these areas produced one of the greatest harvests of my life. I learned to willingly lay my heart bare before Him, to invite Him to reveal my weaknesses and handicaps, and to be unashamed. I also developed daily dependency upon God because my old vulnerabilities had become such habits, practices, and ways of life.

We looked at the sin of the victim in Luke 17:1; now let's zero in on the sin of the trapper. The ramifications of the trapper's sin are so great that he or she becomes the object of *woe*, meaning "disaster, calamity."

Christ issued a woe to anyone who causes another person to sin. But look at the pronounced indictment against anyone who causes one of these little ones to sin. Who are these little ones? The original word is *mikros*. Study the following definition: "of age meaning small, young, not grown up; in the comparative degree meaning less, younger … figuratively, of dignity, authority, meaning low, humble."

By the definition, what kinds of people could be considered *mikros*?

We certainly know Christ's reference to little ones includes literal children because in Matthew's version He actually "called a little child and had him stand among them" before He issued these statements (Matt. 18:2).

Can you think of any ways that the entrapment of a child could cause him or her to be more vulnerable to sin? In the margin list several ways.

Careful attention to the definition of *mikros* suggests that those who are not grown up fall under the category of little ones. A 16-year-old may have the body of an adult, but he or she most assuredly is not grown up. An adult's seduction is entrapment even if the young person "sinned" in any level of willing participation.

Christ's reference to little ones spotlights children in terms of age, but His intent may have wider applications. I believe Christ includes those who are childlike or inferior to the trapper in knowledge, experience, authority, or power—anyone of whom it might be easy to take advantage. That Christ holds the trapper greatly responsible is a gross understatement! He appears to be saying, If you have entrapped a weaker, more vulnerable person in sin, you're going to wish you had drowned in the deepest sea rather than deal with Me.

Most of us have asked, "Why do these things happen?" Luke 17:1 tells us that these atrocities "'are bound to come.'" "But why?" we ask. Matthew's version suggests one reason.

Fill in the following blank from Matthew 18:7:
"'Woe to the world because of the things that cause people to sin! Such things ____________ come, but woe to the man through whom they come.'"

The original word for *must* means "compelling force, as opposed to willingness … as a result of the depravity and wickedness of men, there is a moral inevitability that offenses should come." Add the kingdom of darkness to the depravity of humans and you have a formula for exactly the evil we see in our world.

Why is the work accomplished through *skandalon* particularly important to Satan in targeting Christians?

____

A day of reckoning is coming. No trapper gets away with entrapment—of the human kind nor of the spirit kind. Neither can escape the eyes of *El Roi*, the God who sees. Relief and gratitude is appropriate, but let's not get too smug.

How does Luke 17:3 suggest the trapper is not always the "other guy"?

____

I asked you to identify the audience Christ was addressing. The correct answer is His disciples. Christ wasn't just issuing an assurance of horrible consequences for the trapper. He was also issuing a warning that His disciples better not be among them. If Christ's temperature rises over the godless trapper, can you even imagine how His temperature would rise over the trapper who bears His name? God forbid!

Most of us are not naïve enough to think that these kinds of offenses never happen in church-going families. I'd like to highlight one area that doesn't get much press but where people are at great risk for offense in the church.

In terms of our local church bodies, who might be considered little ones besides those who are young in age?

____

Remember when we talked about spiritual abuses in week 7? We must carefully guard against spiritual abuses of those young or weak in the faith.

What might be some ways a new believer could be entrapped by an older, more experienced believer?

____

New believers are so impressionable. Sometimes their zeal far exceeds their knowledge. They sometimes believe virtually anything a more experienced Christian tells them. Biblical doctrines can be twisted into false teaching to entrap immature believers in all sorts of sins. If God would judge those outside His own household, I think we can rest assured He would discipline His own. Let's not start feeling guilty for some atrocity we may not have committed, but by all means let's be on our guard never to cause another person to sin. The Word is clear we have that potential.

Next, allow me to draw your attention to the forgiveness issue Christ addressed in Luke 17:3-4. Christ suddenly switched to a subject that seems to have no relationship to things that cause people to sin. However, I'd like to suggest a powerful connection between the two. Few things cause people to sin like unforgiveness.

Understanding that unforgiveness itself is a sin, in what ways does it cause further sin?

____

____

Difficult-to-forgive circumstances can set a trap. How does Satan use unforgiveness as bait to entrap us in sin (2 Cor. 2:10-11)?

____

We take the bait when we choose unforgiveness over Spirit-empowered release. Please look back at Luke 17:3.

Who is identified as the one committing sin? ____________________

Please note that Christ's specific prescriptive in Luke 17:3-4 is to fellow believers when we sin against one another. Someone might ask, "Does this mean I have to forgive only other Christians?" No, indeed.

Whom are we to forgive according to Luke 11:4? ____________________

The difference may not be in the forgiveness but in the rebuke. I believe Christ suggests a different method of dealing with a brother's or sister's sin. He issued a directive to rebuke a fellow believer. When dealing with the unsaved, we are still called to forgive—but not necessarily to rebuke. Even though the rebuke of a Christian to a non-Christian could easily fall on deaf ears, we were called to be different in the body of Christ. If we are functioning as a healthy body, ideally we should be able to bring issues that affect us to the table with one another and dialogue and, when appropriate, even rebuke or receive a rebuke. This type of approach demands the maturity expressed by Ephesians 4:14-15. Please read these verses.

What rule of thumb found in verse 15 might apply to rebuking a fellow believer? Check the correct answer.
- ❑ **Let your conversation be always full of grace, seasoned with salt.**
- ❑ **Speak the truth in love.**
- ❑ **Stay away from a foolish man.**

How should a rebuke be given according to 2 Timothy 4:2?

____

Needless to say, a tremendous burden of responsibility falls on the one giving the rebuke. An appropriate rebuke is speaking the truth in love "with great patience and careful instruction." We may not be off base in concluding that a rebuke that invites anger and bitterness might fall under the category of entrapment to sin. Obviously, a huge responsibility also falls on the recipient to rightly accept the rebuke. I am learning that an important part of maturing as a believer is knowing how to receive a rebuke.

Do you know what occurs to me as we wrap up this lesson? If we would learn the art of giving and receiving an appropriate rebuke in the early stages of wrongdoing, we would guard ourselves more effectively against offenses of millstone magnitude! I don't know about you, but I'll be chewing on this lesson long into the night. Thanks for studying so hard with me today. I'm crazy about you.

DAY 2

Where Are the Nine?

We have a family joke. When one of us compliments another, the recipient will tease: "Thank you. But after all, I cannot be less than who I am." It rarely fails to bring a laugh—or a pillow flying across the room. What makes the reply so preposterous is that all four of us are very aware that without Christ, we indeed could not be less!

With Christ we are so much, but we often act like far less than who we are. Christ Jesus, on the other hand, really can't be less than who He is. No matter what was pending, He never set aside His position as Son of man, the Deliverer, and the Healer.

Today we'll catch up with Him on His way to Jerusalem. Christ knew all that would come upon Him. I think even the best of us would be somewhat distracted by pending suffering and death.

Who wouldn't have understood if Christ wanted to travel a remote path to Jerusalem, far from the tugs of the needy? Yet all the way to the city that would scorn Him, Jesus continued to minister, heal, teach, and warn. Why? Because He simply could not be less than who He was. Please read Luke 17:11-19 and complete the following:

At this point, what is Christ's location in His journey to Jerusalem?

____

Today's Treasure

"One of them, when he saw he was healed, came back, praising God in a loud voice" (Luke 17:15).

According to the law of Moses, those with skin diseases were not allowed inside the city to present themselves to a priest unless they had been healed. Read Luke 17:14 carefully.

What hint do you see that Christ required them to exercise faith?

____

How was one of the lepers different from the rest? ____________________

While I ministered in India, I was often stunned by what God empowered me to do. He seemed to raise me above my fleshly senses and allow me to minister in extreme circumstances. I was unable to do only one thing, and it has haunted me ever since. I had confidently planned to minister in a leper colony. The opportunity didn't readily arise, but after passing very close to several colonies, I deliberately did not pursue it.

The reason was not unconcern. I feared I would dishonor them by becoming physically ill. You see, I almost became ill just passing by. Nothing could have prepared me for the sight or the smell. I had been in one squalid village after another without hindrance, but the smell of diseased and decaying flesh was more than I could handle.

I don't know if God was upset with me, but I was definitely upset with myself. My experience helps me to appreciate today's story. Let's highlight several significant pieces of information shared about the lepers in today's reference:

The lepers were outside the city gate. What could be worse than forced isolation? I can hardly stand the thought of the emotional ramifications wrought by this dreadful disease, especially in an ancient society.

What did the law of Moses say about lepers in Leviticus 13:46?

____

Many of us still wear emotional scars as the result of being excluded from certain groups in our youth; yet, by comparison, that was nothing! Try to imagine what this was like. Presumably, the scene is the city gate. Christ met the lepers as He prepared to enter the village. We are told "they stood at a distance" (v. 12). They were obeying the laws meant to control the spread of the highly infectious disease.

Oh, beloved, I'm so grateful we never have to stand at a distance from Christ. Not only is He incapable of catching our "disease," but also He is never reluctant to embrace us.

What does Psalm 34:18 tell you about our Lord?

____

Who could be more brokenhearted, more crushed in spirit, than these outcasts? Even though Christ honored their respect for the law, His healing Spirit had to have drawn close while bathing them with soothing balm.

The lepers cried out in a loud voice. Don't miss the fact that every word attributed to the lepers is "in a loud voice" (vv. 13,15). The distance explains their initial volume. But why did the one who returned and fell at Jesus' feet also cry out in a loud voice?

I'd like to suggest that they were accustomed to having to shout. I asked you to consider Leviticus 13:46. Now I'd like you to read the preceding verse. Leviticus 13:45 is probably as hard for you to read as it is for me.

I was reared by my grandmother and mother to be a cheerleader for the underdog. At my house, a fate worse than death was looking down on someone who could not help his condition. As I read this verse in the Old Testament, I can hardly bear the thought of the excruciating blend of exclusion and publicity.

How did the leper have to identify himself? ______________________

Imagine it. Outside the city gate, unable to work, entirely dependent on charity, yet while excluded they were forced to publicize themselves by crying out: "Unclean! Unclean!" Don't miss the description: ***they cried out.*** They were forced to cover their mouths yet shout continually so that no one would accidentally come near them.

Because of the nature of this ministry and my own testimony, I encounter many people who live like the 10 lepers. They are in bondage either to sin or to the after-effects of sin. Far too often I see actual believers in Christ wearing shame like a cloak, scarlet letters on their chests. Their voices may be silent, but their expressions cry out: "Unclean! Unclean!" They feel excluded from the pretty part of the body of Christ. Yet they feel their shame is displayed for all to see. My heart breaks every time.

In Luke 17:12, the lepers cried out, "Jesus, Master, have pity on us!" Note the definition of the original word for *pity:* "To show mercy, to show compassion, extend help for the consequence of sin, as opposed to *sklerunomai*, to be hardened. The general meaning is to have compassion or mercy on a person in unhappy circumstances … implying not merely a feeling for the misfortunes of others involving sympathy, but also an active desire to remove those miseries." According to this definition, these lepers were not just asking for sympathy.

For what were they asking? ______________________________

Beloved, all the sympathy in the world could not change the miserable condition of these 10 lepers. They needed far more than people feeling sorry for them. They needed someone to change their lives! Jesus was the One and Only who could. Part of my horrible struggle about going to the leper colony in India was an awareness that I could do nothing to help their physical estate.

Sometimes we harden our hearts to shield ourselves from the pain of hurting for others. Better to look and hurt than ignore or grow hard. Pain is part of what reminds us we're alive and still connected. Yes, we wish we could do more, but we know Someone who can. Christ still overflows today with a pity that doesn't just sympathize but changes conditions. Often physically. Always spiritually. Next notice:

The common condition of the lepers eclipsed their differences. The village in today's scene was located along the border between Samaria and Galilee. Both Samaritans and Jews, who actively despised each other, lived in this region. The lepers had to have been a mix of Samaritans and Jews. Christ never would have commented that only a "'foreigner'" returned with thanks if none of the ten had been Jews.

The tragic plight of the lepers gave them far more in common than their differences as Jews and Gentiles. In reality, aren't we the same way? Before we are redeemed, not one of us is better than the other. We are all in the same sad state—lepers outside the city gate. Lost and isolated. Marred and unclean—whether we've lied or cheated, devalued another human being, or committed adultery. Lost is lost. Furthermore, found is found. All of us in Christ have received the free gift of salvation in one way only: grace. When we judge a brother's or sister's sin as so much worse than our own, we are like lepers counting spots. "She has more than I do."

Look at Luke 18:9-14. What evidence do you see of "spot counting"?

____

Let's face it. We've all had leprosy, and our cure cost a life whether we had a dozen spots or a thousand. We separate ourselves in all sorts of ways, but our disease was really the same—as was our cure.

Can you describe an experience with a group of people that eclipsed all the differences and reminded you how much you were all the same?

____

____

The lepers were cleansed during their faith-walk to the priest. Before Christ healed them, He told them to go and show themselves to the priests. Read the Old Testament directive in Leviticus 14:1-9 for those healed of infectious skin diseases like leprosy.

What was the priest to do? ______________________________

____

Instead of waiting for the priest to come and examine them, Christ told them to go to the priests. Mind you, the priests were inside the city gates. The lepers risked expulsion, ridicule, repulsion, and every other kind of human insult. The Word tells us, "As they went, they were cleansed" (Luke 17:14).

Picture them taking their walk of faith, step-by-step. They probably noticed the healing of their feet first because the disease is very disfiguring, making a simple walk awkward if not impossible. Perhaps they noticed their hands next. What a glorious sight! You see, their healing was not simply a matter of the skin clearing. They literally had fingers restored. The numbness in their appendages gave way to the sense of touch.

Can you picture them turning their palms up and down with amazement, running to one another, laughing and expressing their joy in stereo? When they clapped their hands with celebration, they felt the welcome sting of healthy flesh. What an exhibition passed through the simple village that day! Who could have missed it? Ten lepers made whole. Their hair still unkempt and their clothes still torn, but for once they were oblivious. Glad spectacles were they.

As I prepared for this lesson by studying the life of a leper in the ancient Hebrew world, I learned something that really caused me to think. The Mosaic law was very specific about the proper methods of purification after someone with leprosy was cured. Oddly, "the Bible never implies that leprosy can be cured by nonmiraculous means, even though it does contain guidelines for readmitting cured lepers into normal society." Leprosy was incurable.[1]

What does 2 Kings 5:7 imply? ______________________________

Only a handful of references in the Old Testament record lepers being healed, but not one was through natural means. Don't you find it a little odd that the Old Testament law provided such elaborate instructions for purification and reentry to society after healing, and yet it never happened apart from rare divine intervention?

Ah, but did Christ not say He had come to fulfill the law? All those centuries they had been waiting for the cure that the Old Testament law inferred had to be possible. All 10 of those lepers knew what to do after they were healed, yet they never could find a cure—until one day when their cure found them.

I love the way Scripture refers to their healing as being made clean. Oh, dear sister, that's what healing has meant to me. Being made clean! Do you know why I recognize those who wear shame like a cloak? Scarlet letters on their chests? Because I did. But I don't anymore.

What does Acts 10:15 tell us not to do? ______________________

____

You can be fairly certain the village priest had never practiced the purification ritual to pronounce a leper clean. I can almost picture him reading the instructions in Leviticus 14 step by unfamiliar step—like we read a new recipe. What a story he had for the Mrs. that night! Then again, it wouldn't have been like a woman to miss the parade of 10 former lepers dancing their way down Main Street.

One leper returned to give praise to God. I wonder if he tried to get the other nine to come with him. Or, if he suddenly stopped in his tracks realizing he hadn't said thanks, then darted impulsively from their presence to find Christ. The point is, his healing made him think of his Healer, not just himself. Sadly, the rest of them never knew Christ except from a distance. When the one returned, he was unrestrained—falling at Christ's feet and thanking Him.

Just one last thought. I wonder if he was the one with the most spots?

D A Y 3

Lacking One Thing

Today's Treasure

"When Jesus heard this, he said to him, 'You still lack one thing. Sell everything you have and give to the poor, and you will have treasure in heaven. Then come, follow me'" (Luke 18:22).

I know some real heroes of the faith. I'm sure you do, too. Permit me to introduce one to you right now. Her name is Scotty Sanders. She is a beautiful and godly woman, several years my senior. We have the privilege of serving in the same church. Scotty has literally had it all—wealth, prestige, status. She knows celebrities from all over the world. People you and I only read about call her friend. Scotty's passion is inner-city missions. Day in and day out she pours her energy into lives without privilege.

"Why wouldn't she?" someone might ask. "After all, at night she can return to a mansion and her live-in maid." Nope. At night she parks her car in a dangerous area of Houston and returns home to a cracker box apartment in a broken-down complex, right in the middle of the community she serves.

I am honored beyond description to call Scotty my friend. I know many wealthy people who serve God lavishly through their riches. Although I believe He always requires believers with wealth to be excellent stewards of what He's entrusted, He doesn't always require them to give up everything and live among the poor. That's what my friend, Scotty, began to sense Him saying to her. The sacrifice has been tremendous, but you will never hear a hint of martyrdom in Scotty's tone. I want to be standing there in heaven when God presents her with the mansion He's prepared. It's going to be something. But if I know Scotty, she'll move everyone with a lesser mansion into hers.

Please read Luke 18:18-30 and complete the following:

Compare Mark's version in Mark 10:17-31. What additional insight does Mark give regarding the approach of this rich young ruler?

____

Why do you suppose Christ asked the question: "'Why do you call me good?'"

____

Imagine you know this man personally. You may like him. You may not. Based on the information you've read in Scripture, think creatively and add a little fiction to your facts. In the margin describe what he's like.

Why do you think it is so hard for the rich to enter the kingdom of God?

____

What did Jesus say about sacrifices made for the kingdom of God?

____

Keep in mind that this is an actual encounter, not a parable. Although the ruler possessed much of what earth had to offer, he was wise enough to know this life isn't all there is. How gracious is our God to create us with a spirit that somehow knows life must be more. That "knowing" was meant to compel a search for God who promises to make Himself "findable." Let's explore several dimensions of this interesting encounter.

"Why do you call me good?" (Luke 18:19). What an intriguing inquiry! Why in the world would Christ present such a question? I believe He was testing the ruler's knowledge of His identity. When He said, "No one is good—except God alone," I think He was prompting the ruler to think about the root of Christ's goodness. The man may have considered the basis of Christ's goodness to be His good works. Aside from God, no human being is inherently good.

What did the apostle Paul have to say about the human struggle with goodness (Rom. 7:18-25)?

____

Sometimes I can be smack in the middle of seeking and serving God, living beyond all my "self-stuff," when suddenly something will happen to bring out a reaction in me that reminds me, *O, Lord, I know nothing good lives in me, that is, in my sinful nature.* At times an experience like this makes me sob with frustration. Other times, I simply bend the knee and thank Christ again for humbling me and showing me that He alone is good, for He alone is God. Any good thing in me is Him.

When was the last time you saw something in yourself that reminded you of the same thing? Be as specific or vague as you feel comfortable.

____

The rich young ruler did not yet understand the imperative relationship between goodness and God-ness. Christ strongly hinted His deity in this encounter, wooing the man to a place of redefinition. Consider that many of the world religions consider Jesus to have been very good. They just don't consider Him to be God.

In your opinion, why is the difference critical?

____

After Christ redefined goodness, He made a statement to the young man's credit: "'You know the commandments'" (v. 20). Nothing is more dangerous than an earthly ruler who sees himself above all rule. I think this ruler respected God as the real sovereign; I'm just not sure he had a very accurate regard for himself.

Christ began reminding the ruler of the commands he already knew. Interestingly, each one Christ named concerned man's relationship with man.

Without a hint of hesitation, the ruler said he had kept all these since he was a boy. Oh, brother. If I may say, this statement reflects the little piece of information shared by Matthew's version in Matthew 19:20. This rich ruler was young. If he was a rich old ruler, he still may not have given up his wealth, but I don't think he'd be quite as quick to give himself such high marks. When I recall some of the statements I made and thoughts I had in my early 20s, I could nearly die. Talk about self-righteous! And, friend, I didn't have anything to be self-righteous about!

No wonder God had to humble me! And I am so grateful He did. I would be sickening if I had the track record I wish I had. Perhaps others can handle a spotless track record, but I don't think I could do this ministry if I had one.

Actually, I'm not sure the young ruler was dealing with his track record very well either. Look back at the abbreviated list of commandments Christ mentioned. Let's play a game together. The game is not meant to judge this man but to cause us to think about ourselves. Take a look at each command he claimed to have kept since boyhood and give each a mental checkmark for the ruler's probable obedience and an X beside those that seem a little less probable.

"Do not commit adultery" (v. 20). OK, this one may have been a pretty easy checkmark, that is, if he knew nothing about Christ's statement in Matthew 5:27-28.

How did Jesus add a little redefinition to the issue?

____

I am still willing to give the rich young ruler the benefit of the doubt. Perhaps he practiced a very disciplined life and did not feed his flesh with things that spur wrong thoughts. Let's give him a checkmark here.

"Do not murder" (v. 20). Of course, there's that little "anger" issue that Christ discussed in Matthew 5:21-22, but let's go ahead and give him a checkmark on this one, too.

"Do not steal" (v. 20). The kind of stealing intimated by the language in this verse is performed by a *kleptes* as opposed to a *lestes*. A *lestes* steals "by violence and openly. The *kleptes* steals by fraud and in secret." Maybe we've never mugged someone on the street or even swiped candy from the convenience store, but did we ever secretly defraud or steal anything of a less tangible nature from another person? Perhaps so. I'm still willing to give him a checkmark, but let me just say I'm impressed!

"Do not give false testimony" (v. 20). This command is simple: never tell anything false or untrue. Any exaggeration would fall under the category of false testimony. Picture us at age 17, talking to our friends on the telephone, giving our version of this story and that. The rich young ruler's protection may have been that he had never been a 17-year-old girl nor ever owned a phone. Hopefully he never had time to fish, either. We can give him a checkmark if he insists, but you better give me an X.

"Honor your father and mother" (v. 20). Let's see. I hardly ever dishonored mine to their faces, but does it count if, behind their backs, I did a few things they told me not to do? Oops. Go ahead and give the wonder boy a checkmark, but I get another X.

How did you fare throughout our game? Check just one answer.
- ❑ **Just call me perfection personified.**
- ❑ **My halo may be slipping a bit.**
- ❑ **I was thrown out of the game in the first inning, quarter, or whatever.**

Boy, am I thankful for a Savior! The rich young ruler needed one, too. His good track record had certainly fogged up his mirror. Don't get me wrong. I like him. I'm even impressed with him, but I'd rather be saved than be like him! Christ's response to the rich young ruler's claim is best understood in Matthew 19:21.

Fill in the following blank:
Jesus answered, "'If you want to be ___________, go, sell your possessions and give to the poor, and you will have treasure in heaven. Then come, follow me'" (Matt. 19:21).

If this were a game show, the bell indicating the mention of the secret word would have just sounded. Eternal life with God demands perfection. Someone has to be perfect. Either us or someone who stands in for us. This man wanted so badly for it to be him. As good as he had been and as hard as he had tried, he was still lacking. Christ then stuck a pin in the rich young ruler's Achilles' heel: his possessions.

One of the primary purposes of this divine pinprick was to show the man he wasn't perfect nor would he ever be. I really believe a second purpose may have been to offer an authentic invitation for the searching young man to follow Him. Remember, Jesus didn't have only 12 disciples. He had 12 apostles among a greater number of disciples. If the rich young ruler had done what Christ suggested, could he have followed Him? Certainly! He simply needed to lighten his load and be free of wealth's encumbrances. A truck full of possessions would have proved cumbersome.

I also believe Christ had a purely benevolent purpose for the seemingly harsh demand. Jesus looked at this young man and saw a prisoner. The man wasn't really the ruler. His possessions were. Jesus pointed him to the only path to freedom. Sometimes when our possessions have us, we have to get rid of them to be free.

Of course, Christ knew in advance what the young man would choose. When it comes right down to it, we all follow our "god." The ironic part about this story, however, is that rich young ruler was grief stricken over his own choice. He walked away very sad or in Greek, *perilupos*: "severely grieved, very sorrowful." Unless his heart changed somewhere along the way, he lived the rest of his life with all that wealth and an empty heart. The question would have haunted him forever: "What do I still lack?" (Matt. 19:20). Perfection or a perfect Substitute. He had neither. He lacked Jesus.

I wonder if the man stuck around long enough to hear the rest of the conversation between Christ and His disciples. Christ said something like this: Yes, an eternal inheritance involves sacrifice here on earth, but whatever you lay down here for my sake, you will receive a hundred times as much in eternity (see Matt. 19:29).

How could Luke 18:29-30 be misapplied if taken out of context and considered aside from the totality of New Testament teaching?

___

God has called me to make some sacrifices where my family is concerned, but He would never bless neglectfulness on my part as a mom or wife. He has given me the ministry of wife and mother. I can't turn my back on my ministry—in or outside my home. The challenges of both force me to continually seek His will. I certainly don't always get it right, but God keeps me close, and I believe the pure-hearted pursuit of His will is a large part of what God honors. When He sent me to Israel for the taping of this series, I cried over leaving my family. Then God reminded me of these verses. Had I been shirking my responsibility I don't think the verses would have been applicable.

Today's scene draws to a close with a very strong reaction from the disciples, "Who then can be saved?" (Luke 18:26). Do you hear their fear? I think they may have thought something like this: *If a wealthy man who has done virtually everything right has no inheritance in heaven, what will happen to people like us?* Jesus' reply is the glorious hope for every man, woman, and child, no matter how they score on the Ten Commandments: "'What is impossible with men is possible with God'" (v. 27). Thank goodness!

How does 2 Corinthians 8:9 say He has made salvation possible?

___

Only God can change our value systems and truly show us what is lacking. Even when what is lacking is poverty, so that He might make us rich. Just ask my friend, Scotty.

DAY 4

A Wee Little Man

Today's Treasure
"When Jesus reached the spot, he looked up and said to him, 'Zacchaeus, come down immediately. I must stay at your house today' " (Luke 19:5).

I love knowing we have a variety of backgrounds. Some of us grew up in Bible-teaching churches. Others went on Sundays, but know very little Scripture. Some attended only on Easter and Christmas, and some may never have attended and have only recently begun to seek God through Scripture. So many different backgrounds and yet here we are studying together. How awesome! At this moment, however, I wish we could all sit together in those baby-bear chairs and hear my preschool Sunday School teacher dramatize today's encounter. It is one of my very favorite childhood Bible stories.

One reason I like this story so much is that it is equipped with a very theatrical theme song, passed from generation to generation. I taught the same tune to my little girls that my teachers taught to us. I can still see my daughters' tiny, fisted hands with thumb and pointer about one inch apart singing: "Zacchaeus was a wee little man and a wee little man was he. He climbed up in a sycamore tree for the Lord he wanted to see." The dramatic part of the song began when the pointer finger would shake authoritatively while they sang: "Zacchaeus, you come down … for I'm going to your house today. I'm going to your house today!"

I'm not sure I'll tell the story as well as my Sunday School teacher, but I'll give it a try. Please read Luke 19:1-10.

You no doubt picked up on the fact that this little visit caused quite a stir in the community. What might have been the title of the next day's headline if there had been a newspaper called *The Jericho Chronicle*?

____

As a means of creative exploration, let's try to capture a few of the newsiest statements that might have appeared in a newspaper article. Mind you, the bold statements that follow will be strictly fictitious stabs at what a journalist might have written, but the commentary will reflect on Scripture.

"The renowned Jesus of Nazareth passed through Jericho yesterday …" Jesus was just passing through. He couldn't seem to pass through, however, without getting involved. He seemed to attract the dust of every village in His sandals no matter how resolved He was to reach Jerusalem. I wonder if His disciples were ever frustrated that He couldn't go anywhere without getting enmeshed in one way or another. By the time they reached each village, they most likely were tired, thirsty, and famished, yet they encountered one commotion after another. Earlier we saw that He couldn't get through the gate of a border town without healing 10 lepers. I'm sure His followers were thrilled and amazed by all He did, but every now and then we sense a bit of impatience.

Glance at Luke 18:15-17. What evidence of the disciples' frustration do you see in these verses?

____

I'm not sure which got on the disciples' last nerve: the parents or the babies! Their reactive rebuke earned them a sterner one. If Christ's disciples were like most of us, every now and then they probably tried to draw a few boundary lines for Him—lines that soon disappeared beneath His sandal prints as He walked right over them. He passed through, but He couldn't seem to pass by.

"Chief tax collector seen scurrying up a tree …" Zacchaeus was no run-of-the-mill publican. He was their boss. He made a fortune at a business that provided no small opportunity to cheat citizens of their earnings. The locals were often at the mercy of the merciless. The only rule most publicans had to abide was to make sure Rome got their due. Whatever the tax collectors could pilfer in the process was entirely up to them.

That particular day, something caused a greater stir than taxes. Jesus was headed toward their town. Luke 19:3 says Zacchaeus, "wanted to see who Jesus was." Badly enough, in fact, that he went to considerable lengths for a grown man. Mainly because, for a grown man, he didn't have much length. I'm smiling because if my staff and I had attended that Jericho parade, I know exactly which one of us would have been forced to climb the tree. The one with a stool in her office. I have a feeling that Zacchaeus may have been even shorter than she. At least that's the way my Sunday School teacher portrayed him. She measured him right around her elbow, and I always saw her as an expert on those kinds of things.

Picture this grown man running ahead of the parade of people, looking for a tree with a view. Did he have to jump to reach a sturdy branch, or did the sycamore spare him a nice low rung? Either way, this was a scene to behold. The chief of publicans could not have been a young man. He had to work his way up the swindler's list.

Can you hear him huffing and puffing his way up that tree? Clad in a robe, no less? Nothing like climbing a tree in a long dress. How long has it been since you climbed your last tree? Mine was in '65. My older sister and her friend were in our tree house, and I was spying on them. Why do I remember it so well? The branch fell. Thankfully, Zacchaeus didn't perch himself smugly on dead wood during his spy detail.

One of my favorite Old Testament verses is Jeremiah 29:13. How does it bear true in today's scene?

____

"Traveling man requested chief publican's hospitality …" I love verse 5! "When Jesus reached the spot, he looked up and said to him … " Isn't that just like Jesus? He came down to us, all right, but He didn't come to look down on us—not even the least worthy of us. I can almost picture Christ working His way through the crowd as if totally oblivious to a short man in a tall tree.

"Jesus reached the spot." What spot? The spot of His divine appointment. He suddenly looked up with complete familiarity. "'Zacchaeus,'" He said. How in the world did Jesus know his name? Maybe the same way He knew Nathanael's a few years earlier.

What possibilities could the encounter in John 1:43-50 suggest about Jesus and Zacchaeus?

____

We could be under a fig tree, in a fig tree, or up a creek without a paddle; Jesus can still spot us. In fact, Jeremiah 1:4 tells us, "Before I formed you in the womb I knew you." Psalm 139:15 says our frame was not hidden from Him when He wove us together in our mother's womb. God carefully knitted those short legs of a certain tax collector knowing that one day he'd use them to scurry up a sycamore to see His Son.

"'Zacchaeus, come down immediately. I must stay at your house today'" (Luke 19:5).

Why must He? Perhaps because the Son lived to do the will of His Father, and His Father simply could not resist that kind of display of interest in His Son. The Father and Son have an unparalleled mutual admiration society. That day Zacchaeus may have had a pair of skinned knees and elbows that endeared a special dose of the Father's affections.

Luke 19:6 says, "So he came down at once and welcomed him gladly." At once. I'm not sure God honors anything more in a man than a timely response to His Son.

What does Revelation 3:20 say about Christ?

____

When was the last time you stood at a door and knocked … and knocked … and knocked … and knocked? Isn't the repetition even more frustrating when you know someone is home? I praise God that Christ is often willing to knock repeatedly. But that day on Jericho Drive, He didn't have to. Zacchaeus opened the door of his heart. No doubt the chief tax collector had many regrets in life, but among them wasn't the time he wasted between Christ's invitation and his welcome.

"Chief publican caught in the act of rejoicing …" Luke 19:6 tells us Zacchaeus not only came down at once, but also He welcomed Christ "gladly"—and with rejoicing. I don't think we're off base to imagine that his sudden display of glee was slightly out of character. The Word doesn't paint tax collectors as campus favorites. Don't you love how Christ can change an entire personality! Not only can He make the blind man see, but also He can perform a much greater feat: He can make the grump rejoice! Our church pews might not have so many empty seats if we'd invite Him to display such a feat in us. The good news coming from people in a bad mood undermines the message a tad.

Don't you think Christ delights in our glad responses, when we rejoice to obey Him? Let me be clear that God honors obedience even when we're kicking and screaming. Can you imagine how blessed He is when we're anxious to do His will?

Describe the psalmist's response in Psalm 119:14-16.

____

I sense the Holy Spirit leading us to this challenge: let's look for opportunities this week to say, "Lord, I delight to do Your will," opportunities to respond with gladness and welcome Him into a new area of our lives where He desires to stay (see Luke 19:5).

"Noted preacher goes to dinner with a sinner …" I think you'll enjoy the definition of the word for *guest* in Luke 19:7. The word means "to loose or unloose what was before bound or fastened. To refresh oneself, to lodge or be a guest. It properly refers to travelers loosening their own burdens or those of their animals when they stayed at a house on a journey." In effect, Zacchaeus' hospitality said to Jesus: Come to my house and take a load off. Lay your burden down and be refreshed. I'd be honored to have you. What an awesome thought that at the same time, Christ was saying to Zacchaeus: Let me come into your house and take your load. Lay your burden down and be refreshed. I'd be honored to have you.

"Jericho's richest resident gives half his possessions to the poor and repays debts with heavy interest …" Luke 19:8 says Zacchaeus stood up and said to the Lord: "Look, Lord! Here and now, I give … and … pay back." One short man had never been taller. I don't hear a single shred of resistance, do you? He almost seems anxious to get rid of some things. Perhaps the wealth had been less a blessing and more a curse.

What can you glean from Proverbs 15:27; 28:25 about Zacchaeus' wealth?

____

Look at Zacchaeus' example in Luke 19:8. Can you think of any reasons why "here and now" is a good time to act when the Spirit of God moves?

____

____

The moment the Holy Spirit moves, I often sense a greater empowerment to respond generously. The more time I allow to pass, the more my selfishness is apt to well up.

Please realize that Zacchaeus did not receive salvation because he gave to the poor and paid back everyone he owed. Rather, his actions were evidences that a true turn had occurred—the essence of authentic repentance. Earlier we talked about the probable change in the chief publican's demeanor as he responded with gladness.

What is the most marked difference you see that Christ has made in your life, whether in demeanor or life-practice?

____

____

God is amazing, isn't He? I don't remember much about my life before salvation because I was very young, but I can tell you that Christ's authority over my life has dramatically changed both my demeanor and life practices. I was overly sensitive and very fearful, and I would 10 times rather have watched television than studied His Word. My character showed it, too. I have a long way to go; but change is not only possible, it's also gloriously inevitable! He who began a good work will complete it (see Phil. 1:6)!

Student of God's Word, I have waited until now to ask you to reflect on our previous day. Please take a look back at Luke 18:24-25.

How hard was it for Zacchaeus to enter the kingdom of God?

____

A rich young ruler. A chief publican. Both wealthy men. One walked away lost. Salvation lodged at the other's home. Give this question some time:

What do you think the difference or differences might have been?

____

____

Salvation was not impossible for either one of those rich men. Both had the Son of God standing right there in front of them … willing and able to deliver. The difference was that one saw how much he had to lose. The other saw how much he had to gain.

Notice, Christ did not ask Zacchaeus to sell everything he had and give to the poor. Maybe because once he regarded Christ as life's true Treasure, his wealth didn't mean nearly as much to him—which I believe is probably God's primary point to the rich.

A cynic might say, "Why did he only give away half to the poor?" It may have taken every other shekel to pay back all the folks he cheated! Anyway, God isn't looking to take our possessions away. He is looking to make His Son our greatest possession.

Do you have a few scrapes and bruises from trying your hardest to see Jesus? A few tears in your best robe? Have you looked pretty silly to onlookers in your pursuit of Christ at times? If so, good for you.

Let's keep climbing and stretching to places with a view. He'll never be too crowded to spot us in the tree.

DAY 5

Signs of His Coming

Today's Treasure
" 'When these things begin to take place, stand up and lift up your heads, because your redemption is drawing near' " (Luke 21:28).

I love eschatology, a fancy word for end-time events. Few subjects are more exciting to study than the glorious future awaiting us. Just don't lose your head over it! Bible topics are not meant to become our focus—not even critical themes like holiness and service. Jesus is our focus.

Remember, the enemy's primary goal is to disconnect us from the Head. Colossians 2:19 describes the kind of person who becomes more interested in spiritual things than the Spirit of Christ: "He has lost connection with the Head." That's why we must be very careful when dealing with exciting subjects like eschatology. Please read Luke 17:20-36; 21:5-38. Complete the following:

Christ's return will be unmistakable. Two Scriptures in today's reading explain why. Paraphrase the following verses.

Luke 17:24____

Luke 21:27____

According to Revelation 1:7, how do we know that Christ's return to this earth will be impossible to miss?

____

Carefully compare Luke 21:7 with Matthew 24:3. About what two events did the disciples ask?

____

I believe the disciples thought they were asking only one question. In reality they asked about two events separated by millennia—the destruction of the temple and the return of Christ. The temple was destroyed in A.D. 70. We await Jesus' return today.

List some phrases from Luke 21:8-38 that fit each of the three categories:

1. applying to the destruction of Jerusalem ____________________

____

2. applying to the return of Christ ________________________

____

3. applying to either __________________________________

____

I confess that I would like to shake those disciples and tell them to go back and ask better questions. Why do you suppose Jesus didn't choose to be more clear about these events? Wouldn't you like to have a clearer road map or timetable? Whether or not we can answer all the questions, you and I are living in an era on the kingdom calendar that will climax with the visible return of Jesus Christ.

You can see the significance of the dual question in Jesus' words: "'This generation will certainly not pass away until all these things have happened'" (Luke 21:32). The destruction of Jerusalem took place in the generation of Jesus' immediate followers, but He obviously was not referring exclusively to that specific generation. Rather, I believe He referred to the generation they represented. The original word for *generation* literally "means space of time, circle of time, ... a descent or genealogical line of ancestors or descendants." Jesus' words apply equally to the genealogical line through which His witness continues—His spiritual descendants. He will raise up spiritual descendants as His witnesses in every generation until His return.

Let's emphasize a few facts concerning the end of the age and Christ's return:

Christians will long for Christ's return before the world ever sees it (see Luke 17:22). In fact, I believe Luke 17:22 intimates that one of the signs of His return will be a heightened longing. Christ is most assuredly returning, but the Word suggests not as soon as believers may hope as they look upon the tragic state of the earth.

I experience what Luke 17:22 suggests every time I watch a documentary on a starving, suffering people or hear a horrific report of violence and victimization. My only answer is to pray, "O, Lord Jesus, come quickly!" I don't doubt that you also have overwhelming moments when you deeply long for Christ to return and right all wrongs.

When was the last time you remember feeling that way?

____

In both Luke 17:23 and Luke 21:8, Christ warned that as the end of time as we know it hastens, many will come claiming to be Him. The visibility of Christ's return is one reason why believers should never be susceptible to that kind of deception. When Christ returns, people won't have to read about it in the paper. Every eye will see Him. Any rumor of His return is automatically false. The whole world will know it.

Based on your experience, you may think this particular sign has not yet come to fruition. But in fact, false claims of the Messiah occur continually in many different places in the world, and one of the largest cults in the United States teaches that Christ's return has already taken place. Every day people are led astray by false-messiah claims.

There will be dramatic increases in depravity. One key word characterizing the hastening conclusion of this age is *increase*. God's Word describes end-time events like birth pains (see Matt. 24:8), meaning the evidences increase in frequency and strength. Please read Matthew 24:12.

Matthew's version plainly characterizes the end of the age as marked by the increase of____

Why do you think such an increase results in love growing cold?

____

In Luke's Gospel, Christ drew two comparisons; both suggest the dramatic increase in depravity. List the comparison by each reference:

Luke 17:26____

Luke 17:28____

The Old Testament lends some important insight into the condition of the societies surrounding both Noah and Lot. If Christ meant to draw specific parallels between life in the distant past and life in the future, what could life be like before His return based on the following references?

Genesis 6:5,11 (Noah's day) ____________________________

____

Genesis 19:4-5 (Lot's day)_____________________________

____

A staggering measure of human depravity involves sexual sin. I believe the end of time will parallel the days of Noah and Lot in many ways, but among them will be dramatic increase in perversity. Can anyone deny that we are living at a time of dramatic escalation in sexual sin? I believe our society is presently being sexually assaulted by the devil. I am convinced based on multiple characteristics of the last days that they have already begun. However, I'm certainly not date-setting Christ's return.

Based on Luke 12:40, why would forecasting a time of Christ's return be a waste of time?

____

____

Although Christ doesn't want us date-setting, He does want us prepared. Scripture doesn't tell us how long the latter days will last, but we must be primed, like Noah, to be righteous people surrounded by a sea of unrighteousness. Much of it will center on sexuality. We have no other recourse than to radically refuse to cooperate and proactively choose to fight back. If we're going to be victorious in a latter-day society, we must become far more defensive and offensive in our warfare. Peter learned the hard way that we must be ready for Satan to attack. He gave us excellent advice—both defensively and offensively advice.

Defensively, paraphrase 1 Peter 5:8.__________________________

____

Offensively, paraphrase 2 Peter 3:11.__________________________

____

Oh, Believer, let's proactively guard ourselves and our families! The devil is sly and extremely seductive. I believe God is calling upon His church to pro-act rather than react. Depravity won't be the only increase.

God's Word is clear that the latter days will also be marked by: ***a notable increase in violence and cataclysmic events.*** Luke 21:10 tells us "'nation will rise against nation, and kingdom against kingdom.'" Luke 21:12,16 and Matthew 24:9 warn of the escalation in the persecution and martyrdom of Christians. All you have to do is peruse an issue of *Voice of the Martyrs* to see how many Christians are dying for their faith. Those of us who live in the United States like to think persecution and martyrdom are not characteristic of our generation of believers, but we are mistaken. Parts of our body are suffering terribly in many areas of the world.

Had enough bad news for now? Me, too! How about some good news concerning the last days in which there will be: ***an increase in the worldwide witness of the gospel of Jesus Christ.***

What did Jesus say would happen before the end (Matt. 24:14)?

____

Ours is such a God of mercy! He will not judge the wickedness of the earth until the testimony of His Son has reached every nation. What kind of simultaneous increase does this prophecy necessitate? An increase in missionaries! Dr. Jerry Rankin of the Southern Baptist International Mission Board told me that the number of people surrendering to foreign missions is increasing so dramatically that it can be explained no other way than as God fulfilling prophesy. Rejoice in the fact that there will be a soul harvest that no man can count of every tribe, tongue, and nation (see Rev. 7:9)!

According to Acts 1:8, the power to witness with the kind of effectiveness the last days will demonstrate comes from the Holy Spirit. That brings us to the last increase we'll highlight today so that we can conclude our lesson with a spirit of celebration: ***an increase in the activity of the Holy Spirit.***

Fill in the blank from Acts 2:17.
"'In the last days, God says, I will ______________________________
on all people. Your sons and daughters will prophesy.'"

I believe God was hinting at an insatiable appetite to know and share God's Word! Beloved, your love for Scripture is evidence of that harvest. We haven't simply "wised up" in this generation by getting into God's Word. It's the outpouring of the Holy Spirit! Unprecedented numbers of people are becoming armed with the sword of the Spirit because we're entering an unprecedented spiritual war!

I'm so grateful to live during this awesome season on the kingdom calendar. In some ways, we live in the worst of times to date. But in other ways, we live in the best of times. The winds of true worship are blowing. The Spirit of God is moving. I don't want to hold on to my church pew and sing, "I shall not be moved." I want to move with Him!

Behold, He is doing a new thing. Shall we not know it? He's going to make a way in the wilderness and streams in the desert (see Isa. 43:19, KJV).

What's a believer to do? Look for a stream and splash in it.

[1]Ronald F. Youngblood, ed., *Nelson's New Illustrated Bible Dictionary* (Nashville: Thomas Nelson Publishers, 1995), 759-60.

VIDEO RESPONSE SHEET GROUP SESSION 8

Session 8

Introduction: Today we join Christ's disciples on the Mount of Olives. We can only go so far on this journey. We will watch Christ proceed to a place He had to go alone.

Read Luke 22:39-46.

1. The ________ Grasp: At closest proximity, what occurred in that garden will probably remain "about a ________ ________ beyond us."

2. The ________ Location: "Jesus went out ________ ________ to the Mount of Olives." Two reasons why Christ's return to His "usual" place was significant:

- Because ________ was "usual" about the moment.
- See John 18:1-2. Because Judas knew ________ He was ________.

3. The ________ Position: They were there to ________. The original Greek word for *disciples* is *mathetes,* meaning "a ________, ________." The original Greek for *followed* is *akoloutheo,* meaning "to attend, to accompany, to go with or follow a ________." The point? Every true disciple of Jesus Christ will ________ their ________ Gethsemane.

4. The ________ Submission: "He withdrew about a stone's throw beyond them, ________ ________ and prayed." Don't miss two crucial elements involved in His submission:

- The ________ of the ________. More than any other place in Scripture, we see Christ at the full ________ of His dual role as ________-________.

See Philippians 2:5-8. The original Greek word for *servant* is *doulos,* meaning "a slave, one who is in permanent relation of servitude to another, his will being altogether ________ in the ________ of the ________."

See Luke 22:44. The original Greek word for *anguish* is *agonia,* meaning "combat, from which the English *agony* is derived." In the New Testament, it is used for denoting not the fear that ________ ________ and flees, but the fear that trembles in the face of the issue yet ________ ________ to the end.

- The dread of the ________. The four cups of wine taken at the Passover meal represent the four "I wills" of God in Exodus 6:6-7.

5. The ________ of Anguish: Christ knew looking ________ what we still don't comprehend looking ________ (see John 18:4).

6. The ________ Decision: Through ________ ________, God said "Yes!" (see 2 Cor. 1:20).

WEEK 9

The Lamb of God

Day 1

An Available Conspirator

Day 2

The Last Supper

Day 3

Sifted Like Wheat

Day 4

The Kiss of Betrayal

Day 5

A Serious Case of Denial

You and I will be so thankful that our previous week concluded with the reminder of Christ's certain return. Why? Because the next week and a half of our study involves His violent departure. We've known it was coming. Most of us know this portion of the story better than any other event in Christ's earthly life. Yet as we view the events from street level, they will seem more traumatic. After all, we've walked beside Him for eight weeks. Perhaps we'll better understand some of the feelings and reactions of Christ's very human disciples. We may even wonder if we would have hung around as long as they did. This week John 1:11 is going to jump to life before our very eyes: "He came to that which was his own, but his own did not receive him." Not only will we see them reject Him, but also we'll watch as jealousy awakens an insatiable thirst for blood. Hang in there, dear student. If we are to know Christ, we must intimately know the way of His cross.

Principal Questions:

Day 1: How did Judas and the chief priests/teachers of the law become the means to an end to one another?

Day 2: What was Jesus' attitude toward observing the Passover with His disciples?

Day 3: What do you think Christ meant when He used this figure of speech to Peter: "'Satan has asked to sift you as wheat'" (Luke 22:31)?

Day 4: According to Matthew 26:53, what could Christ have done rather than allow Himself to be arrested?

Day 5: Based on your memory of our present journey through Luke, can you identify a few of Peter's encounters with Christ that make his denial more startling?

Ask God to give you a fresh encounter with Him this week. Discover each encounter as if you've never read it before. Beloved, God has something new to show you.

DAY 1

An Available Conspirator

Today's Treasure
"Then Satan entered Judas, called Iscariot, one of the Twelve" (Luke 22:3).

We have arrived at the most critical juncture in our journey. Having accelerated through the parables, we now slow to a crawl, with magnifying glass in hand, to move through the final three chapters. We will spend every moment of weeks 9 and 10 attempting to become eyewitnesses to the events at the conclusion of this Gospel.

Luke 9:51 records that "Jesus resolutely set out for Jerusalem." He performed many miracles and delivered vital messages along the way. In week 7 we witnessed His passionate entrance into Jerusalem. Luke 19:28-48 indicates that Christ's presence was suddenly more than His opposition could stand. In Bethany Christ raised a man who had been dead four days. To the religious establishment, this astounding work was the proverbial straw that broke the camel's back. Before we "catch up" with Christ in His present mode of operation in the city of Jerusalem, let's take a look at Luke 21:37-38.

ILLUSTRATOR PHOTO/BOB SCHATZ

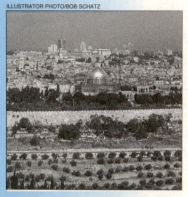

The city of Jerusalem as seen from the Mount of Olives.

What were Christ's habits during this final week in Jerusalem?

____

____

I wish we could all sit together on the Mount of Olives and look at the Holy City for a while. Picture this in your mind. The garden where Christ retreated was on the hill directly across from the altar of sacrifice on the temple mount. Jesus taught at the temple during the day, then at night, He retreated to the Mount of Olives which overlooked the temple.

I recently sat near the place Jesus retreated. I couldn't help wondering what went through Jesus' mind during the days recorded in Luke 21:37-38. On that temple mount God had provided the substitutionary offering for Isaac (see Gen. 22:1-19; see also 2 Chron. 3:1). Paul wrote that through Abraham God provided an "advance showing" of the gospel of grace (Gal. 3:8). "Fast forward" two thousand years to the scene where Christ was camped on the mountain parallel to the place of sacrifice at the temple. He resolved to fulfill the gospel that had been preached to Abraham. In today's reading you will see that the time was imminent. Read Luke 22:1-6 and complete the following:

How did Judas and the chief priests/teachers of the law become the means to an end to one another?

____

Can you think of any way to explain how Satan could have entered one of Christ's own twelve disciples?

____

Who actually came up with the plan (v. 4)? ____________________

How did they respond? ____________________

Why do you think the chief priests and teachers of the law were afraid of the people?

___

My favorite way to study and teach is to expose "a lot about a little" rather than "a little about a lot." Let's take one verse at a time, working our way through this passage.

Verse 1: "The Passover, was approaching." God's timing is never coincidental, but it has perhaps never more deliberate than in the events which unfolded in Luke 22.

What time of year was the Passover and the subsequent Feast of Unleavened Bread according to Leviticus 23:4-6?

___

A new year on Israel's sacred calendar had just begun. Take a look back at Luke 4:18-19 when Christ issued His God-given job description straight from the scroll of Isaiah. If we were to interpret the word *year* in Luke 4:19 as a literal year, it was surely upon them as that particular Passover approached. The most sacred and critical year in all human history was beginning—"the year of the Lord's favor."

God's favor was about to be demonstrated through the offering of His perfect Son. In very literal terms, the most important year of all times had just begun. The age of the completed redemptive work of God was unfolding. Can you imagine the anticipation in the unseen places? The kingdom of God and the kingdom of darkness were rising to a climactic point on the divine calendar.

Verse 2: They "were looking for some way to get rid of Jesus." The same verse also tells us the chief priests and the teachers of the law "were afraid of the people." I think they suddenly felt out of control. They were quite content as long as they were controlling the people, but all the sudden popular opinion had swung in the direction of One who threatened their self-exalted positions.

I find this thought interesting: when Christ is close by, He has an uncanny way of making those people who don't know Him as Lord feel out of control. Since they would rather maintain control over themselves and those around them, they would just as soon get rid of Him. However, people submitted to His authority experience just the opposite—security and peace.

When circumstances suddenly seem out of our control, our reactions may define the nature of our relationship with Christ. Rest assured the chief priests and teachers were feeling very out of control as Christ captivated the attention of their constituency. They needed a plan to deal with their problem. Yet, those same chief priests and teachers would soon discover the hard way how difficult it would be to eliminate their Problem.

Verse 3: "Then Satan entered Judas, called Iscariot, one of the Twelve." I wonder if Judas knew he was inhabited the moment it happened. Perhaps the entrance of the unholy spirit has counterfeit similarities to the entrance of the Holy Spirit. Most of us do not remember "feeling" the Holy Spirit take up residency within us the moment we trusted Christ as our Savior, yet He soon bore some sign of witness through the fruit in our lives. We have no way of knowing if Judas "felt" the unholy spirit take up residence within him, but it certainly wasn't long until the fruit of wickedness was revealed.

If you are new to the study of Scripture, the thought that Satan could enter a disciple might be terrifying. Please understand that just because a person appears to follow Christ doesn't necessarily mean he has placed saving faith in Him.

What do the following references imply about Judas?

John 12:1-6 ______________________________

1 John 2:19 ______________________________

Keep in mind that Satan entered Judas as opposed to Peter, James, or John even though at times each of them had certainly revealed weakness of character. Satan was able to enter Judas because he was available. Judas followed Christ for several years without ever giving his heart to Him. The authentic faith of the others protected them from demon possession, albeit not oppression, just as it protects us. Judas proved to be a fraud, whether or not his tenure began with better intentions.[1]

Verse 4: "Judas … discussed … how he might betray Jesus." In other words, Judas had a plan. I'd like to suggest that it wasn't one he devised on his own. I believe the order of events in Luke 22:3-4 infers he had a little help from his new inhabitant.

Hear this in high volume: Satan has a plan. Ephesians 6:11-12 issues an emphatic "heads up" about the devil's schemes. The meaning of the original word, *methodeia* (schemes), so thoroughly shocked and sobered me that I have made a point of sharing it in almost every study I've written. The definition reads: "Method, the following or pursuing of an orderly and technical procedure in the handling of a subject."

How has the Evil One methodically sought to work in your life recently?

____

____

Satan's methodical planning counterfeits the awesome work of God. Just as our God has a holy plan that He executes in an orderly fashion, the enemy of our souls has an unholy plan he also executes in an orderly fashion.

Satan hasn't enjoyed success for centuries because he's stupid. When I recall the technical procedures he's enacted in my life, I am stunned at his working knowledge of my fairly well-disguised vulnerabilities. By disguised I don't mean just those vulnerabilities I hid from others; I mean some that were even hidden from me. Something new I learned about him is that he possesses a surprising amount of patience to weave seemingly harmless events into disasters while his subject often never sees it coming.

What is our defense? The Word tells us not to be ignorant! Wising up to what the Word has to say about Christ's authority and the devil's schemes has empowered me to throw some holy kinks into Satan's unholy plans for my life.

Verse 5: "They were delighted and agreed to give him money." These events not only demonstrate that Satan is a planner, but also that he is a user. Review the ways Satan used Judas. The enemy convinced Judas that the betrayal was for the fraudulent disciple's own benefit. Judas had a weakness for money, so that's what Satan used.

One of Satan's most successful tricks is to convince his puppets that they have much to gain. In reality Satan makes no real friends. He never uses anyone that he does not ultimately betray. There won't be buddies in hell. Satan will have betrayed every inhabitant by using his or her own self-interest.

Judas is not the only person Satan used in today's scene. Although he did not "enter" the chief priests and teachers, he certainly used them. Again, he capitalized on their personal lusts. He used their appetite for power and control to make them willing parties in an unholy alliance.

Luke 22:5 records that the religious leaders "were delighted" with Judas' proposal and that they "agreed to give him money." They weren't just agreeing with a thief and a betrayer. They were cutting a deal with the devil. The thought sends chills down my spine. Please keep in mind we're talking about the leaders of the religious community. We who fill the church pews cannot afford to be ignorant about the devil's schemes. Hell's most effective attacks often are the result of deals religious people unknowingly make with the devil.

Had they been accused of making a pact with the devil, these religious leaders would have been horrified and would have vehemently denied even the idea of it. Cooperating with the enemy's schemes can easily be unintentional. Do you remember Christ's retort when Peter took Him aside and rebuked Him about going to the cross?

How does Christ's response in Matthew 16:23 illustrate that Satan capitalizes on man's own self-centered interests?

___

Verse 6: "He consented, and watched for an opportunity." Don't you think the concept of Judas' "consenting" is interesting? After all, it was his idea. Sometimes I think that's how Satan works. He tries to make us think the plan was our idea all along, and he's just doing what he can to help. Anything that betrays Jesus Christ in our lives is Satan's idea. Anything. He doesn't have to inhabit people to tempt them to betray Christ. The religious leaders in today's scene are proof. Remember, Satan capitalizes on our lusts—whether for greed, power, control, or sensual pleasure. Let's be careful not to sell out for personal gain, betraying the fact that we have been called to be Christ's disciples. Make sure Satan knows your cooperation can't be "bought."

The curtain drops on this troubling scene with Judas watching and waiting for the perfect opportunity.

Reflect on Luke 4:13. How did Judas model his evil inhabitant's habits?

___

___

Once again, Satan is an opportunist. How does Ephesians 5:11-17 offer a proactive counterattack against Satan's opportunism?

___

___

Biblically we have seen that Satan is a planner and a user. He seeks opportunities to use people to fulfill his plan. He puts on a coat and tie, slicks back his hair, and offers whatever he can to help humans make a personal profit. He's the consummate counterfeit wealth manager. People invest with the intention of drawing high interest, and Satan ends up extorting the profit. He's the betrayer's betrayer. Buyer beware.

D A Y 2

The Last Supper

Today's Treasure
"He took the bread, gave thanks and broke it, and gave it to them, saying, 'This is my body given for you; do this in remembrance of me'" (Luke 22:19).

On a fresh spring morning, the sun rose over the Mount of Olives and cast a spotlight on a city preparing for the most cherished celebration on the Jewish calendar. No other day held the same significance as the fourteenth of Nisan. The Passover feast had arrived.

Scripture assures us Christ knew everything that would happen to Him. I wonder if He closed His eyes a single time that Passover eve? Jesus' vantage point gave Him a bird's-eye view of the temple and all the pilgrims entering the city. In fact, when the sun rose that morning, appropriately, it rose right over His head. Malachi 4:2 says the "sun of righteousness [would soon] rise with healing in its wings." On this day the Son of righteousness began His walk to the cross. Surely Christ's tent of flesh had never been less comfortable to wear.

As the last spoonfuls of sand slipped through the hourglass, surely the blood pumped harder through His veins, overworking His heart. Would God have allowed Him to forego the tightness of dreadful anticipation in His chest? Would He have interfered with His Son experiencing the full gamut of the human body's involuntary anticipation? Did God allow His Son's hands to shake? Oh yes, I think Christ felt every bit of it.

Dread is not sin. Disobedience is. I believe Christ's humanity had never been more constricting or alarming. And it was only just beginning. Please read Luke 22:7-23:

How were Peter and John to identify the place to prepare the Passover?

____

What was Jesus' attitude toward observing the Passover with His disciples?

____

The people of Israel had observed the Passover for approximately 15 centuries. But that particular night, a change occurred. Christ not only observed the ancient memorial of the Passover, but also He instituted something new.

Describe the new observance Christ instituted. ____________________

____

That Jesus had given much thought to the approaching feast is evident in verse 15: "'I have eagerly desired to eat this Passover with you before I suffer.'" If we were to read the statement with the strong double construction of the original language, it would more accurately be reflected by the words, "with desire I have desired."[2] Even if we never fully grasp the significance of the evening, our perception can be deeply marked by the fact that Jesus considered it to be enormously profound.

Nothing about the evening was trivial or accidental. With the same omniscience He exerted to arrange the circumstances of the chosen venue, Christ also chose His two ambassadors. Until now, we have rarely seen Peter and John as a pair. We have seen Christ encounter each of them individually, but when they were grouped apart from the twelve, it has almost always been as a threesome with James, John's brother.

I don't believe Christ simply glanced up, saw Peter and John, and decided they'd be as good a choice as anyone to prepare for the Passover. Quite the contrary, this profound work was prepared in advance for them to do (see Eph. 2:10). It's likely the two men may have wished someone else had been chosen for the tasks, some of which were usually assigned to women. The Passover involved a fairly elaborate meal with a very specific setting. They may have grumbled, as we often do. Why? Because we may have no idea as to the significance of the work God has called us to do. Give some thought to the preparations Peter and John made. Read about the original Passover in Exodus 12:1-14.

What three symbolic foods were to be eaten during every observance of the Passover meal (v. 8)?

____

What is the significance of the unleavened bread (1 Cor. 5:6-8)?

____

The bitter herbs symbolized the bitterness of the suffering memorialized in the Passover observance: the bitterness of slavery, the bitterness of death, and the bitterness of an innocent lamb's substitution. The herbs, eaten intermittently during the meal, would intentionally bring tears to their eyes as a reminder of the associated grief.

While every part of the meal was highly symbolic, it had no meaning at all without the lamb. The most important preparation Peter and John made was the procuring and preparing of the Passover lamb. They had knowledge or understanding that the detailed preparation involving the lamb would soon be fulfilled in Jesus Christ. They may not have grasped the significance of it at the time, but eventually they "got it."

Who wrote the following verses under the inspiration of the Holy Spirit and, in essence, what did they say?

1 Peter 1:18-20 ______________________________________

Revelation 5:6-8,12-13 ________________________________

Peter and John are the only two of the twelve who were recorded referring to Jesus as the Lamb. Coincidental? Not on your life. Christ's ultimate goal in any work He assigns to us is to reveal Himself, either through or to us. The tasks He assigned them that day were used by the Holy Spirit to reveal to them the Lamb of God. The images and remembrances were deeply engraved in John's mind. Many years later he was inspired to refer to Jesus as the Lamb at least 30 times in the Revelation. Beloved, the tasks God gives you are never trivial. More than anything else, His desire is to reveal Himself to you and through you.

Can you think of ways He has revealed Himself to you through any of your assignments? ❑ Yes ❑ No If so, describe what you learned in the margin.

When the hour came, Jesus and His apostles reclined at the table. The Passover was a celebration for families and those closest to them. Christ was surrounded by His closest family. They may have been weak, self-centered, and full of unfounded pride, but they were His. He desired to spend this time with them.

Capture this meal with your imagination. I think we've inaccurately pictured the last meal as moments spent over the bread and the wine. Christ and His disciples observed the entire Passover meal together. Then He instituted the new covenant, represented by the bread and the wine.

As they gathered around the table at sundown, Christ took the father role in the observance. Soon after they gathered, He poured the first of four cups of wine and asked everyone to rise from the table. He then lifted His cup toward heaven and recited the Kiddush, or prayer of sanctification, which would have included these words or something very close: "Blessed art Thou, O Lord our God, King of the universe, Who createst the fruit of the vine. Blessed art Thou, O Lord our God, Who hast chosen us for Thy service from among the nations … . Blessed art Thou, O Lord our God, King of the universe, Who hast kept us in life, Who hast preserved us, and hast enabled us to reach this season."[3] This is very likely the blessing He recited in Luke 22:17.

Read back over the words of the Kiddush. Which part of it seems especially meaningful as you imagine the words coming from the mouth of Christ? Why?

____

____

If Christ and His disciples followed tradition, they took the first cup of wine, asked the above blessing, observed a ceremonial washing, and broke the unleavened bread. These practices were immediately followed by a literal enactment of Exodus 12:26-27. The youngest child at the observance asks the traditional Passover questions, provoking the father to tell the story of the exodus. Many scholars believe John may have been the one who asked the questions at the last supper because of his position at the table.

Where was he during the observance according to John 13:23? (John is the one called the "disciple whom Jesus loved.")

____

Look at the very next verse. What did Simon Peter want John to do?

____

Early church tradition cited John as the youngest apostle.[4] In all likelihood, John assumed the role of the youngest child in the family, asking the traditional questions that provoked Christ to tell the story of the Passover. Might this be the reason Peter nudged John to ask one more question?

The four cups of wine served at the Passover meal represented the four expressions, or "I wills" of God's promised deliverance in Exodus 6:6-7. At this point in the meal, Christ poured the second cup of wine and narrated the story of Israel's exodus in response to the questions. Oh, friend, can you imagine? Christ, the Lamb of God, sat at their table and told the redemption story! He recounted the story as only He could have—and then, at the very next sundown—He fulfilled it! Oh, how I pray He will tell it again for all of us to hear when we take it together in the kingdom!

The One sent "'to proclaim freedom for the prisoners'" (Luke 4:18) told the story of captives set free, spared from death by the blood of the Lamb. Oh, the perfect plan of redemption, secured before God ever breathed a soul into man. Do you see, Beloved? The creation of humankind would have been pointless without this awesome plan of redemption. Before we ever lived to see our first temptation, God procured a "way of escape" for all who would choose it. Indeed, the redemptive decision was sealed and Christ was named the Lamb slain before the creation of the world (see Rev. 13:8). Hallelujah!

They ate the meal between the second and third cups. Now note the timeframe recorded in Luke 22:20.

When was this cup taken? ______________________________

Although all four cups would have been observed at the last supper, not all four cups are specified in Luke's Gospel. We know, however, exactly which cup is specified in Luke 22:20 because of its place of observance during the meal. The third cup was traditionally taken after the supper was eaten. It is represented by the third "I will" statement of God recorded in Exodus 6:6-7.

Fill in the third "I will" statement: "I will ______________ with an outstretched arm and with mighty acts of judgment."

This is the cup of redemption. I am convinced this cup is also the symbolic cup to which Christ referred only an hour or so later in the garden of Gethsemane when He asked God to "'take this cup from me'" (Luke 22:42). This was a cup He could partake only with outstretched arms upon the cross.

The imminent fulfillment of the cup of redemption signaled the release of the new covenant that would be written in blood. We know Christ did not literally drink this third cup because He stated in Luke 22:18 that He would not drink of another cup until the coming of the kingdom of God. Instead of drinking the cup, He would do something of sin-shattering significance. He would, in essence, become the cup and pour out His life for the redemption of man.

Whose Passover was it according to Exodus 12:11? ______________

That most holy weekend, the Passover was completely fulfilled. "For Christ, our Passover lamb, has been sacrificed" (1 Cor. 5:7). God instructed the Hebrew people that they were to continue the Passover feast, celebrating it as an ordinance (see Ex. 12:14). As Gentile believers, we have much to learn and appreciate about the Passover, but we have been commanded to remember the death of Christ every time we observe the Lord's Supper (see 1 Cor. 11:26).

How seriously are we to take this observance (1 Cor. 11:27-31)?

____

Christ never took anything more seriously than the cup of redemption He faced that last Passover supper. His body would soon be broken so that the Bread of life could be distributed to all that would sit at His table. The wine of His blood would be poured into the new wineskins of all who would partake. It was time's perfect night—a night when the last few stitches of a centuries-old Passover thread would be woven onto the canvas of earth in the shape of a cross. Sit and reflect.

O perfect Lamb of Passover,
Let me not quickly run.
Recount to me the blessed plot,
Tell how the plan was spun
That I, a slave of Egypt's lusts,
A prisoner of dark dread,
Could be condemned unto a cross
And find You nailed instead.

DAY 3

Sifted Like Wheat

Today's Treasure
"'Simon, Simon, Satan has asked to sift you as wheat'" (Luke 22:31).

Today, we pull up our chairs to the Passover table. The meal has been eaten. The third cup of wine has been distributed among the disciples as a representation of His blood poured out for them. Rather than sip the cup of redemption, Christ soon will become the drink offering.

Once again I am caught off guard by the awesome love of Christ. He knows the battles we fight with our egos. He knows our every secret vulnerability. He knows the outcome of every conflict. At a time when His own imminent suffering could understandably have consumed Christ's attentions, we find Him still thinking of the others. Let's climb the stairs, return to the upper room, and once more sit down at His table. To capture the context, today's reading will slightly overlap day 2. Please read Luke 22:14-38.

In the margin list the conversation themes that occurred before they left the table reflected in verses 24 through 38.

What does verse 23 imply about how Jesus treated Judas?

____

I am intrigued by the fact that the disciples had no idea Judas was the betrayer. Obviously, Christ never treated Judas any differently than the others. Jesus fellowshipped with him, ate with him, prayed with him, laughed with him, and loved him as the rest … knowing all the while Judas would betray Him. Amazing.

I don't know about you, but if I worked every day with someone I knew had no affection for me and would betray me, I'd have a little trouble not differentiating. Oh, how I want to be like Jesus, but how I resist the painful conflicts that hasten the process!

Are you like me? Do you want to be made like Him—but more through His victories than His sufferings? Thankfully, we have a Savior who is willing to steadfastly walk with us even when we take three steps forward and two steps back. Today we'll see the colors of that willingness painted like a mural on the walls of the upper room.

If we often find ourselves in contrast to Jesus' perfect character, we're not so unlike His original disciples. Their inability at the Passover table to pinpoint who was the worst among them led to a dispute over who was the greatest. Had not Christ already dealt with them over this issue? Before we are too judgmental of the disciples, however, we'd better see if their sandals fit our feet. I ask this of you gently—but of myself a little less gently: how many lessons have we learned from Christ the first time He presented them?

I suppose if the disciples' sandals fit our feet, we'd better wear them. But, praise God, not for long. Please read John 13:1-17. These events occurred at the very same meal.

How did Christ's demonstration provide an unforgettable contrast to the disciples' concept of greatness?

___

The remedy to our ego problems isn't found in simply admitting we're self-centered, ego-driven status seekers who, like the original disciples, are slow to learn and quick to judge. "Guilty as charged" only condemns us. Left alone, it does nothing to change us.

When we recognize that the disciples' sandals fit our feet, let's allow Christ to kneel in front of us, slip them off, and wash our feet. Oh, how we need Jesus to minister humility to us. Without it, He will vastly limit how much He ministers through us.

As effective as the lesson was, Christ still hadn't settled the issue of greatness. He knew that the matter was so critical that He would need to prove on a field trip what He had taught in class. I could kick myself all over the room for forcing a few lessons into field trips instead of learning them in the classroom, but, I don't mind telling you, field trips are effective! I fear the lesson on greatness is rarely learned in the classroom alone.

Within hours each of those disciples would encounter just how "great" they were. All would desert Christ and flee (see Matt. 26:56). However, the lesson taught and demonstrated in the upper (class)room, then confirmed during the field trip, would eventually "stick." Christ turned those 11 status seekers into humble servants.

Again I find myself so amazed at the character of Christ. Just when we wouldn't have blamed Him if He had thrown water all over them, He washed their feet. And just when they argued over who was the greatest, He paid them their greatest compliment.

What did He say about them in Luke 22:28? ___

___

Now look at the next two verses. In essence, wasn't He saying, You can kneel and wash a few feet now, because one day you're going to sit on thrones in my kingdom! He really didn't owe them that kind of positive motivation, did He?

Please don't lose sight of the fact that as surely as Christ knew Judas would betray Him, He knew all those disciples would desert Him. He knew every move each disciple would make. Immediately following the conferral of the kingdom, He directed His attention to Peter and said, "'Simon, Simon, Satan has asked to sift you as wheat'" (v. 31).

What do you think this figure of speech means?

___

My most reliable commentaries say that the word *you* in verse 31 is the Greek plural *hymas,* while the word *you* in verse 32 is the Greek singular, *sou.*[5] The implication is that Satan asked to sift the disciples as wheat in verse 31 and that Christ specified Peter's own encounter in verse 32. I tend to think the Scriptures imply Christ permitted Satan to attack Peter with greater force than the others. If so, we might want to ask ourselves why. I believe these few verses intimate several reasons.

1. Peter was very likely the natural leader among the disciples. Christ seemed to be singling him out as a leader in Luke 22:31 as He directed the statement concerning all the disciples (plural "you") to Peter: "'Simon, Simon, Satan has asked to sift [all of] you [disciples] as wheat.'" Very likely, Christ thought that Peter, as a leader among the disciples, could either take the extra heat or needed the extra heat. I have a hunch both apply. Please be encouraged that Satan can't just presume to sift a believer like wheat. I believe this New Testament precedent suggests he must acquire permission from Christ. (Compare Job 1.) Christ will not grant the devil permission to do anything that can't be used for God's glory and our good—if we let it.

I'd also like to believe, based on the same precedent, that if Christ gives the enemy a little extra leash where we're concerned, He prays for us. The word for *prayed* in Luke 22:32 is *deomai,* meaning "to make one's need known." This particular word for prayer involves the petition for what one lacks. I don't think Christ's petition for Peter's need referred only to what he needed to be victorious in this sifting season. I believe Christ saw that this sifting season itself was something Peter needed.

What things might someone in Peter's position lack that a serious sifting season could supply?

❑ strength ❑ patience ❑ power ❑ humility

❑ honesty ❑ empathy ❑ other ________________

Although I can think of many things, humility as a servant of God and alertness as a target of the enemy most readily come to my mind. Peter was a natural leader and might have led in the flesh ... if he were not taught its terrible weakness and danger. In about 51 days, Christ would transform him into a powerhouse among the disciples (see Acts 2). He needed a crash course only a fierce sifting could supply.

Those in critical positions aren't the only ones who can benefit from a good sifting. Please know if ever I put on a shoe that fits, it would be this one. I, too, as a servant, badly needed a sifting and, I assure you, God was faithful to permit it. Being sifted like wheat is not your regular brand of temptation. It's an all-out onslaught by the enemy to destroy you and cause you to quit. It surfaces what you detest most in yourself and reveals the ugliness of self. Not everyone has or needs such an experience.

Have you had a sifting or do you know someone who has? ❑ Yes ❑ No

If so, what was the outcome? ________________

The horror of my sifting season remains as real as yesterday, but, I pray, so is the grain left behind. The method of sifting wheat is to put it through a sieve and shake it until the chaff, little stones, and perhaps some tares surface. The purpose is that the actual grain can be separated and ground into meal.[6] You see, Satan's goal in sifting is to make us a mockery by showing us to be all chaff and no wheat. Christ, on the other hand, permits us to be sifted to shake out the real from the unreal, the trash from the true. The wheat that proves usable is authentic grain from which Christ can make bread.

Praise Christ's faithful name! Satan turned Peter's field trip into a field day, but he still couldn't get everything about Peter to come up chaff. Satan's plan backfired. He surfaced some serious chaff, but Christ let Peter have a good look at it. Then Christ blew the chaff away, took those remaining grains, and demonstrated His baking skills. Christ had a few other reasons for allowing Peter to be sifted like wheat.

2. *Christ knew that Peter would turn back.* "'But I have prayed for you, Simon, that your faith may not fail. And *when* you have turned back'" (Luke 22:32). Not *if,* but *when.* We're somewhat like books Satan can read only from the outside. His book review is limited to assumptions he makes about what's inside, based on what he reads on our "book jackets." He cannot read the inside of us as Christ can.

At times Satan observed Peter's apparent audacity, his overconfidence, and his propensity toward pride. He surmised that, when the sifting came, every page would come up chaff. He was wrong. Christ knew Peter's heart. He knew that underneath Peter's puffed-up exterior was a man with a genuine heart for God. Jesus knew that Peter could deny Christ to others, but he could not deny Christ to himself. He would be back—a revised edition with a new jacket.

3. Christ knew how Peter's return and "revision" could be used for others. "'And when you have turned back, strengthen your brothers'" (v. 32). The word for *strengthen* means "to set fast, to fix firmly, ... stands fixed." From falling, Peter was about to learn how to stand. Note Peter's response to Christ's warning in Luke 22:33; then read Mark's amplified version of the conversation in Mark 14:27-31.

How would 1 Corinthians 10:12 apply to Peter at that moment?

____

Peter would indeed fall, but his faith would not fail. The wonderful words of Micah 7:8 would prove true in Peter's life: "Do not gloat over me, my enemy! Though I have fallen, I will rise." Rise, he would. And he would use everything Christ taught him to strengthen his brothers. You see, Christ didn't want to take the leader out of Simon Peter. He just wanted to take Simon Peter out of the leader. His goal was to let Satan sift out all the Simon-stuff so Christ could use what was left: a humble jar of clay with no confidence in his flesh. Did the plan work? Look for yourself in 1 Peter 5:6-11.

List every hint you see that he used what he learned to strengthen fellow brothers and sisters like you and me, helping us to stand.

____

____

Not everyone has to learn to stand by falling. Better ways to learn exist, but I'm afraid that I learned a similar way. I finally learned to stand on Christ's two feet because my feet of clay turned out to be so unstable.

I was not so unlike Peter. I was young when I surrendered my life to Christ and completely confident that nothing could shake my commitment. Excuse my bluntness, but I was an idiot. I cannot recall ever learning a more difficult lesson than that which my own sifting season taught me, but neither can I recall a lesson more deeply ingrained. Many years have passed, and I still do not live a day without remembering it and fearing another departure from Christ's authority more than I fear death.

In light of today's lesson, if you've never experienced a sifting season, what might be a few good ways to avoid one?

____

____

I wouldn't wish a sifting on a single soul, but if that's what a life of harvest requires, may God use it so thoroughly that the enemy ends up being sorry he ever asked permission. Beloved, commitments can be shaken, but Christ cannot. When the shakedown comes, may the fresh winds of God's Spirit blow away the chaff until all that is left is the bread of life.

DAY 4

The Kiss of Betrayal

Today's Treasure
"Jesus asked him, 'Judas, are you betraying the Son of Man with a kiss?' " (Luke 22:48).

Tens of thousands of Jews celebrated the Passover that year in Jerusalem, gathered around a table set with roasted lamb, unleavened bread, and bitter herbs. For many, this year's observance was indistinct from the last. They had no idea that nearby the Lamb of God lifted the cup of redemption and offered it to all. In the upper room the disciples' stomachs were full, their recollections rekindled, and their feet washed by the Son of man. "Having loved his own who were in the world, he now showed them the full extent of his love" (John 13:1). The One who created time submitted Himself to it. In the same perfect order that the heavens and earth were created, salvation's story must unfold like a book already written … penned before the foundation of the world. The Spirit of God blew the next page open to the chapter called "Agony." The garden awaited.

"When they had sung a hymn, they went out to the Mount of Olives" (Matt. 26:30). Jesus singing! How I would love to hear that sound. When He sang, did the angels of heaven hush to His voice? Or did they cease their song and join in His? Did He sing tenor? bass? Did Christ and His disciples sing in harmony, or did they all sing the melody? Did Jesus sing often or was this a moment of rarity?

How fitting that on this very night Christ, the coming King, would give voice to songs penned centuries earlier just for Him. Traditionally, every Seder or Passover celebration ended with the latter half of the Hallel, Psalm 115—118. Very likely Christ and His disciples sang from these psalms.

Fill in the following blanks, imagining the Son of God singing these words as the seconds ticked toward the cross. In the margin, write any significance you think the verse might have had to Christ at this exact time of His life.

Psalm 116:12-14: "How can I repay the Lord for all his goodness to me?

I will lift up the ________________ and call on the name of the Lord.

I will ____________ to the Lord in the ______________________."

Psalm 118:6-7: "The Lord is with me; I will not be afraid.

____________________ ______________________________?"

The Lord is with me; he is my helper.

I will look in ________________ on my enemies."

Psalm 118:22-24: "The stone the builders ____________ has become the ____________; the Lord has done this, and it is ____________________ ________. This is ____; let us rejoice and be glad in it."

How many times have you sung "This is the day that the Lord has made"? Did you realize that in context the psalm speaks specifically of the day Christ was facing? The day "the stone the builders rejected" became "the capstone." Imagine Christ, fully aware of all that was coming, singing, "This is the day the Lord has made."

Whatever Christ sang as the Passover meal concluded that night, the words had significance for Him that the others could never have comprehended. I wonder if His voice quivered with emotion? Or did He sing with exultation? Perhaps He did both, just as you and I have done at terribly bittersweet moments when our faith exults while our sight weeps. One thing we know: Christ, above all others, knew that He was singing more than words. That night He sang the score of His destiny.

In our own ways, many of us have experienced something similar. Perhaps we've sung a hymn or chorus a hundred times. Then suddenly the words mean so much we can hardly get through them.

Can you remember a time in your life when the familiar suddenly fell on you with fresh meaning? ❑ Yes ❑ No If so, describe the situation.

____

Now read all three of the synoptic records of Christ's agony in the garden so you can focus your lens to the panoramic view. Matthew's Gospel probably offers the most detail. Read Matthew 26:36-46. Then compare Mark 14:32-42 and Luke 22:39-46. Please record any pieces of information Mark's and Luke's Gospels add to Matthew's portrait.

Mark:	**Luke:**
____________________	____________________
____________________	____________________
____________________	____________________
____________________	____________________

Without Mark's Gospel, we would not know Christ cried out to His Father using the name, "Abba." I don't often give you an extensive quote, but this one captured my soul with rich meditation; I hope it will yours. *The Dictionary of New Testament Theology* explains:

> In Aram. *'abba* is originally … a word derived from baby-language. When a child is weaned, "it learns to say *'abba* (daddy) and *'imma* (mummy)." … also used by adult sons and daughters. … *'abba* acquired the warm, familiar ring which we may feel in such an expression as "dear father." Nowhere in the entire wealth of devotional literature produced by ancient Judaism do we find *'abba* being used as a

> way of addressing God. The pious Jew knew too much of the great gap between God and man to be free to address God with the familiar word used in everyday family life. ... we find only one example of *'abba* used in reference to God. It occurs in a story recorded in the Babylonian Talmud: "When the world had need of rain, our teachers used to send the schoolchildren to Rabbi *Hanan ha Nehba* [end of the 1st cent. B.C.], and they would seize the hem of his cloak and call out to him: "Dear father (*'abba*), dear father (*'abba*), give us rain." He said before God: "Sovereign of the world, do it for the sake of these who cannot distinguish between an *'abba* who can give rain and an *'abba* who can give no rain."[7]

When Christ Jesus fell to His face and cried out "Abba, Father," He cried out to the Abba who can give rain. The Sovereign of the world was His Daddy. Everything was possible for Him ... including removing the cup of dread.

Never minimize the moment by thinking God couldn't have removed the cup. To make a severely uneven comparison, consider that removing God's freedom of choice would be toward us somewhat like removing our freedom of choice toward God. Indeed, did not God create humanity with the freedom to choose? Ah, yes. And in this way we are created in the image of our God. He wants and woos, but He does not force Himself or His creation. The fullness of joy is in the choice. Obviously God never chooses sin, but He most assuredly has freedom of choice. "In him we were also chosen" (Eph. 1:11). "For we know, brothers loved by God, that he has chosen you" (1 Thess. 1:4). Do not subtract God's freedom of choice from this picture. God can relent if He chooses. After all, He is the Sovereign of the world.

What is your reaction when you consider that God could have spared Jesus' suffering and chosen to let us bear the consequences of our own sin?

____

____

That God could have stopped the process yet didn't is a matchless demonstration of love. Can you think of anyone for whom you'd watch your only child be tortured to death? "'Abba, Father,' he said, 'everything is possible for you. Take this cup from me'" (Mark 14:36).

The request Christ placed before the Father ought to make us catch our breath. It ascended to heaven through wails of grief. God's Beloved was overwhelmed with sorrow to the point of death. Luke's Gospel tells us His sweat dropped like blood, a condition almost unheard of except when the physical body is placed in more stress and grief than it was fashioned to handle. Do we think God sat upon His throne unmoved?

Our hearts ought to miss a beat. Christ could have walked past the cross. He could have—but He didn't. Luke 22:47 tells us, "While he was still speaking a crowd came up." Imagine the scene they walked into that day.

Please try to grasp Christ's physical condition just before the crowd headed up the Mount of Olives to seize Him. Like a body that rejects a transplanted organ, the human body of Jesus Christ was practically tearing itself apart. The full throttle of divine impact and emotion was almost more than one human body could endure. The stress had nearly turned Him inside out. I do not make this point to emphasize His weakness. Quite the contrary. Please view the scene recorded in John 18:1-6.

What happened when Christ answered "I am he" to the crowd's request for Jesus of Nazareth?

____

Even overwhelmed with sorrow to the point of death, the proclaimed presence of Jesus Christ knocked them to the ground. Don't read any further yet. Stop and meditate.

Dear Sweet Jesus. We really have no idea who You are, do we? Your God-ness could not be diminished for a moment, in or out of that prison of flesh. Lord, don't let us forget. You, who submitted Yourself to the hands of sinful men, were very God.

As we allow the Holy Spirit to escort us to a place of fresh insight and gratitude, we're considering not only what God has done that He didn't have to do, but also what He didn't do that He could have. God deserves our praise both for what He has done and hasn't done.

What could Christ have done according to Matthew 26:53?

____

According to Matthew 26:54-56, why didn't He?

____

The reminder of Christ's immense power and complete God-ness makes Judas' betrayal even more audacious. Go back with me and capture the scene. Luke 22:47 tells us Judas "approached Jesus to kiss him." With the precision of a doctor, Luke shared his version of the events in the garden, but Matthew, the tax collector, collected evidence far more like that of a lawyer establishing premeditation. Read Matthew 26:47-49. Isn't it enough to make you nauseous? Betrayal is bad enough. Betrayal with a comrade's kiss on the cheek is almost too much to stomach.

In the margin note what Christ called Judas immediately after he betrayed Him with a kiss (Matt. 26:50).

How do the words of Psalm 55:12-14, 20-21, written by a man after God's own heart, lend a familiar ring to that night's scene at the Mount of Olives?

____

Few things rend the heart like betrayal. Christ's knowing eyes ripped the smiling facade off Judas so fast his adrenaline probably plummeted. I would be interested to know just how long Satan hung around in Judas' body. The devil is such a user. he probably dumped the fraud the moment the betrayal was complete. Imagine Judas being on his own with the realization of what he had just done. It proved to be more than he could stand. The devil had not "made him do it," but he had certainly empowered him. Another inside job—Satan's favorite. In the most literal sense, Judas came near to Christ with his mouth that night, but his heart remained far from Him (see Isa. 29:13).

Today's lesson concludes dramatically. Peter sliced off an ear before the rest of the disciples could even ask if they should draw swords. If Christ were not omniscient, I could almost picture Him thinking, *Remind me not to let Peter hold the sword next time.*

Luke never names the sword-wielding disciple, but Peter's friend John tattles on him. You can almost hear Peter: "I was going for his head!" The servant must have seen the sword coming and tilted his head to his left shoulder, leaving only his right ear exposed to the blade. I don't doubt he got a shave and a haircut, too.

Dr. Luke is careful to tell us that Jesus "touched the man's ear and healed him" (v. 51). Don't overlook this action. Reflect on the fact that the servant of the high priest knew without a doubt that Jesus was no ordinary man, let alone a vicious criminal. Do you realize how many people confronted the truth that this lynching was wrong as they came face-to-face with right? Only heaven knows how many people never slept peacefully again.

The hour had come—the one in which darkness would reign (see Luke 22:53). Even in the dark, however, many knew that what they were doing was wrong. One thing about God: we can always depend on Him to turn the light back on. "He will bring to light what is hidden in darkness and will expose the motives of men's hearts. At that time each will receive his praise from God" (1 Cor. 4:5).

DAY 5

A Serious Case of Denial

Today's Treasure
"The Lord turned and looked straight at Peter. Then Peter remembered the word the Lord had spoken to him: 'Before the rooster crows today, you will disown me three times' " (Luke 22:61).

Our next scene doesn't "unfold"—it bursts with a moment so highly charged that our minds must work overtime to comprehend it. Like a film clip of frenzied activity, it must be viewed over and over to absorb the details. If God were to raise a video camera above the city of Jerusalem on this night of nights, we would see several scenes within a scene. We will attempt to capture some of those. Our reading will slightly overlap day 4 in order to reestablish context. Please read Luke 22:47-62.

You may be familiar with the story of Peter's denial. Having been so involved in the story line this time, does anything about the account strike you with added force? ❑ Yes ❑ No If so, explain.

____

____

We know that Christ and His disciples dramatically encountered the entire detachment of soldiers, priests, and Pharisees somewhere on the Mount of Olives. While Luke's Gospel simply says they seized Him and led Him away, John's Gospel gets a little more specific. Please read John 18:12-14.

How and where did they first take Jesus? ____________________

Who was Annas?________________________________

Who was Caiaphas? ______________________________

Did you catch the terminology? This huge detachment of soldiers bound Jesus (see John 18:12). They couldn't know that all the ropes in Israel couldn't bind Him unless He chose to be bound. The time had come for Him to submit to a plan that included them. Jesus did not need to be bound. He resolutely set out for Jerusalem for such a time as this.

John's Gospel tells us Christ was first taken to Annas, the father-in-law of Caiaphas, the high priest. The trials can be very confusing, especially because they are not all recorded distinctively in each of the Gospels. Keep in mind that Christ was subjected to six trials—three religious trials and three civil trials. Perhaps the following list of trials in the order of their occurrence will help. You'll probably need to glance back at it several times before our focus on the hours leading up to Christ's crucifixion concludes.

Religious Trials

Before Annas:	John 18:12-14,19-23
Before Caiaphas, Sanhedrin:	Matthew 26:57-68; Mark 14:53-65; Luke 22:54,63-65; John 18:24
Before the Sanhedrin:	Matthew 27:1-2; Mark 15:1; Luke 22:66-71

Civil Trials

Before Pilate:	Matthew 27:2,11-14, Mark 15:1-5; Luke 23:1-7; John 18:28-38
Before Herod:	Luke 23:6-12
Before Pilate:	Matthew 27:15-26; Mark 15:6-15; Luke 23:13-25

Annas was high priest when John the Baptist began his ministry (see Luke 3:2). By this time he had been deposed and succeeded by his five sons, one grandson, and son-in-law, but still was extremely influential. Christ was first taken to Annas, who then sent Him to Caiaphas, his son-in-law, the high priest who presided over these proceedings.

God obviously considered Peter's denial so significant that He inspired its record in all four Gospels. We will, therefore, give ample attention to this "scene within a scene." Luke's Gospel picks up in Luke 22:54 at the house of Caiaphas.

I am convinced that one reason God placed the account of Peter's denial in all four Gospels is so we'd sober to the reality that if Peter could deny Christ, any of us could. Never lose sight of the fact that Peter was certain he could not be "had." Please don't let the magnitude of Peter's departure get past you for a single second. Take in these words with a fresh awareness: Peter denied he even knew Christ. Not once. Not twice. But three times. Denying Christ is huge.

Based on your memory of our present journey through Luke, in the margin list a few of Peter's encounters with Christ that make his denial more startling.

At Christ's arrest the disciples scattered like scared rabbits. John 18:15-16 tells us Peter and John followed Christ to the high priest's house, but Peter had to wait outside. He was not known to the high priest as John was. Strangely, Peter's presence suggests a confession of sorts that he knew Christ, but he denied it with his mouth.

Notice the other nine were nowhere to be found. Followers of Christ can deny they know Him in a variety of ways. Although I have never said, "I don't know Him," with my mouth, I've no doubt suggested something similar with my life and even at times with my silence.

In what other ways besides Peter's can we deny Christ?

____

____

Do you think the blows Christ later endured from the whip stung any more than Peter's denial? I believe the Holy Spirit is deeply grieved when our lives "deny" Christ.

I very much want us to relate to Peter's actions and to apply the challenge personally, but I don't want us to minimize the sin in that courtyard. Peter adamantly and repeatedly denied even knowing Christ. At the beginning of our lesson, I asked you if anything about Peter's denial struck you with added force. The following elements seem particularly significant to me. As we consider each one, I hope we'll recognize those factors that set up Peter for failure so we can avoid similar pitfalls.

Peter was willing to kill for Jesus, but he was reluctant to die for Him. Keep in mind the time element. Only an hour or so before Peter denied Christ to save his own skin, he drew a sword and cut off a man's ear. Maybe Peter's haste to use the sword was not just motivated by his desire to defend Jesus but by his concern to defend himself.

Nothing displays our self-love like a crisis. Christ's disciples, both then and now, are called to live above that human baseline of self-importance.

What had Christ called Peter and His disciples to do in Luke 9:23-24?

____

If Peter had denied himself, he would not have denied Christ. God had a future mission for Peter, so He would not allow Peter's self-denial to have disastrous consequences. Peter, of course, had no way of knowing that confessing Christ would not lead to his capture or death, but Christ had unquestionably called him to follow at all costs.

We can "forget" about ourselves because Christ never forgets us. We can afford to be less important to ourselves because we are vastly important to God. We can willingly be crucified with Christ because we are raised to walk in resurrection life. Biblical self-denial will never fail to be *for* us rather than *against* us, whether here or in eternity. When Peter chose to deny Christ rather than himself, he really chose human limitations over divine intervention.

Practice a little "holy speculation." In the margin describe what you think might have resulted if Peter had chosen not to deny Christ.

Peter followed Jesus, but at a distance. Obviously, if Peter had been holding onto Jesus' shirt sleeve, he probably wouldn't have denied Christ. Even though Christ asked the soldiers to let His disciples go (see John 18:8), after all the miracles and proofs the twelve had seen, why didn't even one insist upon staying? From a divine standpoint the answer is most likely God's sovereignty in fulfilling prophecy that Christ would be deserted and forsaken. From a human standpoint the answer is pure fear.

The scene reminds me of 2 Kings 2 when God was about to take His prophet, Elijah, up into a whirlwind. Elijah had several stops to make on his way to the Jordan and continued his attempt to say farewell to his servant, Elisha. All three times, Elisha said, "As surely as the Lord lives and as you live, I will not leave you." If Peter had been as insistent as Elisha, Satan would not have had the room to come between him and his master with a sieve to sift him like wheat. Elisha's actions showed sheer determination to follow his master to the ends of his earthly life.

Picture two sets of footprints in each scene: Elijah's and Elisha's in scene 1 and Christ's and Peter's in scene 2. In scene 1 the second set of footprints (Elisha's) was close and deliberate. Scene 2 depicts a second set of footprints (Peter's) at a much greater distance from the first. The prints appear tentative, almost as if they were cast on tiptoes. I believe we can safely say that we are far more likely to trip and fall from tiptoeing behind Christ than we are by stomping loudly and deliberately in a set of steel-toed boots.

Consider the following two statements. Choose one, circle it, then explain why you believe the statement to be true.

1. **A tentative (tiptoeing) walk leads to an almost certain detour.**
2. **Distance creates room for denial.**

____

____

When we tiptoe to keep from being too obvious or to obscure ourselves in safe places and remain unidentifiable, we are already bounding toward denial.

Peter sat down with the opposition and warmed his hands by the same fire. John 18:18 identifies who Peter joined at the fire in the middle of the courtyard.

Who were they? ______________________________

I assure you the night was indeed cold; I've been in Jerusalem in the early spring. The semi-desert climate may heat a spring day, but the temperature drops dramatically when the sun goes down. Since fear also has a way of quickening the senses, we're probably picturing him accurately as a young man who trembled nearly uncontrollably as he stood at that fire. I believe Peter made a very poor choice of company in the courtyard. However unintentionally, he ended up surrounding himself with others who, in effect, denied Christ. The risk of failure heightened dramatically at that moment.

Can we ever note a point of application here! Being sent by God to be a witness to those who "deny" Christ is one thing. Warming our hands by the same fire is another.

Can you think of an example of when you heightened the risk of denying Christ by a poor choice of companions? ❑ Yes ❑ No If so, describe it.

____

____

Read John 18:25-27. Once again, Peter's buddy John brings up the ear incident. Who happened to be warming his hands by the same fire?

____

Peter ended up doing the last thing he expected. He denied Christ. Satan most assuredly had sifted him like wheat. Needless to say, the enemy was hoping for "three strikes and you're out." Thankfully, he discounted Christ's mercy.

Peter's repetitive actions went beyond the realm of excuses. Rationalizing his choice to deny Christ and gaining sympathy from the others would have done nothing to help Peter become a man Christ could "crucify" and then use. Peter had to come face-to-face with the fact that in him no good thing dwelled. Only then would he be willing to deny himself and exist for the sole purpose of Jesus' renown.

I cannot help but relate some of my own seasons of defeat to Peter's. I will regret some of my choices every day of my life. Like Peter, I also made some choices in my past that went beyond rationalization. How thankful I am now that I couldn't just make excuses for my behavior! Any part of me I could have "excused" would still be "alive and kicking." Listen to my heart carefully: I want no part of myself. None. I want Jesus to so thoroughly consume me that "I" no longer exist. "I" am far too destructive. "I" would do far too much to deny His lordship. One regret I never will have is that God got me "over myself" by letting me confront the truth that in me dwells no good thing.

Are you relating with Peter on any level at this point? ❑ Yes ❑ No If so, share how.

____

____

The scene ends in Luke 22:61-62 with an invisible sword piercing Peter's heart in a way no soldier's blade could have severed him. The Lord turned and looked straight at Peter. In Peter's attempt to shield himself from the piercing sword, he fell to a far more piercing one: the look of Jesus into his eyes. Oh, I don't think the stab resulted from a look of condemnation. Rather, I imagine Peter's heart hemorrhaged from Christ's penetrating look of unveiled reality and love.

I do not doubt that Christ's face was painted with pain when their eyes met in the courtyard, but I think the conspicuous absence of condemnation tore through Peter's heart. I wonder if Christ's fixed gaze might have said something like this: "Remember, Peter, I am the Christ. You know that and I know that. I called you. I gave you a new name. I invited you to follow Me. Don't forget who I am. Don't forget what you are capable of doing. And, whatever you do, don't let this destroy you. When you have turned back, strengthen your brothers."

Surely nothing leads to repentance in those who are tender like the kindness of God (see Rom. 2:4). Peter was devastated. As we conclude today's lesson, sit just a moment and listen to him cry. Is anything more painful to hear than the uncontrollable cries of a grown man? Peter went outside and wept bitterly. The original language suggests he took on every external form of grief. He wailed. He probably tore his robes. He may have grabbed a handful of sand and thrown it over his head.

The conflict of his soul surged in a tidal wave of grief, betraying his true identity. His belief had not been a sham. His denial had.

---

[1]Ronald F. Youngblood, ed., *Nelson's New Illustrated Bible Dictionary* (Nashville: Thomas Nelson Publishers, 1995), 714.
[2]Frank E. Gaebelein, ed., *The Expositor's Bible Commentary* (Grand Rapids, MI: Zondervan Publishing, 1984), 1026.
[3]Kevin Howard and Marvin Rosenthal, *The Feasts of the Lord* (Orlando, FL: Zion's Hope, Inc., 1997), 55.
[4]Ibid., 57.
[5]Gaebelein, *Expositor's Bible Commentary*, 1029.
[6]Fred H. Wight, *Manners and Customs of Bible Lands* (Chicago: Moody Press, 1953), 185.
[7]Colin Brown, *The New International Dictionary of New Testament Theology* (Grand Rapids, MI: Zondervan Publishing, 1986), 614.

VIDEO RESPONSE SHEET GROUP SESSION 9

Session 9

Introduction: Without the events we're studying today, humanity might have benefited from the life and ministry of a man called Jesus of Nazareth, but we would still be lost. At best, He would be revered as a great prophet. A good man. He was far more than either one. Jesus Christ was the One John the Baptist proclaimed, "Look, the Lamb of God, who takes away the sin of the world!" (John 1:29).

1. A ______ ______. (see Luke 22:53). Three words offer helpful insight:

- **Hour:** The original Greek word is *hora,* which means "figuratively, of a season of life, the fresh, ____ ______ and beauty of youth, the ___________ and _________ of manhood."
- **Darkness:** The original Greek is *skotos,* which can mean "physical darkness or spiritual darkness." In this verse, it most likely applies to ______. The *Complete Word Study Dictionary of the New Testament* specifies the word is used in Luke 22:53 in reference to "the infernal _________ as the opposite of Christ, the sun or light of righteousness."
- **Reigns:** The original Greek word is *exousia* meaning "__________, authority, right, liberty, ________ to do something." Please understand that the only reason why the kingdom of darkness was allowed to "reign" to this degree was because God was using it to accomplish His own purposes (see Matt. 26:50-56).

2. A ______ ______. Read Luke 23:45-46. Compare Matthew 27:51. The curtain of the temple was torn in two from ____ to _________. See Hebrews 10:19-22.

3. A ______ _______. Read Luke 23:46. Remember that Jesus Christ was "the ______ made flesh" to dwell among us. While the writers of the Old and New Testament books were inspired by God, Christ was the One and Only to give Divine ______ human ________. Let's compare the first and last word recorded from the human vocal chords of Jesus Christ: See Luke 2:48-49.

4. A ______ _______. See Luke 23:46. Reflect upon Genesis 2:7.

5. A ____________ _______. Read Luke 23:50-53.

6. A ___________ _________. Read Luke 23:49.

WEEK 10

The Risen Hope

Day 1
The Ultimate Mock Court

Day 2
To the Cross

Day 3
He Has Risen!

Day 4
A Burning Heart

Day 5
Jesus Himself

As I meditate on the week ahead, the words of the apostle Paul consume my thoughts: "May I never boast except in the cross of our Lord Jesus Christ, through which the world has been crucified to me, and I to the world" (Gal. 6:14). The cost for each of us to be a new creation was far beyond anything we can fathom. Even though we will see only a glimpse, may a fresh wave of faith bring us face-to-the-floor. May a fresh look at the cross cause us to be more crucified to this world. A warning: there is nothing pretty about this week's immediate venture, but it was necessary to overcome the grave. Let's not be tempted to run from the cross as did Jesus' original disciples. Let's go with Him, step-by-step. Let's carry it for Him instead of letting Simon do it. Let's hear the nails, the cries. Let's stand by until He draws His last breath. Then let's help Joseph take His body off the cross and carry it to the tomb. We'll then wait with the women. As sure as the earth will quake on Friday, a stone will roll on Sunday. Oh, beloved. Don't miss a moment of it.

Principal Questions:
Day 1: Why was Pilate necessary?
Day 2: According to Colossians 2:13-14, what was nailed to His cross?
Day 3: What did Mary Magdalene and the other Mary find at the tomb?
Day 4: What was the mood of Cleopas and his companion when Christ asked what they were discussing?
Day 5: What special significance do Christ's words in Luke 24:36 have as conveyed in Ephesians 2:14?

Even if we have each walked to the cross to be saved, Galatians 2:20 invites us to walk to the cross and be crucified. Not so we can live like the dead—but so we can die to death and live in the power of Christ's resurrection. Let's not just read this week's study, my friend. Let's live it with Him.

DAY 1

The Ultimate Mock Court

Today's Treasure
"They all asked, 'Are you then the Son of God?' He replied, 'You are right in saying I am' " (Luke 22:70).

We're going to have one of those lessons today that causes us to hang our heads and whisper, "God, have mercy on humanity." Given over to our natural urges and instincts, we are more violent and dangerous than the beasts of the field.

I remember a childhood game I tried to avoid at all costs. It was called "King of the Mountain." The players established a high place of some kind as the "mountain." The "king" was the one who could defend his territory by kicking or pushing anyone who came near him. It was a mean game. We play lots of mean games, though, don't we? Not just when we're little. The games may appear more sophisticated and acceptable in adulthood, but they are also much meaner.

I wish we could skip this lesson, but we can't because Christ didn't skip it. Brace yourselves. We're going to see the inhuman side of humanity. Read Luke 22:63—23:25; then read the events immediately following in Matthew 27:27-31. Complete the following:

Counting the Matthew passages, how does the scene begin and end?

____

In the space below, list in their order the primary occurrences involved in the mock trials according to Luke 22:66–23:25.

______________ ______________

______________ ______________

______________ ______________

______________ ______________

Did you catch a detail this time that you've never noticed before? Or, did a fresh insight or reaction come to you this time? If so, describe it.

____

____

How many times did Pilate say or imply that he found no basis for charges against Christ? _______

Write a brief character analysis of Herod. What was he like in your opinion?

____

____

Who was Barabbas? ______________________________

Let's first analyze Luke 22:66—23:25 and conclude with a look at the "bookend" events in Luke 22:63-65 and Matthew 27:27-31. We'll analyze the scene by spotlighting the leaders of the opposition in each stage, but don't overlook the role of the crowd.

The council of elders. By the time Luke 22:66 unfolds, Christ has been kept awake all night long and subjected to illegal proceedings. The sun rose that morning over the Mount of Olives like a spotlight on the council of the elders—the chief priests and teachers of the law. Their robes of self-righteousness looked particularly ill-fitted. They had a harder time than usual hiding their flint foreheads behind their phylacteries. They demanded in verse 67: "If You are the Christ, tell us." Christ immediately pointed out three truths:

1. *"If I tell you, you will not believe me"* (v. 67). In other words, "My answer would make no difference, would it?"

2. *"If I asked you, you would not answer"* (v. 68). I believe this statement referred to the messianic prophecies of healing and miracles. Christ was saying that if He asked if He had fulfilled those prophecies, they would refuse to answer.

3. *"The Son of Man will be seated at the right hand of the mighty God"* (v. 69). In other words: "What you think makes no difference anyway. The mission will be accomplished, and I will reign with my Father over the kingdom."

The council of the elders then asked the question they hoped would provoke the incriminating answer they needed. "Are you then the Son of God?" (v. 70).

As you picture every moment of the proceedings, don't lose sight of those words. Imagine every event unfolding on a large-screen TV. During the entire ordeal the words scroll boldly across the bottom of the scene: "the Son of God." The irony is this: the only reason Christ was standing in front of them was because He was exactly who they "tried" Him for being. Though His accusers couldn't see the truth for themselves, Christ was found guilty of being the Son of God. They would end up releasing the insurrectionist and crucifying the Savior of the world.

I love Christ's answer: "'You are right in saying I am'" (v. 70). Christ repeated words to them not so unlike His Father's to Moses in Exodus 3:14: "I am who I am."

Aren't you thankful humanity can "try" Christ for being anything they choose, but He is who He is? No amount of disbelief can change Him or move Him. Why did the chief priests and teachers of the law disbelieve? Why couldn't they accept their Messiah? Because they wanted to be king of the mountain.

Their retort sends chills down my spine: "Why do we need any more testimony? We have heard it from his own lips" (v. 71). They were right. They needed no more testimony. Those who believe have all the proof we need; those set on disbelief had the evidence they needed to incriminate Him. Neither side needed more testimony. Heaven and hell were both armed for the showdown of all times.

Pilate. Luke 23 introduces us to Pilate, who was the fifth Roman prefect of Judea, ruling from A.D. 26-36. John 18:31 tells us exactly why the religious leaders took Christ to Pilate. I hope you receive a bolt of fresh shock from it.

Why was Pilate necessary? ____

Don't let this get past you: Pilate offered several times to simply punish Jesus with a severe beating, but the religious leaders (read those two words over and over) would not have it. They wanted Him dead. That's pretty serious hatred. Jesus so greatly threatened their spot on the "mountain" that injuring Him wasn't enough. The only way to keep Him off their mountain was to kill Him. Pilate had the authority they needed.

In Pilate we see the consummate unprincipled politician. He simply wanted power. He wasn't driven by conviction or creed—just by need—that which he needed to stay in business. Pilate read the situation with amazing clarity. First of all, he clearly recognized that he had encountered nothing less than a mob lynching, but he lacked the guts to challenge it. Mark 15:9-10 records something else he clearly recognized.

What was it? ______________________________

In the margin list a few things about Christ you think might have surged such vehement envy in the religious leaders.

The original word for *envy* in Mark 15:10 is *phthonos*, meaning "envy, jealousy, pain felt and malignity conceived at the sight of excellence or happiness." Compromising people can't stand the sight of excellence, and miserable people can't stand the sight of happiness. The definition proceeds to explain that *phthonos* ... is incapable of good and always is used with an evil meaning. Nothing is benign about envy. Like a cancer left untreated, it will consume us. Envy is deadly. It can kill anything from contentment to relationships to people.

Have you personally seen envy kill? ❑ Yes ❑ No If so, how?

____

Pilate not only discerned personally the malignancy in the religious leaders, but also he had several other sources which caused him to question the unfolding events. The first reason for Pilate to exercise caution is recorded in Matthew 27:19.

What warning did Pilate receive and from whom? ______________________________

____

I wonder what kind of conversation Pilate and the Mrs. had over dinner that night. Pilate resisted a word from his wife that confirmed his own sense of Christ's innocence. Now look at an interchange recorded in John 19:8-11. Pilate asked Jesus two questions, one He didn't answer and one He did. The first question was, "Where do you come from?" (v. 9). The fact that Christ knew the answer gave Him the courage and motivation to stand before such a mock court.

What did Christ know according to John 13:3? ______________________________

____

Pilate's second question must have echoed irony through the heavenlies. "Don't you realize I have power either to free you or to crucify you?" (v. 10). I can almost see the angels looking at one another in shock and hear them screaming in voices Pilate could not hear: "No, Buddy. It's the other way around. Don't you realize He has the power to free or to crucify *you*?" Based on what he did "from then on" (John 19:12), I believe Pilate's insides told him that Jesus was exactly who He said He was.

What did Pilate do "from then on"? ______________________________

____

So why did Pilate give in to the demands of the religious leaders and the crowds? He was afraid that if he didn't, he would no longer be king of the mountain on his little hill.

Herod. The Herod in Luke 23 was one of the sons of Herod the Great. His name was Antipas, and he's the one who put John the Baptist's head on a platter.

Herod absolutely epitomizes human arrogance. His contributions to the kangaroo court appear in Luke 23:8-12. He plied Jesus with questions. Why didn't Jesus answer him? Probably for the same reason He didn't supply the miracles Herod wanted. Herod wanted a performance, not proof. He had no intention of believing Christ.

Christ's silence reminds me of Matthew 7:6: "Do not throw your pearls to pigs." The longer Christ stood silent, the more the chief priests and the teachers of the law accused Him (see Luke 23:10). Isn't their response typical of humans? If we have a lot banking on being right, we can't afford to be silent, and sometimes we feel we can't afford to be wrong. This passage reminds me of the evil that dwells in me apart from Christ.

I'm sure you saw that in the midst of the frenzy, a new friendship was born. What do you see as the basis of this "friendship" (Luke 23:12)?

____

Neither Pilate nor Herod could find a basis for the charges (see Luke 23:14-15). Herod sent Jesus right back to Pilate, but not until he did the unimaginable. He mocked the Son of God just to feel like the king of the mountain. For a few very difficult moments, please visit the scenes depicted in each of the following passages.

Record what each of the following Scriptures describes:

Luke 22:63-65 ______________________________

John 19:1-3 ______________________________

Matthew 27:27-31 ______________________________

How does Isaiah 52:14 describe His appearance when they finished?

____

Stripped. Mocked. Spat on. Struck … again and again. Flogged. Beyond recognition. The fullness of the Godhead bodily. The bright and morning Star. The Alpha and Omega. The anointed of the Lord. The beloved Son of God. The radiance of His Father's glory. The Light of the world. The Hope of glory. The Lily of the valley. The Prince of peace. The Seed of David. The Son of righteousness. The blessed and only Potentate, the King of kings, and Lord of lords. Immanuel. The With of God.

The most terrifying truth a mocking humanity will ever confront is that no matter how Jesus is belittled, He cannot be made little. He is the King of the mountain.

> "'On my holy mountain, the high mountain of Israel, declares the Sovereign Lord, there in the land the entire house of Israel will serve me, and there I will accept them'" (Ezek. 20:40).

DAY 2

To the Cross

The time had come when the seconds would not tick by but would pound to the rhythm of a hammer. Since a flaming sword flashed back and forth disbarring humanity from entrance to the garden of divine intimacy, God had crossed days off the kingdom calendar preparing both heaven and earth for this one. The worst and the best day of all. Join me as we journey to the cross. Please read Luke 23:26-49 and complete the following.

Today's Treasure
"When they came to the place called the Skull, there they crucified him" (Luke 23:33).

What kinds of things might Simon have been thinking or feeling as he carried Jesus' cross?

____

Take another look at Christ's words in Luke 23:34. The religious leaders had been conspiring against Jesus for a while and had simply been waiting for the perfect time to seize Him. Scripture is also clear that their goal was not His punishment but His death. Humanly speaking, they seemed to know exactly what they were doing.

What do you think Christ meant when He said they did not?

____

John's version gives us some interesting information about the "written notice above him, which read: "THIS IS THE KING OF THE JEWS" (Luke 23:38). John had connections the others lacked, which may explain his added insight (see John 18:15).

What happened behind the scenes concerning the inscription according to John 19:19-22?

____

In the margin contrast the responses of the two thieves who hung nearby. How much difference did their responses apparently make (Luke 23:39-43)?

What explanation does Luke 23:45 give for the darkness?

____

What added detail does Matthew 27:51 share about the curtain that tore around the time of Christ's last breath?

____

Compare Luke 23:20,23,35 with Luke 23:48. How might you explain the crowd's sudden change of mood?

____

As the story unfolds, we are told an innocent bystander on his way in from the country was forced to carry the cross. Luke 23:26 tells us they forced Simon to carry the cross behind Jesus. Can you imagine the horror of walking behind a man whose back had been torn to shreds by whips laced with jagged metal? Christ had been beaten so badly that He could hardly stand under the weight of the cross. The severity of the beating administered prior to crucifixion often depended upon how long the officials wanted victims to live. They could live up to six days. Quite possibly, Christ's beating demonstrated the full extremity of severity, not to spare Him a lengthy death, but to allow the religious leaders to be home for supper. After all, it was a holiday weekend.

Throngs of people joined the procession as if part of a parade. The path twisted through the city and to Golgotha. Luke 23:32 tells us two other men also were led out with Him to be executed. Scripture's only description of these two men is that they were criminals, fulfilling Isaiah's prophecy that Christ "was numbered with the transgressors" (Isa. 53:12). Then, with startling brevity, Luke 23:33 records the most critical event of all: "When they came to the place called the Skull, there they crucified him."

According to ancient custom, the cross, or at least the crossbeam, was placed upon the ground, then Christ was stretched out upon it. I cannot imagine being the one who actually targeted the nail to the proper place in the skin and struck the blow. Do you think he at all costs avoided Christ's eyes? They probably secured His hands before His feet so that His arms would not flail when His feet were nailed. We often picture the nail wounds in the palms, but the bones in the hands could not hold a victim to the cross. The nails were usually driven through the wrist. In Hebrew, the wrist was considered part of the hand rather than the arm.

Without becoming more graphic than necessary, crucifixion, almost always preceded by a near-death flogging, was unimaginably painful and inhumane. This kind of capital punishment was targeted as a deterrent for rebellious slaves and was forbidden to any Roman citizen no matter how serious his crime.

Crucifixion was a totally inhumane way for even the two criminals to die. But this was the King of glory! They took a hammer and nails to the "Word made flesh."

I want you to sit and "listen" to the sound of the hammer striking. I'm not trying to be melodramatic. I just want us to come as close as possible to being eyewitnesses. You don't have to open your eyes and "look," but I want you to open your spiritual ears and listen. Move close enough to hear the conversation of the marksman as he positions the nail at the wrist of Christ. You'll have to fight the crowd to get close enough. Then listen to the hammer hit the nail—several times at each hand and foot to make sure the nails are securely in place. I'm not trying to make you wince. I only want you to hear the sound as the nails are driven securely into the wood.

Now I want you to read the words that apply so beautifully to Christ at this moment. In their immediate sense, they were written about Eliakim, but you will see their ultimate significance in terms of the cross of our Christ. Please read Isaiah 22:20-25.

How did God say He would give His servant the key to the house of David, opening a door no one can shut according to Isaiah 22:23?

"I will ____."

The passage foreshadows Christ in a remarkable way. As unfathomable as the process is to you and me, the cross was the means by which God chose to position Christ in the seat of honor for the house of His Father. The cross is the open door no man can shut.

Isaiah 22:23 says, "I will fasten him as a nail in a sure place" (KJV). The original word for *firm* in the NIV and *sure* in the KJV is *aman:* "in a transitive sense to make firm, to confirm ... to stand firm; to be enduring; to trust."

Nothing was accidental about the cross of Christ. The Son of God was not suddenly overcome by the wickedness of man and nailed to a cross. Quite the contrary, the cross was the means by which the Son of God overcame the wickedness of man. To secure the keys to the house of David and open the door of salvation to all who would enter, God drove His Son like a nail in a sure place. A firm place. An enduring place.

As horrendous as the pounding hammer sounds to our spiritual ears, please read Colossians 2:13-14 and record what was nailed to His cross.

____

My sin—oh, the bliss of this glorious tho't:
My sin not in part, but the whole
Is nailed to the cross and I bear it no more,
Praise the Lord, praise the Lord, O my soul![1]

I will never fully grasp how such human atrocities occurred at the free will of humanity, while God used them to unfold His perfect, divine, and redemptive plan. Christ was nailed to the cross as the one perfect human. He was the fulfillment of the law in every way. When God drove His Son like a nail in a firm place, He took the written code, finally fulfilled in His Son, and canceled our debt to it. With every pound of the hammer, God was nailing down redemption.

After the soldiers nailed Christ's body to the wood, either the crossbeam was hoisted to a timber prepared with an adjoining slot, or the entire cross was raised with ropes, then dropped with a thud into a socket securing it upward. Imagine the cross raised over the heads of the people, placing Christ in full view.

In terms of Christ's own words in John 12:31-32, what did Christ say to show the kind of death he was going to die (v. 33)?

____

As if the physical wounds Christ suffered were not enough, they were not the killers in crucifixion. Death crept in slowly through exhaustion and asphyxiation from an increasing inability to hold oneself up to draw breath. If you've ever experienced anything close to "excruciating" pain, can you imagine how difficult talking would be?

Regardless of how many times you've heard sermons preached on Christ's next words, don't hear them casually. The moment words formed on His tongue and His voice found volume, He said, "'Father, forgive them, for they do not know what they are doing'" (v. 34).

Not, "Father, consume them," but, "Father, forgive them." This may be the most perfect statement spoken at the most perfect time since God gave the gift of language. As unimaginable as His request was, it was so fitting! If the cross is about anything at all, it is forgiveness. Forgiveness of the most incorrigible and least deserving.

I don't believe the timing of the statement was meaningless. It was the first thing He said after they nailed Him to the cross and hoisted it into view. His immediate request for the Father's forgiveness sanctified the cross for its enduring work through all of time. His request baptized the crude wood for its divine purpose.

Please understand, the cross itself had no power. Neither was it ever meant to be an idol, but it represents something so divine and powerful that the apostle Paul said, "May I never boast except in the cross of our Lord Jesus Christ, through which the world has been crucified to me, and I to the world" (Gal. 6:14).

Dr. Luke was the only one God inspired to record the forgiveness statement. How appropriate that a physician would be the one to pen such healing words. Surely, in the days to come, many involved were haunted by their consciences. No doubt many in the crowd at the crucifixion were saved on the Day of Pentecost, since both events occurred in Jerusalem only weeks apart and on major feast days. The main reason to believe these were the same people, however, is because God doesn't ordinarily refuse the request of His Son. Can you imagine how many of those sorrowing over their part in the crucifixion found healing in Christ's request for their forgiveness?

The curtain drops on our scene in the form of darkness which lasted three hours. Christ said in Luke 22:53 that this would be the "'hour—when darkness reigns.'" That Luke included the fact that the sun stopped shining is poignant. The Light of the world was about to be extinguished, if only for a brief time. Just before He breathed His last, Jesus cried out with a loud voice, "'Father, into your hands I commit my spirit'" (23:46). How appropriate that He would use His last breaths to utter the trust upon which His entire life had rested. I'm not sure we can properly appreciate those words of faith unless we consider the ones spoken by Him only moments before.

Fill in the words first prophesied in Psalm 22:1 and recorded by Matthew in Matthew 27:46:
"'My God, my God,____?'"

I believe this cry marked the exact moment the sins of all humanity—past, present, and future—were heaped upon Christ and the full cup of God's wrath poured forth. Somehow I believe that to bear the sin, Jesus also had to bear the separation. Though Christ had to suffer the incomparable agony of separation from the fellowship of His Father while sin was judged, I am moved that He breathed His last breath with full assurance of His Father's trustworthiness.

The human body of the Life-giver hung lifeless. It was finished. He gave up His last human breath so He never had to give up on humanity. Try to absorb what had just happened. Jesus Christ, "being in very nature God, did not consider equality with God something to be grasped, but made himself nothing, taking the very nature of a servant, being made in human likeness. And being found in appearance as a man, he humbled himself and became obedient to death—even death on a cross!" (Phil. 2:6-8).

Recently I had the privilege of participating in a solemn assembly of 30,000 college students gathered on a huge field in Memphis, Tennessee. We heard a powerful message about the cross. As we responded with songs of worship, two young men began to walk down the hill carrying a large wooden cross. The two students, bent under the weight, carried the heavy cross through the crowd to a place just in front of the platform and then erected it as a visual aid. We couldn't possibly have planned what happened next.

Students began running to the cross with an urgency I can neither possibly describe nor recall without sobs. They sprinted from every direction throughout the crowd. Their sobs echoed in the open air. They lifted the cross out of the ground and began to pass it with their hands lifted high above their heads all over the crowd. They passed it from hands to hands all over the crowd and up the hill. I am covered with chills as I recall the scene when the repentant found refuge in the shadow of the cross.

In our sophistication and familiarity, have we been away too long? Run to the cross.

DAY 3

He Has Risen!

Today's Treasure
"'Why do you look for the living among the dead? He is not here; he has risen!'" (Luke 24:5-6).

By the time I knew Jesus was crucified, I also knew He rose from the dead; yet, I am sitting here bawling like a baby. How I wish I could put my feelings into words. The underdog in me wants to stand up and cheer that the good guy wins. The romantic can't bear the man of my dreams being in that tomb another minute. The weakling in me longs desperately for resurrection power; the optimist fails without its hope.

The event we study today means everything to us! Pause and meditate during your reading. Try to picture it. Hear it. Feel it. We will read in two segments: Luke 23:50-56 and Luke 24:1-12. Please read Luke 23:50-56 and complete the following:

What kind of man was Joseph according to this segment of Scripture?

❑ old ❑ good ❑ religious ❑ upright ❑ quiet

Luke 23:52 tells us Joseph of Arimathea went to Pilate to ask for Jesus' body. Stop here for a minute. Allow your imagination to help you picture some of the dynamics in the room where they met. Two men of position faced one another: one a man of principle and the other a man of self-promotion.

What do you think each was thinking about the other at that meeting?

Joseph about Pilate: ________________________________

Pilate about Joseph: ________________________________

Imagine the difficulty and courage of Joseph's task. I ask again: *How does one take down a body from a cross? Especially this One?* I can hardly bear the thought. This broken human frame had housed the fullness of the Godhead, the radiance of the Father's glory. These fixed eyes had looked through everyone He met. These lips, cracked from fever, thirst, and death, had spoken nothing but Truth. Hands, trained in carpentry, had rebuilt lives and raised the dead, then succumbed to a hammer and nails. Don't lose sight of it. This former "House" of the fullness of the Spirit was precious.

Imagine with what care Joseph tenderly took the body down into his arms. I wonder if he wept. Did he prick his fingers as he removed the crown of thorns embedded in that head? Did he brush hair out of that face? Did he speak to Jesus like I spoke to my mother as I stroked her lifeless hand? I have no idea what Joseph thought, felt, and experienced, but it could have been nothing less than profound. He wrapped the body of Jesus in linen cloth and placed it in a cleft of the rock as the Sabbath was about to begin.

How the Sabbath hours must have dragged for the women. They had prepared the spices and perfumes but were forced to rest on the Sabbath. They had come with Jesus from Galilee, so we can assume they were guests in others' homes. Surely the time seemed to be an eternity. Women two thousand years ago were not so unlike we are today. We want to do something. Feeling needed is sometimes the very thing that keeps a woman going. For months they "had followed him and cared for his needs" (Mark 15:41). Now all that was left to do was to serve Him in memorial. They *needed* to get to the tomb and do the one last thing they could for their Lord.

How about you? When was the last time you had to wait and "rest" in the midst of a crisis when you desperately wanted to do something?

____

____

As the moments crawled by, I'm sure these women recounted with horror the last few days' events. Surely, at times, they sat in silence, each one weeping in painful solitude as she remembered every encounter with Him. Jesus had a way of making a person feel like the apple of His eye. He still does.

Now read Luke 24:1-12. Even if you've heard of the empty tomb a hundred times, in the margin note anything that jumps out at you this time.

The women "rested" through a Sabbath dusk that frustratingly gave way to night (see 23:56). More waiting. They probably never slept a wink and were on their way to the tomb before a cock could crow. John 20:1, spotlighting Mary Magdalene, tells us "it was still dark."

What were the women wondering on the way to the tomb (Mark 16:1-3)?

____

The women were hoping the officials would allow someone to roll away the stone so they could apply the spices and perfumes to the body. To their astonishment, they saw the "very large" stone had been rolled away. The women had no way of knowing at that moment what Matthew 28:2-4 records.

What had happened? ______________________________

I love the wording in Matthew 28:2: "An angel of the Lord came down from heaven and, going to the tomb, rolled back the stone and sat on it." Can you fathom the angels' horror when humans mocked, spat on, beat, flogged, and crucified the Son of God?

Imagine the joy of the angel whose thunderous arrival caused the ground to shake. God chose him to be the one who rolled back the stone—not to free Jesus—but to reveal Him already missing! Can you picture the angel's gleaming face as he perched on that stone? The guards were so afraid that they shook and became like dead men. The graveyard needed a few folks acting like dead men since a number of the formerly dead were suddenly walking the streets (see Matt. 27:52-53). I'm about to have to shout hallelujah! The women entered the tomb, but they did not find the body.

Read Acts 2:24. Why was Christ raised from the dead?

____

Some things are simply impossible—and death keeping its hold on Jesus is one of them. Mind you, the women didn't yet understand. Luke 24:4 tells us "while they were wondering about this, suddenly two men in clothes that gleamed like lightning stood beside them." John's version hints at these two celestial ambassadors' assignment.

When Mary Magdalene looked inside the tomb, how were the angels positioned according to John 20:12?

____

Quite possibly, these angels also guarded the body of Jesus while it lay "in state" in the sepulcher. The Old Testament tabernacle contained a marvelous picture foreshadowing this moment. The ark of the covenant represented the very presence of God. In Exodus 25:17-22, read the instructions for the "mercy seat" (KJV) or "atonement cover" (NIV) on the ark of the covenant.

What was the position of the cherubim? ______________________________

Do you see the picture? No, I can't be dogmatic that the cherubim prefigured the angels at Christ's head and feet—but I am convinced. Jesus has always been the means by which God would "meet with" humanity (Ex. 25:22).

If the cherubim prefigured the angels in the tomb, can you imagine how they guarded the body through the wait? With their wings overshadowing Him, they faced each other, looking toward the cover. Picture their reactions when the glorified body of Jesus sat up from the death shroud and walked out of the tomb, right through the rock. Wouldn't you have loved to hear as Christ thanked them for their service?

Glory to God! Though the news echoed throughout the heavenlies at the moment of Christ's resurrection, the angels probably longed for God to turn on their volume in the earthly realm and announce it to the mortals. At the sight of the angels, the women fell on their faces. The celestial guards announced to them, "Why do you look for the living among the dead?" The what? The living! "He is not here" (Luke 24:5-6).

I give you the joy of finishing the sentence: ______________________________

Oh, Glorious, Merciful, Omnipotent God! He is risen indeed! I cherish the next five words of the angels: "Remember how he told you" (v. 6). Beloved, have you forgotten something He told you? Christ, our Lord, is faithful to His promises. If you're not presently "seeing" Him at work in your situation, do not live as if He's lifeless and you're hopeless. Believe Him and expect Him to reveal His resurrection power to you!

The angels reminded the women of three facts Jesus foretold, not just to His disciples, but obviously to them as well.

List the three facts recorded in Luke 24:7. "The Son of Man must be … "

1. ____

2. ____

3. ____

All things had to go exactly according to the plan. No point was negotiable. After the heralds delivered their three-point sermon, "they remembered his words" (v. 8). Luke leapfrogs immediately to their departure and intent to tell the eleven, but Matthew shines a flashlight on something that happened en route.

What happened according to Matthew 28:8-10?

____

I hope God recorded that scene so we can watch the replay in heaven. As hard as pulling themselves away from the visible presence of Christ must have been, the women did as He commanded them. Luke 24:9 records one of my favorite reasons why I believe God might have chosen to reveal the empty tomb first to this group of women.

What did they do when they came back from the tomb?

____

If I may say with a chuckle, one possible reason God chose to reveal the resurrection first to women is because He can trust us to get the word out! Telling what we've been told is our specialty! However, nothing can deflate the spirits of an enthusiastic woman like an apprehensive audience. Luke 24:11 records that the apostles "did not believe the women, because their words seemed to them like nonsense."

Sisters, don't be insulted by this scene in Luke 24:11. Rather, be blessed that God was up to something awesome even in this seemingly insignificant detail. You see, "the witness of women was not [even] acceptable in that day."[2] They couldn't testify as witnesses.

Now isn't this just like my Jesus! He threatened the status quo in countless ways, not the least of which concerned women. He invited them into Bible class (see Luke 10:39) after they had spent centuries learning what little Scripture they could from their husbands. He honored their service during a time in which men were the only ones who ministered publicly (see Mark 15:41). He healed, forgave, delivered, and made whole the very ones society shunned. Women of ill repute.

Appointing these women as the first to share the news of Jesus' resurrection was a definite "custom shaker." Jesus knew the apostles wouldn't believe them, but perhaps He felt that the pending discovery of their authenticity would breed a fresh respect. After all, look at the first roll call we have in the post-ascension New Testament church, and you'll see who comprised the first New Testament cell group (see Acts 1:13-14).

For centuries the synagogue kept men and women separate. Suddenly they would be working, praying, and worshiping shoulder-to-shoulder. Christ built His church on a foundation of mutual respect. Don't misunderstand. Christ wasn't prioritizing women over men. He simply took the ladder down to the basement where society had lowered women. With His nail-scarred hands, He lifted them to a place of respect and credibility.

The last thing we women should want to do in the body of Christ is take men's places. They have far too much responsibility for my taste! But by all means, let's take our places! We have also been called to be credible witnesses of the Lord Jesus Christ.

Oh, how I have enjoyed our lesson! I could almost see Him. I could feel the hair stand up on the back of my neck as Mary gazed in the tomb and saw two angels. I could smell the earth as the women fell on their faces at the sight of the angels. I could race down the streets this minute and proclaim to every doubter, "He is risen!" And, if I should run into Him on the way, my knees would buckle involuntarily. I would drop to the ground, clasp His feet, and wash them in my tears. I would grab Him, worship Him, and never want to let Him go. Someday, my dear friends, we will get our chance.

Until then, "Don't be afraid. Go and tell."

DAY 4

A Burning Heart

Today's Treasure
"They asked each other, 'Were not our hearts burning within us while he talked with us on the road and opened the Scriptures to us?' " (Luke 24:32).

Reading the Bible is like taking a wild ride through a vast land, but instead of wondering about the stories of those you pass, you get to stop off and see them face-to-face. I've tended sheep in the desert with Moses. I've laughed my head off with Sarai in Abraham's tent. I've shouted with Joshua at the walls of Jericho. I've danced with David down the streets of Jerusalem, and I've been shipwrecked with Paul. What a ride! Today the track will take us down the road to Emmaus where we'll hop off the roller coaster and walk for a while. Please read Luke 24:13-35 and complete the following:

Luke 24:13 begins with the words, "Now that same day." Check your context. What day was it?
❑ Saturday ❑ Sunday ❑ Monday

What was the distance to their destination? ____________________

Describe their mood when Christ asked what they were discussing.

____

How did Christ respond to their narration of the recent events (vv. 25-27)?
❑ great joy ❑ a Bible lesson ❑ a rebuke ❑ a commendation

At what point did the men recognize Jesus? ____________________

I love this story! Let's get a little sand in our shoes and walk with Cleopas and his companion on the very Sunday of Christ's resurrection. I can't help but wonder if Christ had the time of His life that day surprising people. Apparently the two men we're joining were followers of Christ. They described the women who discovered the empty tomb as "some of our women" (v. 22). We can also assume they were members of the same group Christ told about His capture, crucifixion, and even His resurrection.

The scene unfolds with a pair of mouths traveling faster than their feet. Luke 24:15-16 tells us that Jesus joined them on the road but kept them from recognizing Him. Christ may not make a habit of walking up to us in human form, but I think He sometimes "joins us" in our circumstances in ways we don't recognize.

Can you think of a time when Christ walked beside you but you did not recognize Him until "after the fact"? If so, share briefly.

____

____

The next scene is mind-boggling. Christ asked what they were discussing. With downcast faces they answered Him. Freeze the frame for a moment. Trade places with Cleopas and paste his expression on your face. Can you imagine how ridiculous we look with hopeless, downcast faces while the immortal Son of God stands right beside us?

Imagine that God has decorated your mansion in glory with a number of framed pictures of two of His very favorites: you and Christ. The pictures capture the two of you during momentous earthly occasions. You could not see Him with your eyes, but He was there every moment in living color. Hopefully, we've each walked with Him long enough to have a few treasured photos with expressions suggesting we chose to see with the eyes of faith rather than the eyes of humanity.

Reflect back on some victorious moments in your journey. In the margin describe a highlight picture of you with your Christ.

I can almost imagine Christ sitting around heaven with small groups of us, pulling out the photo album, pointing out a few sour expressions. Picture us covering our faces with good-humored embarrassment, turning as red as beets. No doubt the still shot of Cleopas in Luke 24:17 is one that would spur a little good-natured, heavenly ribbing. Christ, however, didn't find it nearly so amusing this side of heaven. Note that the events surrounding Christ's crucifixion were so well publicized that Cleopas implied Christ would have to be a visitor to be unaware of the recent happenings. He then proceeded to tell Christ … about Himself. Can you imagine being in Cleopas' sandals? Wouldn't you hope you got the facts straight? Let's draw another pretend scenario. Christ spent much of His earthly tenure in the role of teacher.

If Christ had been a teacher grading Cleopas on his oral report, what grade do you think He would've given him and why?

____

If I were grading Cleopas' oral report, I wouldn't have subtracted points until the "kicker" in Luke 24:21: "But we had hoped that he was the one." Picture the downcast face, the sagging posture. Listen to the tone in his voice. For a clue, see Christ's indignant response in Luke 24:25. Cleopas seemed to be saying, "We had hoped … but He let us down." Cleopas needed a good dose of Psalm 43.

I love how the psalms reveal the thought processes of a writer. The psalmist, while feeling rejected by God, sunk into mourning. In Psalm 43:5 the psalmist wrote his own prescription for a downcast soul: "Put your hope in God, / for I will yet praise him, / my Savior and my God." The Word of God often couples a downcast soul with feelings of hopelessness. In the Greek the word *hope* encompasses far more than wishful thinking. It means confident expectation. Christ told His followers what to "expect" and reminded them that a victorious ending would follow the tragic means. When Christ gives us His Word, He wants us to live in absolute expectation of it, trusting that whether it happens sooner or later, it will happen.

Read the following Scriptures and write your own prescriptions for hope.

Romans 15:4 ____

Romans 15:13 ____

Ephesians 1:18 ____

What is Christ called in 1 Timothy 1:1? ______________________________

Cleopas and his friend had allowed the very evidence that could have ignited them with hope to instead make them hopeless. Remember now—the women had shared the testimony that Christ was alive. I realize I'm taking the next statement out of context, but I get a kick out of Cleopas' words in Luke 24:22: "In addition, some of our women amazed us." There you have it. Women are amazing. It's absolutely scriptural. Of course, *amazing* can mean many things. The most common colloquialism we have which matches the word for *amazing* is to say something has "blown our minds." I blow Keith's mind all the time—but it's not always a good blow. Sometimes he just stands there and gives me that, "She's blonder than she pays to be" look.

Christ clearly showed His displeasure over the men's disbelief. He rebuked them but followed the rebuke with some of the most amazing moments in Scripture: "Beginning with Moses and all the Prophets, he explained to them what was said in all the Scriptures concerning himself" (v. 27). What I would give to hear that comprehensive dissertation! Christ began with the books of Moses, went straight through the prophets, and explained what was said in all the Scriptures concerning Himself. Part of heaven for me will be hearing a replay of this sermon! The entire Old Testament was written about or toward Christ. Imagine Jesus Himself explaining the hundreds of ways the Scriptures predict and prepare for His coming. I could teach on this subject for hours, and I don't know a fraction of the ways Christ is taught in the Old Testament.

In the margin list ways you know that the Scriptures predicted Christ.

Take another look at Luke 24:27. Luke's use of the word *explained* in reference to Christ's teaching approach means "to interpret, translate. To explain clearly and exactly." I can't wait to know exactly what some Scriptures mean. Unlike me, Christ never had to say, "I think ..." or "I believe this means ... ." He knew. What a Bible lesson those two men heard! A lesson that would have taken 40 years of wilderness wanderings for me, Christ delivered with glorious precision over a few Emmaus miles.

No wonder the two men hated to part with Jesus! "Jesus acted as if he were going farther. But they urged him strongly, 'Stay with us'" (vv. 28-29).

Don't you love the part in a movie when the surprise is revealed? We have now arrived at that climactic moment. Allow me to set the table for you. The men invited Jesus into one of their homes. A simple meal was prepared. They reclined at the table. Christ took the role as server. He broke the bread and called down divine favor through a benediction. He handed each of them a portion of the small loaf. As if the veil of the holy of holies was torn again before their very eyes, they recognized Him! Then He disappeared. Talk about a photo I want to see in a heavenly album! Can you imagine those expressions? I have a feeling "downcast" wouldn't be an adequate description.

I relish few things more than witnessing someone's fresh reaction to Jesus Christ. How blessed we are that God chose to tell us what the men said after they picked up their chins off the floor. "'Were not our hearts burning within us while he talked with us on the road and opened the Scriptures to us?'" (Luke 24:32). Oh, this question is so chock full of riches, I'm almost too excited to teach it! First, did you notice that spiritual heartburn is scriptural? You bet it is! "Did not our heart burn?" (KJV).

The word *burn* means exactly what you think it does: "to make to burn, ... flaming ... to consume with fire." Beloved, if you have ever paid any attention to anything I've ever written about the key to a passionate relationship with Christ, pay attention now. Your heart means far more to Christ than anything. That your heart is utterly taken with Christ is more important than any amount of service you could render or rules you could keep. If Christ has your heart, He will have your obedience (see John 14:21). God wants to completely captivate your heart and cause it to burn with passion for Him. It is His absolute priority for you according to Mark 12:30; joy and satisfaction will elude you in its absence. Two immutable keys exist that turn our spiritual ignition and enflame godly passion. Both are tucked like rubies in the embers of Luke 24:32.

Fill in the blanks: "'Were not our hearts burning within us while he

(1.) ________________________ on the road and

(2.) ______________________ the ________________________ to us?'"

To me, "talked with us on the road" is a wonderfully personal and tender representation of prayer and "opened the Scriptures to us" is a perfect representation of Bible study. Beloved, we may do many other things to fan the flame of our spiritual passion for Christ, but all other efforts are in vain without the two sticks of prayer and Bible study rubbed together to ignite a fire.

Tomorrow we will conclude our present adventure and our paths may not cross again this side of heaven. Our hearts have burned together like a raging fire and I will miss you terribly, but you certainly don't need me. You can always know what causes a heart to burn in the presence of Jesus Christ.

Some may say, "But I've said prayers before and attended Sunday School many times and my heart didn't burn." I'm not referring to popcorn prayers and drive-thru lessons. I'm talking about entering into a love affair of prayer with Jesus Christ, where you talk to Him throughout the day as if He, the unseen One, is a far greater reality than those within your vision. I'm talking about opening up the Word, throwing back your head, face toward heaven, and saying, "Thrill me with Your Word!" (see Ps. 119:18). Evolving into this kind of intimacy with God takes time, but the road trip is half the excitement!

Don't confuse a passionate relationship with God with an unrealistic state of perpetual chill bumps. I'm talking about the meshing of two lives, yours and Christ's, increasingly engulfing and igniting the whole of heart, soul, mind, and strength. God is more than anxious to give you a heart full of fire for His Son. Tell Him you want it more than blessing or your daily bread. Beloved, promise me you will not settle for mediocrity! When Jesus, the Alpha and the Omega, the Author and Finisher of our faith, takes the wheel, you won't lack excitement, amusement, or a seat with a view. He has nothing less in mind for you than a great adventure. A wild ride awaits you. All aboard?

DAY 5
Jesus Himself

Today's Treasure
" 'Look at my hands and my feet. It is I myself! Touch me and see' " (Luke 24:39).

Our last day? How can this be? The months seem to blow off the calendar faster and faster these days. In a flash, our lives on earth will evaporate like a cloud, but every moment we've spent in the Word is an eternal investment in the treasury of heaven. Stay in God's Word! Study under biblically sound teachers so you develop into a follower of Christ and not a follower of the world. Worship Christ alone. Stay connected to a local body of believers and serve God with contagious joy. I commit to you that I will do the same. If we never meet here on earth, I cannot wait to get to know you in heaven. Please drop by my house and share a heavenly cup of java with me. Come tell me how you love Him and what you felt when you saw Him face-to-face.

I am at a loss for words to express my gratitude to you. That a person of your character would choose to walk through the Word of God with someone like me—a former pit dweller with so much left to learn—is so humbling, I cannot assimilate it. I simply cast the privilege like a perfect rose at the feet of my Savior. As always, my eyes sting with tears as we meet on a well-worn page of God's Word for our final reading together. Please bask in Luke 24:36-53 and complete the following:

How would you title and subtitle the scene described in verses 36-49?

______________________:______________________

What is your favorite part and why? ______________________

____

Why do you think Christ ate at a time like this? ______________________

____

What had the Father promised (Acts 2:32-33)? ______________________

Why do you think Christ said to wait on the coming of this promise?

____

What was Christ doing at the very moment He departed?

____

In Luke 24:51, a very human band of followers enjoyed the last glimpse of their Leader. Why do you think they were filled with such great joy even though He had departed from their physical sight?

____

Let's set the stage for the events described in Luke 24:36. After Christ revealed Himself at their table and then disappeared, Cleopas and his companion walked what was perhaps the fastest seven miles of their lives, right back to Jerusalem. By the time they reached the eleven, the disciples were swept up in the excitement of Christ's appearance to Peter. Finally, they were proclaiming: "It is true! The Lord has risen" (v. 34).

I love Christ's dramatic timing. "While they were still talking …" (v. 36). Who? The chaps from Emmaus! They kept getting caught giving their testimony about Jesus, but I think they received a much better grade on this one. Jesus Himself stood among them. Oh, glorious day! After all the conjecture, all the doubt. Not Gabriel. Not the heavenly hosts. Not a vision. No apparition. Jesus. Beloved, when our eyes are unveiled to heavenly sight, we will see Jesus Himself. "For the Lord himself will come down from heaven … And so we will be with the Lord forever!" (1 Thess. 4:16-17). Be still, my heart!

What were the first words out of Christ's mouth when He interrupted the scene in Luke 24:36? ______________________________

Peace or *Shalom* is the most common greeting among the Hebrew people, but nothing was common about this greeting that resurrection night.

What special significance do these words carry based on Ephesians 2:14?

____

I have to laugh out loud from the delightful irony that Christ's greeting of peace nearly scared the disciples to death (see Luke 24:37). John 20:19 helps explain why Christ's surprise visit incited such fear. The disciples were locked in for fear of the Jews.

Luke 24:37 translates two very strong original words to describe the terror of the disciples. Suffice it to say, they could not have been more frightened. I think they would have run for their lives if they could have moved. Notice that just minutes earlier they were cheering, "It is true!" But somehow when they came face-to-face with Jesus, the sight was almost more than they could bear. I delight in knowing our future will be somewhat similar. You and I have banked our entire lives on the fact that Jesus Christ is very much alive, yet I have a feeling when we actually behold Him, it will only be eternal life that keeps us from dropping like dead men. Christ responded to the fright of His disciples by asking, "'Why are you troubled, and why do doubts rise in your minds?'" The original word for *troubled* implies a sudden disturbance of all sorts of emotions.

Fear is an obvious emotion the disciples felt. Can you think of any others that might have suddenly erupted within them? Explain.

____

____

The original word for *doubts* in Luke 24:38 is *dialogismos*. You see in it the word *dialogue*. The Greek word means *thoughts* and *directions* and can also mean *debate*. I think their minds went on instant overload, dialoguing all sorts of debates between what their eyes suddenly saw and what their brains could not rationalize. I can almost hear Christ saying: "Boys, you don't have a mental file already prepared to stick this information in. This one won't compute intellectually. Quit trying. Just behold and believe." Christ's willingness to continue to draw us to belief totally astounds me. At no time did He say: "You bunch of idiots! I'm sick of trying to talk you into believing Me!" When the sight of Him wasn't enough, Jesus said: "'Look at my hands and my feet. It is I myself! Touch me and see; a ghost does not have flesh and bones, as you see I have'" (v. 39).

Christ did not have to retain the scars in His resurrected body. In the margin write why you think He did.

I wear a bracelet on my wrist as a visible reminder that I am the Lord's. In such a poignant way, I believe the nail scars represent something precious to Christ. The scars are ways you and I have been engraved on His very hands and feet (see Isa. 49:16).

The nail scars weren't the only ones He retained. To what other wound does Christ refer in John 20:27?________________________________

Many believe the spear wound in Jesus' side pierced His heart. The wound suggests a picture of the bride of Christ. His betrothed has come from His side like the first woman came from Adam's. Not from His rib, however, from His heart.

Unlike His first disciples, you and I have never looked upon Christ's touchable hands and feet. At first, it may seem the disciples had such an advantage over us. After all, they saw the risen Christ with their own eyes. Christ, however, announced that we are the ones with a special advantage.

What did He say in John 20:29 that applies to you and me?

____

Oh, Sister! We who believe, yet have never seen, are blessed because it is faith that pleases Him so (see Heb. 11:6)! We have often seen His hands through constant provision and glorious intervention. We have often seen His feet as He's gone before us. Surely we have beheld the hands and feet of Christ with eyes of faith!

The English version of Luke 24:41 paints an almost disturbing picture of the disciples until we grasp what I believe God is implying. After the disciples saw His hands and feet, we are told "they still did not believe." But I don't think the implication is that they were stiffnecked and obstinate, demanding further proof.

They still did not believe because of________________________________

Have you ever been so excited over a piece of news that it didn't seem real until later? That's how the disciples felt! They were thinking something like, *Is this too good to be true?* Christ's response marvelously implies what was going through their minds. He immediately asked for something to eat, demonstrating that He was real. This was no ghost! Can you imagine the resurrected body of Christ? He walked through walls and ate real food. His resurrected body had complete form and firmness, yet was unrestrained by earthly boundaries. For the most incredible part, read 1 John 3:2.

What will we be like?________________________________

This incredible verse suggests that while we don't yet know what we will be in our glorified state, we know what we will be like. We shall be like Him. I believe this Scripture implies that the physical properties of our glorified bodies will be much like His. How thrilling! Among many other more spiritual things, I am delighted we will be able to eat! But, if it's all the same to Jesus, I think I'd rather have the fried fish instead of the broiled since I'll have a heavenly body.

Someone might be thinking, *This is no time for fun and games!* But I think Jesus had a bunch of fun with His disciples when He saw their joyous disbelief and asked for a piece of fish to prove the point! No one can tell me that behind those closed doors there wasn't hilarity, replete with unreligious laughter and unsophisticated jumps for joy. We have been created in the image of our God. Ecstatic joy is His gift, and what better time to share it than dancing in the moonlight on resurrection night? I am convinced that the brief moments between Luke 24:43 and 44 were filled with celebration. Somewhere between those lines, the disciples saw and believed!

Christ then reminded the disciples in verse 44: "'Everything must be fulfilled that is written about me in the Law of Moses, the Prophets and the Psalms.'" That includes His return. The Old Testament is perfectly clear that the Messiah will return to earth and occupy the throne of David. He entered Jerusalem before as a humble servant on a donkey.

Based on Revelation 19:11, how will He next make His entrance?

____

Hallelujah! My dear sibling in Christ, as surely as Jesus died and rose again, He will return. Everything must be fulfilled. After Christ's adamant reassurance, Luke 24:45 records something magnificent.

What did Christ do? ______________________________

I'm not sure original definitions get much better than the one for *understand* in Luke 24:45. Meditate on this definition: "The comprehending activity of the mind denoted by *suniemi* entails the assembling of individual facts into an organized whole, as collecting the pieces of a puzzle and putting them together. The mind grasps concepts and sees the proper relationship between them." Beloved, I believe Christ can do the same thing for you and me! No, we will never be infallible in our understanding.

But what does the Holy Spirit urge us to pray for as New Testament believers according to the following references?

Colossians 1:9-10 ______________________________

Colossians 2:2-3 ______________________________

Ephesians 1:17-18 ______________________________

That's plenty to ignite our excitement! For the rest of our days, let's ask Him to open our minds, putting one puzzle piece after another in our hands, causing the unspeakable joy of seeing how they fit together. May we shout for joy at times! Weep with wonder at others! May we spend the days of our lives fitting together one piece after another until all we lack is the vivid picture of His perfect face. Oh, happy day!

As the curtain drops on resurrection night, the disciples finally saw the puzzle pieces coming together. They began to comprehend why the plan necessitated Christ's suffering and His resurrection from the dead. Like a small battalion of soldiers, they received their marching orders. Preach "'repentance and forgiveness of sins … in [My] name to all nations, beginning at Jerusalem.'" I love the next statement: "'You are witnesses of these things'" (v. 48). And so are we. What they saw with their eyes, we have seen with our hearts. I pray that nothing can keep us from telling.

Luke's account of the evening concludes with the promise of the power and presence of the Holy Spirit. "'I will ask the Father, and he will give you another Counselor to be with you forever—the Spirit of truth. … I will not leave you as orphans; I will come to you'" (John 14:16-18). Very soon Christ's words would be fulfilled. With their minds freshly opened, perhaps they wondered when, but I think they no longer wondered if.

Luke's Gospel pen, filled by the ink of the Spirit for 24 glorious chapters, appropriately runs dry on a priceless scene. A small band of motley men, whose lives had been turned every-which-way-but-loose by Jesus of Nazareth, strained for their last earthly glimpse of Him. From the first page to the last, Luke's entire Gospel has been about glory interrupting the ordinary. They never asked for Jesus. He asked for them—and their lives would never be the same. The last thing they saw was the scars on His feet.

Thirty-three years earlier, the feet of God toddled their first visible prints on earth, a young mother's footprints chasing close behind. The walk grew rough, the path strewn with stones and thorns. Now God Incarnate stepped off this planet with feet scarred and bruised. As God predicted at the fall, the ancient serpent struck Christ's heel, but on the day He ascended, all things were under His feet. Jesus Christ walked the way of humanity so humanity could walk the way of God. How beautiful the feet that brought good news.

Not one of those disciples was sorry He had come their way. Their losses were incalculable. Most of their friends. Much of their family. Their jobs. The blessings of their fathers. Physical safety. And now, a Leader they could see. Yet they left the Mount of Olives with great joy, continually praising God, for their ordinary lives had been interrupted by Glory.

The words of Romans 8:18 became their reality long before each disciple fell prostrate on heaven's floor. The sufferings of this world simply could not compare to the glory He had revealed to them. They, like no others, could say: "The Word became flesh and made his dwelling among us. We have seen his glory, the glory of the One and Only, who came from the Father, full of grace and truth" (John 1:14). It sustained and swelled them long after the visible became invisible. You and I are the spiritual descendants of Peter, James, John, and all the others who offered their lives, not for what they thought or what they hoped, but what they knew. Who they knew. Our faith is based on fact, beloved. Never let anyone convince you otherwise.

Jesus the One and Only—the title is His forever. He was the One and Only long before He breathed a soul into humanity, and He will continue to be the One and Only long after the last soul has been judged. He is changeless. But you and I were destined for change. So determined is God to transform us, we cannot draw near Him and remain the same.

As we conclude our 10-week journey through Galilee, Jerusalem, and Judea, the question is not, "Is Jesus the One and Only?" Our vote cannot elect Him to a position He already occupies. The question is this: Has Jesus become your One and Only? Is He transcending all else in your life? Is He beyond compare? Your one and only Savior? Your one and only Deliverer? The one and only Lover of your soul? If so, my dear friend, you are being transformed from glory unto glory like Moses who descended the mount of God with face radiant. You may not see it, but others do. That's God's way. May our lives be obscured by the glory of Christ, hidden in the shadow of His cross. And when all is said and done, may our tenure on this planet be characterized by one simple word: *Jesus.*

There is a Name above all names
Let mine be lost in His
Hide me in His crimson heart
O, way of secret bliss!
One life alone is worth the find
Nail mine onto the tree
Till Jesus ever shining here
Is all beheld in me.

Bring Him forth each day I live
And leave me in the tomb
I seek no other glory here
Make not the smallest room.
Blessed anonymity!
Count my life but loss.
—Jesus the One and Only—
Tread over me, Dear Cross.

---

[1]Horatio G. Spafford, "It Is Well with My Soul," *The Baptist Hymnal* (Nashville, TN: Convention Press, 1991), 410.

[2]Frank E. Gaebelein, *The Expositor's Bible Commentary* (Grand Rapids, MI: Zondervan Publishing, 1984), 1049.

VIDEO RESPONSE SHEET **GROUP SESSION 10**

Session 10

Introduction: Today we join the disciples on the Mount of Olives for our last earthly glimpse of Jesus Christ. Christ's physical departure from this earth ushered in a new era. Why is this era so important to you and me? It's the one in which we live. Some call it "The Church Age." But no matter what this present era is called, it is the age in which God chooses to act primarily through His disciples. In the first generation, it was Peter and the others. In this generation, it's you and me. We have the invitation, therefore, to join the disciples for Christ's basic instructions before leaving earth, not just as spectators but as recipients.

Read Luke 24:49-52 and Acts 1:1-11.

1. We, too, have reason to return to our worlds with ________ ________ (see Luke 24:52; 1 Pet. 1:6-9).

2. We, too, have been chosen by ________ ________ (see Acts 1:1-2).

3. We, too, have been given ________________ through the Holy Spirit (see Acts 1:2).

4. God has also supplied our generations with "many ________________ proofs" that He was alive. (see Acts 1:3).

5. We, too, receive the awesome ________ of the Holy Spirit (see Acts 1:8; Eph. 1:18-21).

6. We, too, are His ________ in our cities, our regions, our ________, and the ends of the earth (see Acts 1:8). The original word for *witnesses* is *martus*. In the New Testament, *martus* represented two things:

   - Those who announce the ______ of the gospel and tell its ________.
   - Those who have suffered __________ in consequence of confessing Christ.

7. We, too, await the __________ and __________ return of the Lord Jesus Christ. (See Acts 1:10-12. Compare Zech. 14:3-4.)

CHRISTIAN GROWTH STUDY PLAN

In the **Christian Growth Study Plan (formerly Church Study Course)**, this book *Jesus the One and Only* is a resource for course credit in the subject area Personal Life of the Christian Growth category of diploma plans. To receive credit, read the book, complete the learning activities, show your work to your pastor, a staff member or church leader, then complete the following information. This page may be duplicated. Send the completed page to:

Christian Growth Study Plan
One LifeWay Plaza; Nashville, TN 37234-0117
FAX: (615) 251-5067

For information about the Christian Growth Study Plan, refer to the Christian Growth Study Plan Catalog. It is located online at www.lifeway.com. If you do not have access to the Internet, contact the Christian Growth Study Plan office (1.800.968.5519) for the specific study plan you need for your ministry.

Jesus the One and Only
COURSE NUMBER: CG-0525

PARTICIPANT INFORMATION

Social Security Number (USA ONLY-optional)	Personal CGSP Number*	Date of Birth (MONTH, DAY, YEAR)
_ _ _ - _ _ - _ _ _ _	_ _ _ _ - _ _ _ - _ _ _ _	_ _ - _ _ - _ _

Name (First, Middle, Last)	Home Phone
	_ _ _ - _ _ _ - _ _ _ _

Address (Street, Route, or P.O. Box)	City, State, or Province	Zip/Postal Code

Please check appropriate box: ☐ Resource purchased by self ☐ Resource purchased by church ☐ Other

CHURCH INFORMATION

Church Name		
Address (Street, Route, or P.O. Box)	**City, State, or Province**	**Zip/Postal Code**

CHANGE REQUEST ONLY

☐ Former Name		
☐ Former Address	City, State, or Province	Zip/Postal Code
☐ Former Church	City, State, or Province	Zip/Postal Code

Signature of Pastor, Conference Leader, or Other Church Leader	Date

*New participants are requested but not required to give SS# and date of birth. Existing participants, please give CGSP# when using SS# for the first time. Thereafter, only one ID# is required. **Mail to:** Christian Growth Study Plan, One LifeWay Plaza, Nashville, TN 37234-0117. Fax: (615)251-5067.

Rev. 3-03

Nurture Your Spiritual Growth

If you've enjoyed this study, catch your breath and get ready for another: ***Beloved Disciple: The Life and Ministry of John; Breaking Free: Making Liberty in Christ a Reality in Life; A Heart Like His: Seeking the Heart of God Through a Study of David***; or ***A Woman's Heart: God's Dwelling Place.***

Similar in design and format, these Bible studies will encourage and challenge you and your friends to apply practical Bible truths with life-changing results.

Each study features a personal study workbook; a leader kit that includes the Member Book, leader helps, and six videotapes with administrative help plus Beth Moore's teaching presentations. Audiotapes that feature the audio portions of the videotapes and a listening guide are available for purchase separately.

Two additional studies that include leader helps and group study guides do not require videos. ***Living Beyond Yourself: Exploring the Fruit of the Spirit*** is a 10-week study of the fruit of the Spirit (Gal. 5:22-23). ***Living Free: Learning to Pray God's Word*** is a 6-session study that combines key concepts from the best-selling *Breaking Free* with prayer practices Beth teaches in *Praying God's Word* for a more in-depth look at Christian freedom.

Whispers of Hope is a unique prayer and devotional journal designed to help women develop consistent, daily prayer.

Ask your church to schedule these studies soon—they're ideal for reaching and ministering to women of all ages.

Additional women's enrichment resources:

Women Reaching Women: Beginning and Building a Growing Women's Enrichment Ministry
Chris Adams, compiler; foreword by Anne Graham Lotz—A comprehensive leadership resource for beginning and expanding your church's women's ministry.
ISBN 0-7673-2593-1

Journey: A Woman's Guide to Intimacy with God
This monthly devotional magazine helps women grow closer to God by addressing their unique needs and issues. Available in multiple copies.

For a complete listing of Bible studies and books by Beth Moore, visit our Web site at www.lifeway.com or see the LifeWay Church resources catalog. To request a catalog, call 1-800-458-2772.

To order resources:

- WRITE LifeWay Church Resources Customer Service Center; One LifeWay Plaza; Nashville, TN 37234-0113
- FAX order to (615) 251-5933
- PHONE (800) 458-2772;
- EMAIL to customerservice@lifeway.com.
- ORDER ONLINE at www.lifeway.com
- VISIT the LifeWay Christian Store serving you.

To learn about opportunities for women's enrichment training, visit our Web site at www.lifeway.com, fax (615) 251-5058, or email chris.adams@lifeway.com.

To learn about women's enrichment events, visit our Web site at www.lifeway.com or call 1-800-254-2022.

Promo #A613099